IMAGES
of America

DRACUT REVISITED

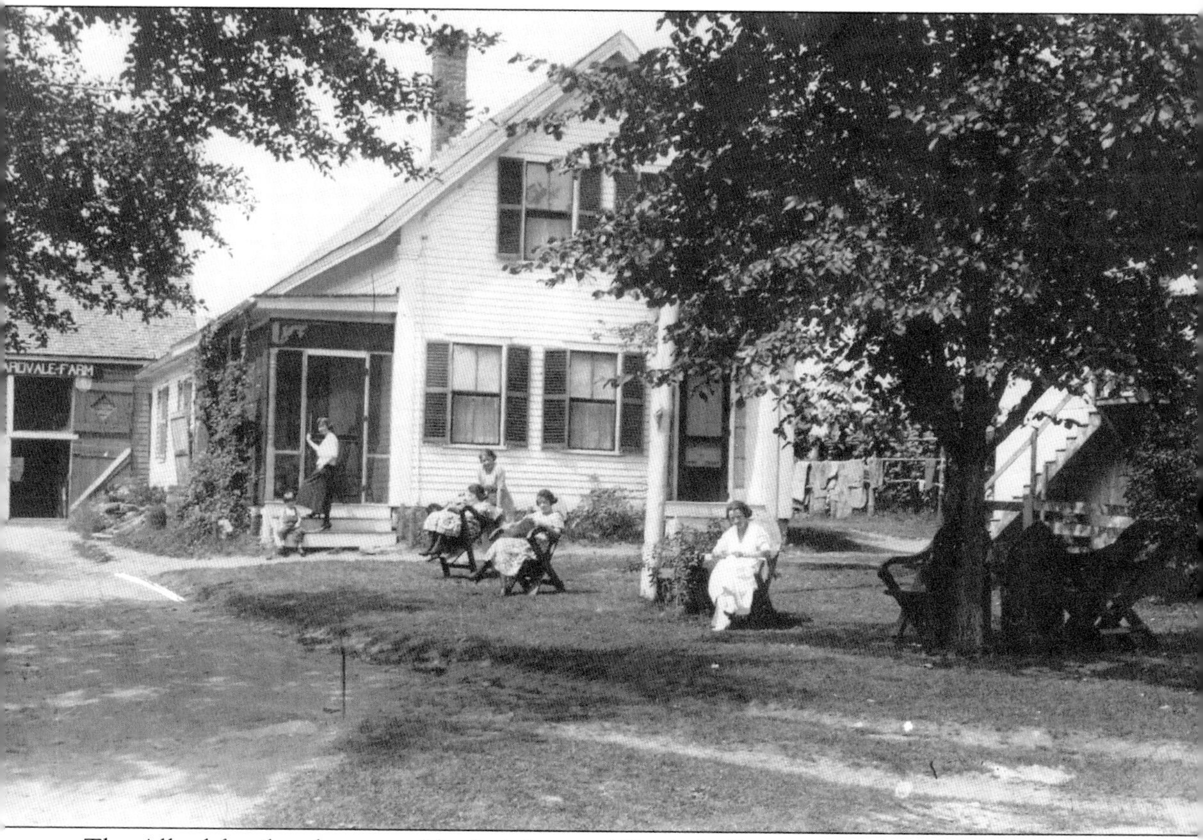

The Allard family relaxes outside their home, Allardvale Farm, on Nashua Road. (Courtesy Dracut Historical Society.)

On the Cover: The Allardvale Store, owned by the Allards, is seen here around 1910. The Allard family farm and store were both on Nashua Road. The Allardvale Farm is gone now, and a housing development stands in its place. (Courtesy Dracut Historical Society.)

IMAGES
of America

DRACUT REVISITED

Rebecca A. Duda

ARCADIA
PUBLISHING

ISBN 978-0-7385-9151-3

Published by Arcadia Publishing
Charleston, South Carolina

Printed in the United States of America

Library of Congress Control Number: 2011940257

For all general information, please contact Arcadia Publishing:
Telephone 843-853-2070
Fax 843-853-0044
E-mail sales@arcadiapublishing.com
For customer service and orders:
Toll-Free 1-888-313-2665

Visit us on the Internet at www.arcadiapublishing.com

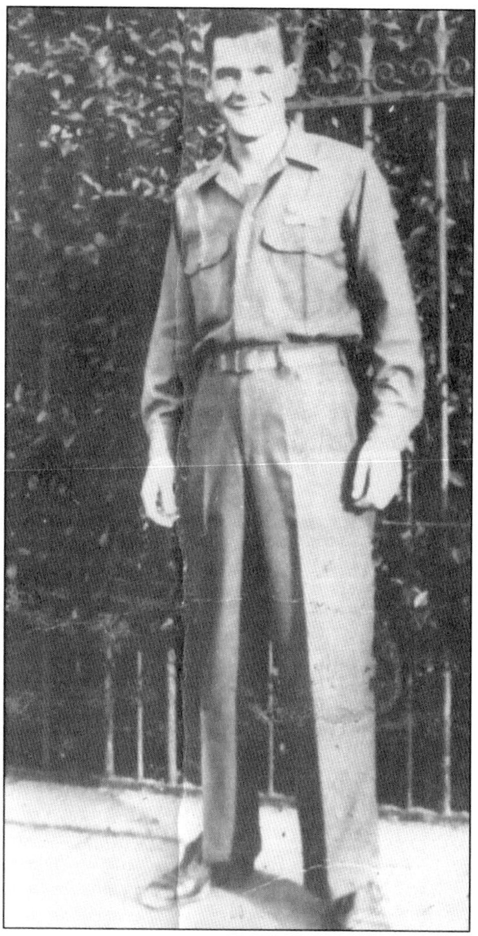

This book is dedicated to my grandfather Louis C. Wilson, a shining example of the "Greatest Generation." Pictured here in his World War II uniform, he took part in the invasion of Normandy and was awarded the Purple Heart. (Author's collection.)

CONTENTS

FOREWORD

No history of the Dracut community would be complete without mention of the Dracut Scholarship Foundation (DSF), a most successful local charity, which has awarded thousands of scholarships to deserving Dracut High School (DHS) graduates. At its inception, only 20 percent of DHS graduates, most raised in the homes of farmers or mill workers, went to college. As the town of Dracut has grown, the foundation has increased scholarship support to DHS graduates, 80 percent of whom now pursue further studies at various institutions of higher education.

The Dracut Scholarship Foundation was established over 50 years ago by a group of successful Dracut businessmen organized by Dr. Christos Daoulas, superintendent of schools. Established and chartered to provide scholarship assistance to outstanding graduating DHS scholars, the foundation has awarded over $2 million to deserving students. The first scholarships equaled tuition for one semester at Lowell State College. Today, over 25 DHS graduates receive scholarships ranging from $500 to $3,500.

In the early years of the foundation, members raised funds by going door to door in the community and from business donations. In addition, some scholarships were funded from interest earned in established trusts and memorial funds. In the 1980s, the scholarship's board of directors established two major fundraisers: the annual Fall Craft Fair and the DSF "four nights in March" telethon, which is broadcast on local television. Both of these events, especially the telethon, are unique and popular fabrics of life in Dracut. Endowed funds, combined with the proceeds from the craft fair—featuring more than 100 crafters—and the telethon, allow the foundation to award approximately $100,000 annually to deserving DHS graduates. The author's proceeds from the sale of this book will go to the Louis C. Wilson Memorial Fund, which is endowed with the Dracut Scholarship Foundation.

—Bruce Hutchins

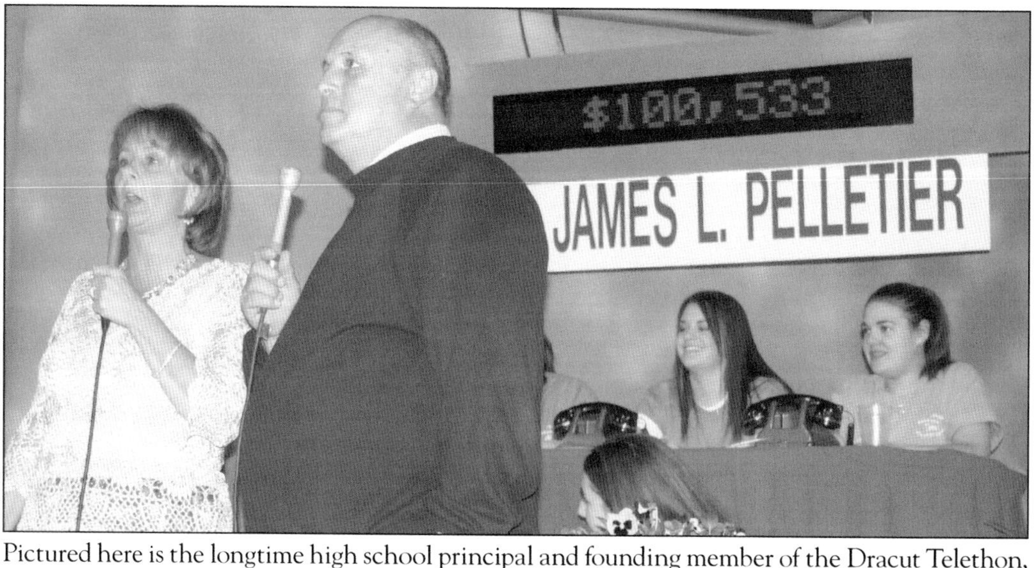

Pictured here is the longtime high school principal and founding member of the Dracut Telethon, Bruce Hutchins, with former DSF president Darlene Ducharme at the 2006 Dracut Telethon. Hutchins is now retired and is a director emeritus for the Dracut Scholarship Foundation. (Courtesy Gary Meuse.)

Acknowledgments

Since I first began teaching in Dracut eight years ago, I have had the pleasure of meeting many people who have been willing to share with me their knowledge of Dracut's history. Bud Paquin was among the first to introduce me to this rich history. I will always remember the first time he brought me out to the Claypit Cemetery behind the Brunswick Bowling Alley to show me the town's first burying ground. He was also kind enough to visit my class one day and do a presentation on Dracut's old homes. It was these early lessons on Dracut that spurred my interest in learning more about the town of which I was now a part.

When I took on this project, numerous people supported me to make this a successful endeavor. One of the first to share his father's collection of photographs and postcards was William Dumont. Eleanor Duda, no relation, of Peperrell, contacted me with photographs she had from her childhood in Dracut. Paul and Bonnie Elie also provided photographs from their family collection, and Warren Shaw allowed me access to the photographs at Shaw Farm. Ken and Rhonda Wojtas provided me with information related to the Dracut Fire Department and the history of Firefighter's Day. Of course, the Dracut Historical Society is owed a tremendous debt of gratitude for allowing me access to their collections throughout the summer. Norma Taplin and Harvey Gagnon were invaluable, helping to explain the history behind many of the photographs. Unless otherwise noted, the images in this book are from the Dracut Historical Society's collection.

I also wish to especially thank Brian Duff for his countless hours of technical help with the scanning and cropping of virtually all of the photographs. There would be no book without him, and I cannot fully express my gratitude for his help and patience. Marietta Paquette and her brother Frank Gorman were very helpful with providing me information about Veterans' Memorial Park and Beaver Brook Village. Mrs. Paquette saved me countless research hours. Lastly, a thank-you is owed to Dr. Michael McNamara for proofreading the manuscript and offering many helpful critiques.

Introduction

Dracut was officially incorporated as a town in 1701, but settlers were here much earlier. The town's first settler was John Evered Webb, who purchased land on the northern side of the Merrimack River from Jonathan Tyng but did not attempt to establish a permanent settlement. He built a home on what is now Old Ferry Road but returned to Boston. His widow sold his land to Samuel Varnum and Edward Colburn, both of Ipswich. They began a permanent settlement in the 1670s, and by 1701 Dracut was officially incorporated as a township by the Massachusetts General Court. The Varnums and Colburns built their town on the frontier, and the settlers encountered fighting during King Phillip's War in 1675–1676, building a garrison house for protection. It stood on what is now Riverside Street in Lowell until it was torn down in 1887. A replica of the garrison is featured at the Dracut Historical Society.

It did not take long for Dracut to establish its place in the history books. The town sent a third of its population to fight during the American Revolution, and numerous Dracut residents distinguished themselves with their service. Among them were Joseph Bradley Varnum, who fought at Lexington and Concord and later served as the Speaker of the House of Representatives; African Americans Barzillai Lew, who fought at Bunker Hill, and Tony Clark, who fought at the Battles of Monmouth and Saratoga; Moses B. Coburn, who was injured during the Battle of White Plains; and Col. Louis Ansart, a French nobleman who helped improve American artillery and after the war renounced his French title and settled in Dracut. Ansart died in 1804 and is buried in Woodbine Cemetery. His house still stands on Varnum Avenue in Lowell.

Dracut residents returned to their farming lives after the American Revolution, and the town's population gradually grew. In 1790, there were 1,217 residents; in 1820, there were 1,407 residents; and by the outbreak of the Civil War in 1861, Dracut's population was 1,881. The Civil War gave Dracut another opportunity to fight on behalf of the country, and many Dracut residents enlisted. Most notable among the enlisted was Moses Greeley Parker, a Dracut native who enlisted as an Army doctor in 1864 after graduating from Harvard Medical School. During the war, he helped supervise the construction of an Army hospital. Today, he is best remembered for creating the Parker lecture series and the Dracut Public Library, which is named in his honor. With the end of the Civil War, Dracut residents began to see their farming community industrialize. In 1862, construction on the Merrimac Woolen Mills in the Navy Yard District began. The Merrimac Woolen Mills were so successful that they had an exhibition at the 1893 world's fair in Chicago. In 1886, Michael Collins built the Collinsville Mills, which are known today as the Beaver Brook Mills. At its peak, Collinsville Mills employed 260 mill workers and produced approximately 230,000 yards of cloth annually. Today, the Beaver Brook Mills are home to local businesses, restaurants, and apartments. The homes along Mill Street were originally built for the workers in Collins's mills.

Even with industrialization, Dracut retained its farming roots. There were still numerous farms in the town as the 20th century approached, including the Richardson farm, the Curtis farm, the Wiggin farm, the Willet farm, and the Little farm. Today, few of these farms remain, but Shaw Farm, established in 1908, recently celebrated its centennial and is still very successful, continuing to offer home delivery. However, when the people of Dracut were not working their farms or in their mills, they had the premier regional resort destination on the shore of Lake Mascuppic—Lakeview Park, established in 1889. The Willow Dale Park on Lake Mascuppic already existed at the time, but the Lowell and Suburban Trolley Company wanted to attract more riders. Building a second resort on the lake would help achieve that. Lakeview Park had an ideal location, with trolley connections extending as far south as Boston and as far north as Nashua. The park proved to be a very popular destination and in 1893, a theater was built at Lakeview, followed by other attractions, including swimming, boating, bowling, restaurants, and a dance hall. The dance hall burned in 1928, but owner Harry Kitteridge replaced it. A large new roller coaster was built as well. In 1935, the last streetcar ran from Lowell to Lakeview, marking the end of an era. Gradually, Lakeview Park received fewer and fewer visitors and eventually closed in the 1970s. The famous carousel has been preserved and is still in operation in New York. The history of the famous park has also been preserved at the Dracut Historical Society. There is an entire room dedicated to Lakeview Park at the town's museum. As the 20th century progressed, other recreational areas appeared in Dracut. In the 1930s, Belle Grove provided picnic areas as well as boating and swimming along the Merrimack River. The Dracut Speedway was established just after World War II and remained a popular spot until it was finally closed in the 1950s.

As the town grew, so did the need for an expanded school department. The town had several one-room schoolhouses. The Collinsville Grammar School, built in 1891, received honorable mention at the 1893 world's fair as an "ideal country school and grounds." Students who continued with their secondary education were sent to Lowell High School until 1936, when Dracut High School was established. Today's Greenmont Elementary School was the home to Dracut's first high school. Dracut takes great pride in its school department, and the 20th century has seen some remarkable accomplishments in the town's schools. The longest-serving superintendent in Massachusetts was Dracut's Dr. Christos Daoulos, who served as superintendent from 1962 until his retirement in 1998. The town honored him for his remarkable service to the town's schools in 2005, dedicating the school complex on Lakeview Avenue as "The Dr. Christos Daoulos Education Complex." In addition to having an icon heading the schools, Dracut established something unique to the town to help students who wished to continue their education after graduation: the Dracut Scholarship Foundation. In 1957, the first two scholarships were awarded to graduating students to help with college expenses, amounting to $350. The foundation was incorporated in 1959 and, since then, has awarded $1.3 million to 1,304 graduates. The foundation is run by a board of 29 volunteers. The highlight of the year's fundraising is the annual telethon, which began in 1984. The first telethon was produced by longtime Dracut High School principal Bruce Hutchins, with the help of board members and students. One of those students, Gary Meuse, now serves on the current board of directors for the scholarship foundation. The 2011 telethon raised a record-setting $120,391 for the foundation. The continued success of the telethon and the Dracut Scholarship Foundation is a true testament to the strong commitment the town has for its schools. Support for the schools continued under Dr. Daoulas's successor, Elaine Espindle. Under her leadership, the town voted to build Lakeview Junior High School, named for the town's famous lakeside resort, which opened in September 2001.

In addition to supporting academics, Dracut has a storied sports history and is best known for its football program. Legendary coach Ed Murphy headed the football program from 1946 to 1992. Coach Murphy was a 1937 graduate of Lowell High School and graduated from Holy Cross. Before coming to Dracut, Coach Murphy served in the Marine Corps during World War II. In 1946, he became the head football coach and won the Division II Super Bowl against Beverly in 1988. Dracut again won the Super Bowl in 2008. The current head football coach, Jason Houston, is continuing the tradition of having an outstanding football program. Dracut has had numerous other sports teams earn recognition; more and more students participate in the sports programs offered at Dracut High each year.

Dracut played a major role in the American Revolution, and its citizens continued to serve their country as the nation engaged in other conflicts. The residents who served have been remembered by Dracut with memorials throughout the town. In the 1920s, a monument was erected in Hovey Square to honor those who served during World War I, and the residents of Collinsville created an honor roll during World War II for their loved ones while they were fighting in Europe and in the Pacific. Later, that honor roll was taken down and replaced with a memorial at the high school to honor all Dracut servicemen and women. During the Vietnam War, Dracut lost Michael Monahan, and the town remembered him by naming Monahan Park on Pleasant Street after his sacrifice for the nation. Most recently, Dracut lost Capt. John Ogonowski during the attacks on the World Trade Center on September 11, 2001. Two memorials have been erected at the intersection of Broadway and Jones Avenues, across from his parent's farm, in his honor.

Throughout its history, the people of Dracut have been characterized by a commitment to their community and to their country. The town has evolved from a small farming hamlet on the edge of the New England wilderness to a New England mill town and now to a thriving town of 30,000. Dracut's past accomplishments are simply a prelude to a future filled with unlimited possibilities.

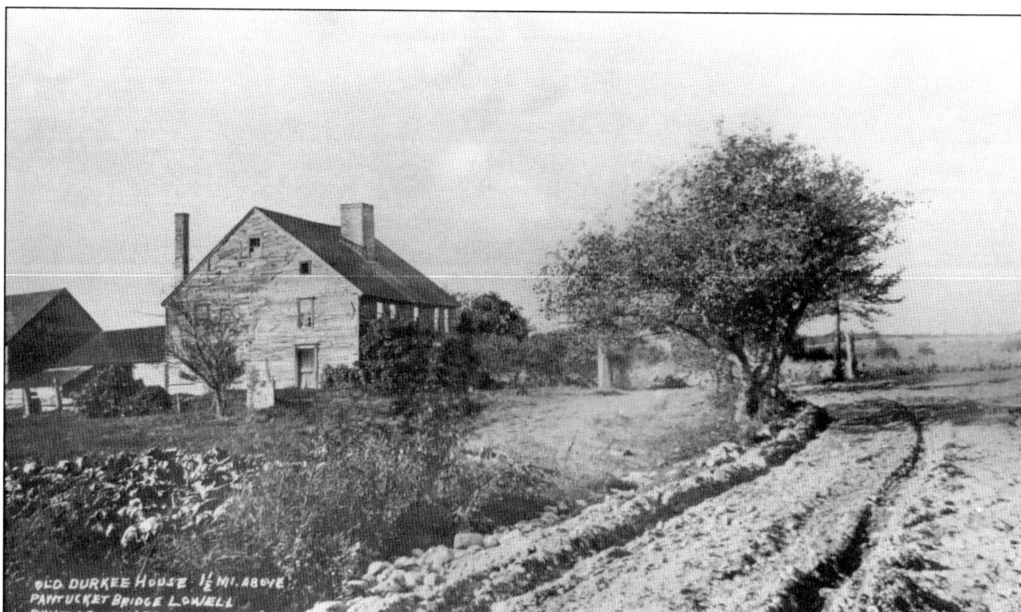

Dracut's first home, the Webb-Durkee House, was located on what is now known as Old Ferry Road. It was built by John Evered Webb, Dracut's first settler. Webb sold his land to Dracut's first permanent settler, Samuel Varnum of Ipswich, and Dracut was incorporated as a town in 1701. The house stood until the 1950s, when it was razed after suffering severe damage in a hurricane.

One

The Century Begins 1900–1930

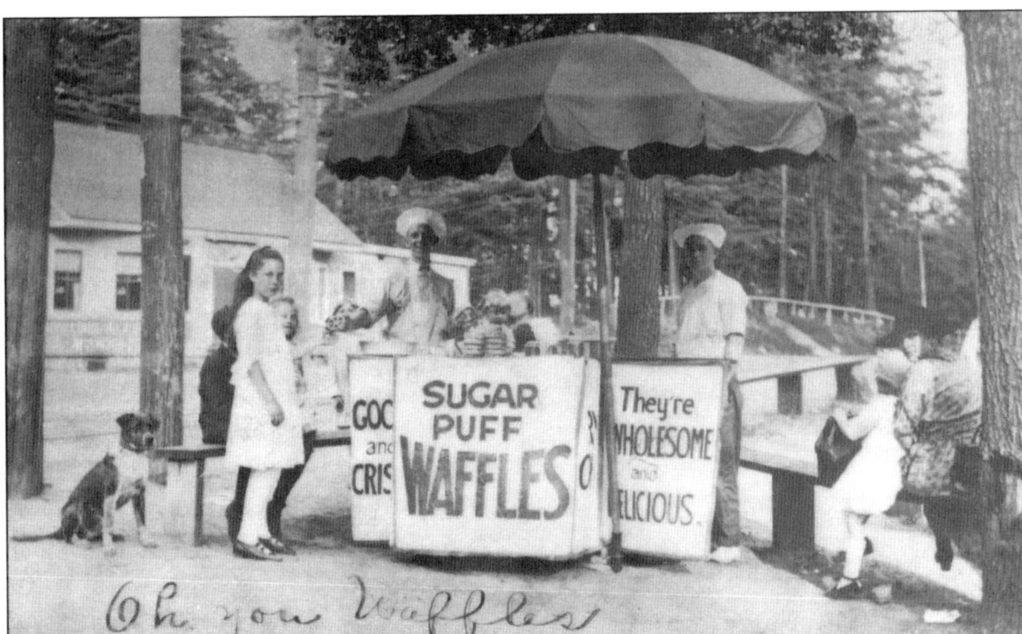

Lakeview Park was established on the shores of Lake Mascuppic in 1889. Visitors to the park had an array of activities in which to indulge. From swimming and dancing to riding the "flying horses," there was entertainment for all ages. Here, children enjoy homemade waffles, one of the popular treats served at Lakeview.

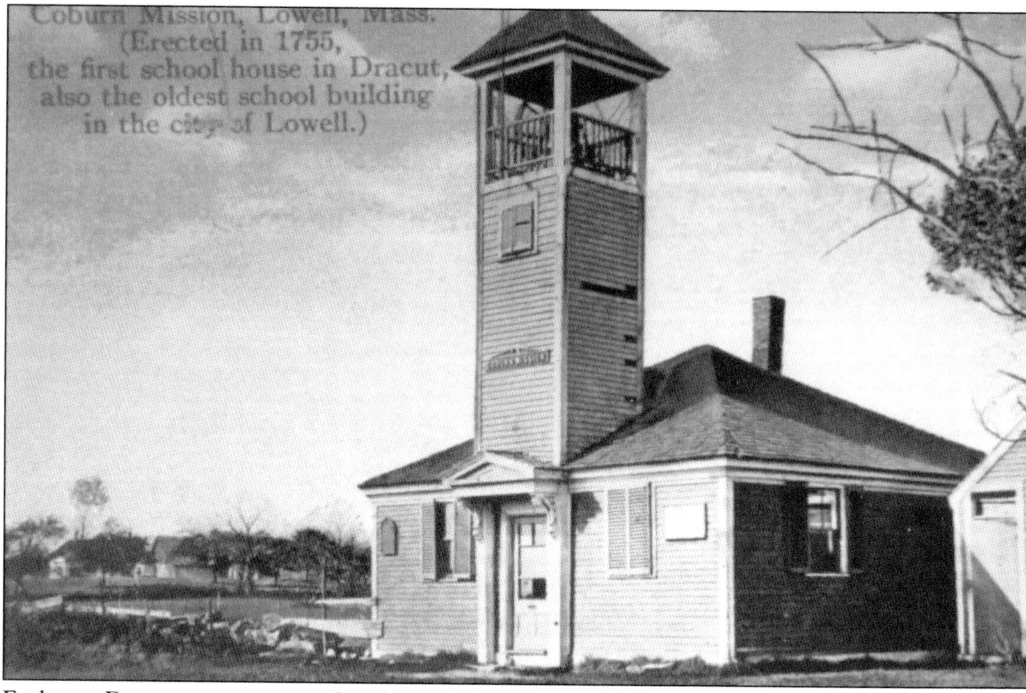

Early on, Dracut was concerned with ensuring education for the town's children. On October 1, 1736, the selectmen voted to hire Phineas Stevens of Andover to establish a school in Dracut to teach reading and writing. The first schoolhouse was erected in 1821 on land given to the town by Ephraim Coburn. Known as the Coburn Mission and located in what today is Pawtucketville, Lowell, it was torn down in 1965. Pawtucketville was annexed to Lowell in 1874.

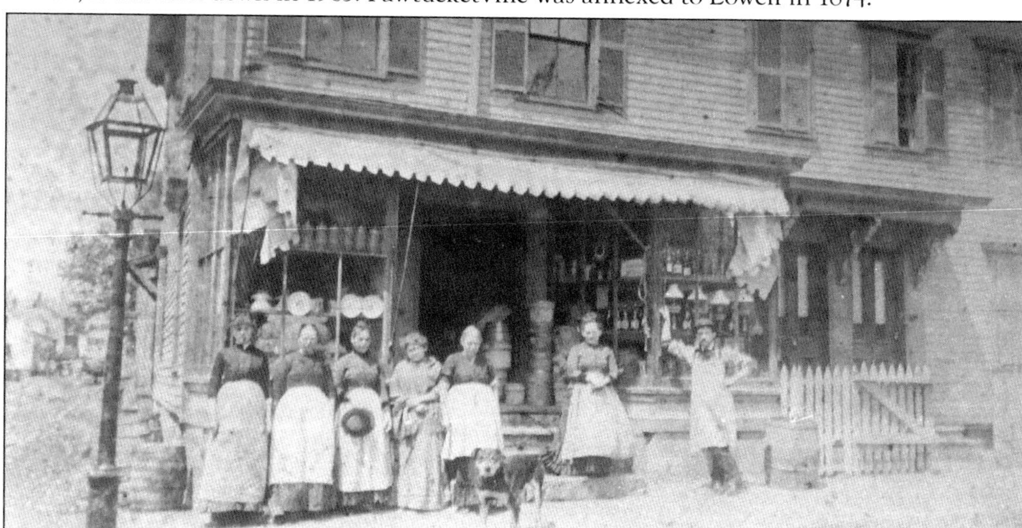

This c. 1875 photograph shows Cassidy's Store on Chapel Street in Lowell. Standing in front of the store are the grandparents of George Englesby, who was born on April 21, 1907, and became a very well-known educator in Dracut. He held various positions, including teacher, principal, assistant superintendent, and superintendent. The Dracut Junior High School was renamed the Englesby Junior High School in his honor in June 1972. The dedication committee was chaired by John Harvey. Today, grades five through six are housed at the school.

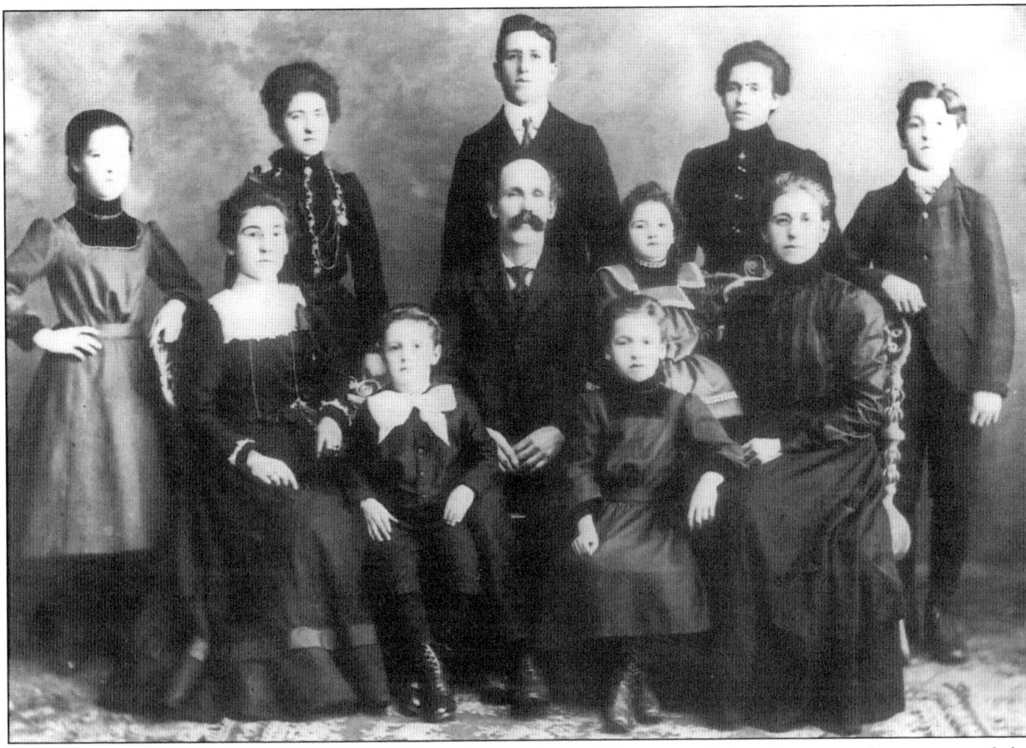

The family of Clovis and Elizabeth Elie is shown here. Their son John Elie was the owner of the Golden dairy farm at 68 Loon Hill Road before becoming an insurance salesman for Met Life. The Elie family included, from left to right, (first row) Henry and Bibianne; (second row) Agnes, Clovis, Cecile, and Elizabeth; (standing) Emma, Anna, Joseph, Mary, and John. (Courtesy Paul and Bonnie Elie.)

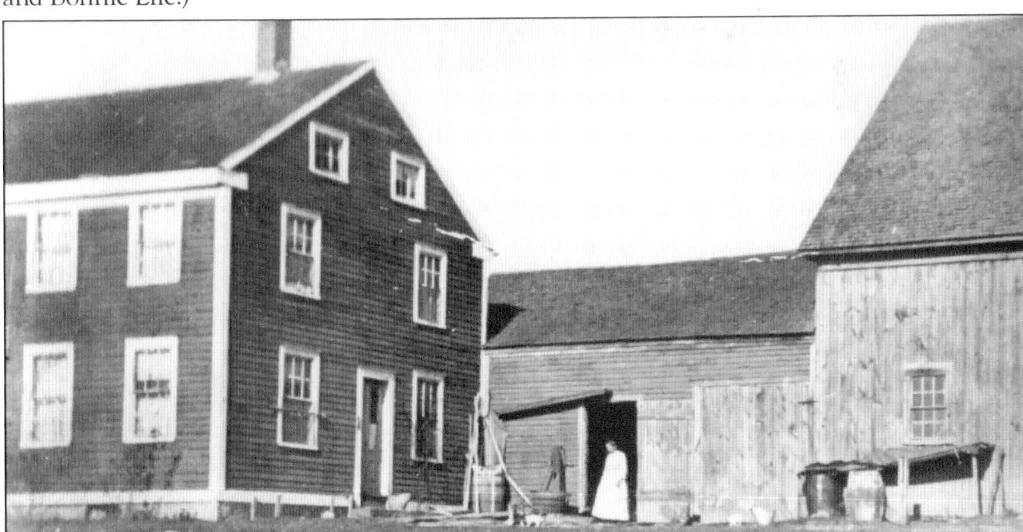

This house was built in 1726 by John East, who settled in Dracut to partner with Joseph Varnum in a nickel mine. The mine was located near the Methuen boundary and is today surrounded by the Brox Quarry. East sold his share of the mine but remained in Dracut. The house still stands on Pelham Road. (Courtesy Robert and Melanie Peach.)

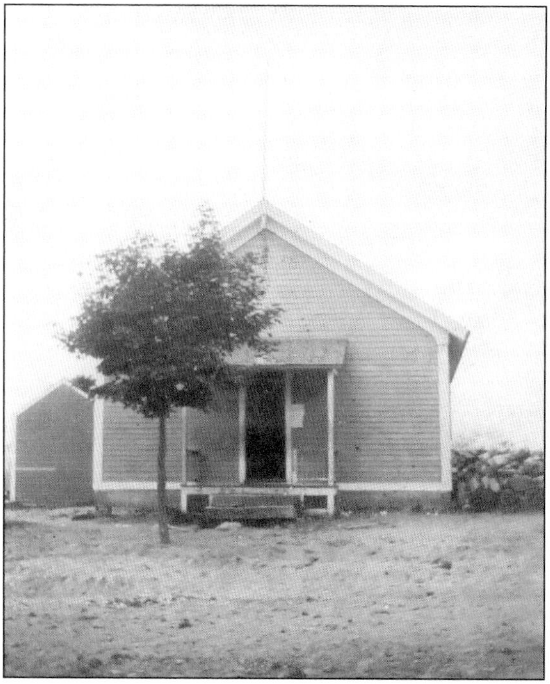

The East Dracut schoolhouse is seen here around 1900. By 1911, students could deposit money they had saved in savings accounts, which were in each school. They were given a deposit book in which to mark their deposits. By 1919, the town appropriated $31,800 annually to operate the town's schools. By 1922, Dracut had seven schools: Center School (today's Town Hall Annex), Collinsville (today used by the School Department as the district's central office), Parker Avenue, Kenwood, Goodhue (today the Goodhue Professional Building), East Dracut, and Broadway.

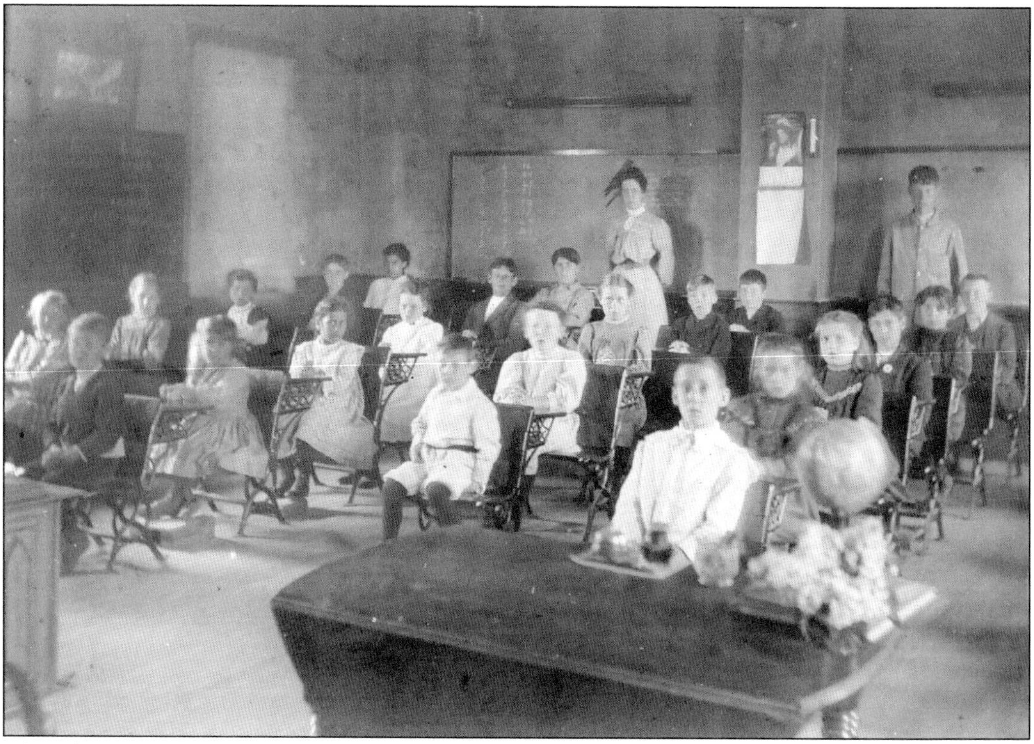

This photograph was taken in the early 1900s in the East Dracut schoolhouse. The system of administering the schools with a superintendent and a school committee was adopted by Dracut in 1881. The school department also employed a truant officer and a supervisor of music. Besides reading, writing, and arithmetic, basic trade skills were also taught.

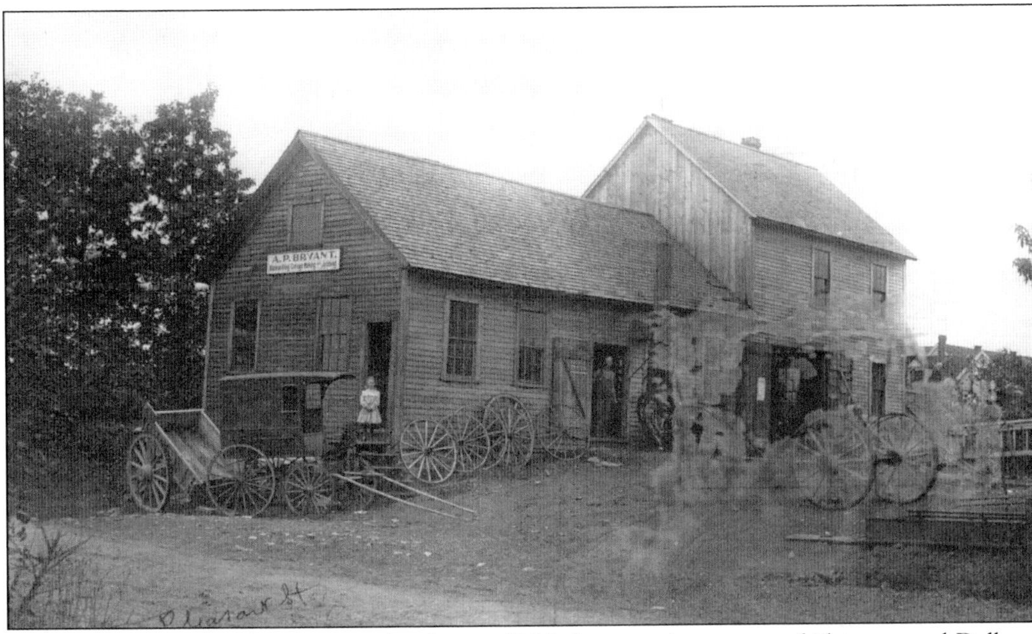

Few would recognize this scene today, but in 1904 this was the corner of Pleasant and Delbert Streets. Pleasant Street is the dirt road in the forefront. This wheelwright shop was owned by the father of Helen Hibbard, a longtime secretary for the school department. The wheelwright shop is gone, but the family's c. 1895 home is still located there. (Courtesy Willard Hibbard Jr.)

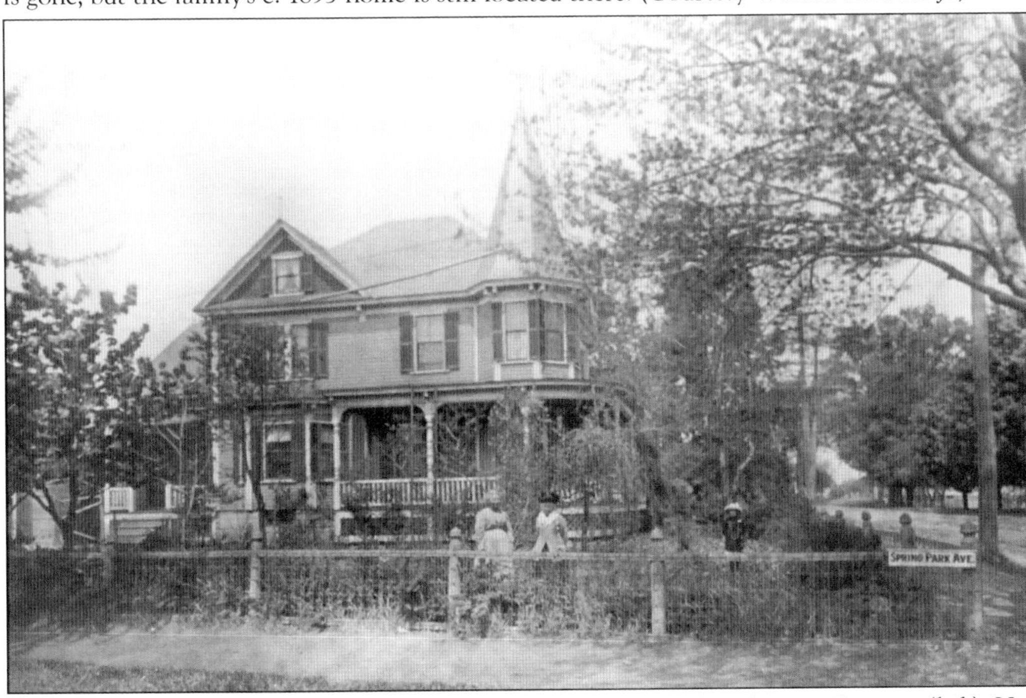

The Barnett home, seen here around 1905, was built in 1887 for Florence Barnett (left). Her brother George Barnett, a Civil War veteran, lived in the home after his sister. George Barnett's daughter Florence Atwell lived in the home until 1969. The home was torn down in 1971 and is currently a convenience store.

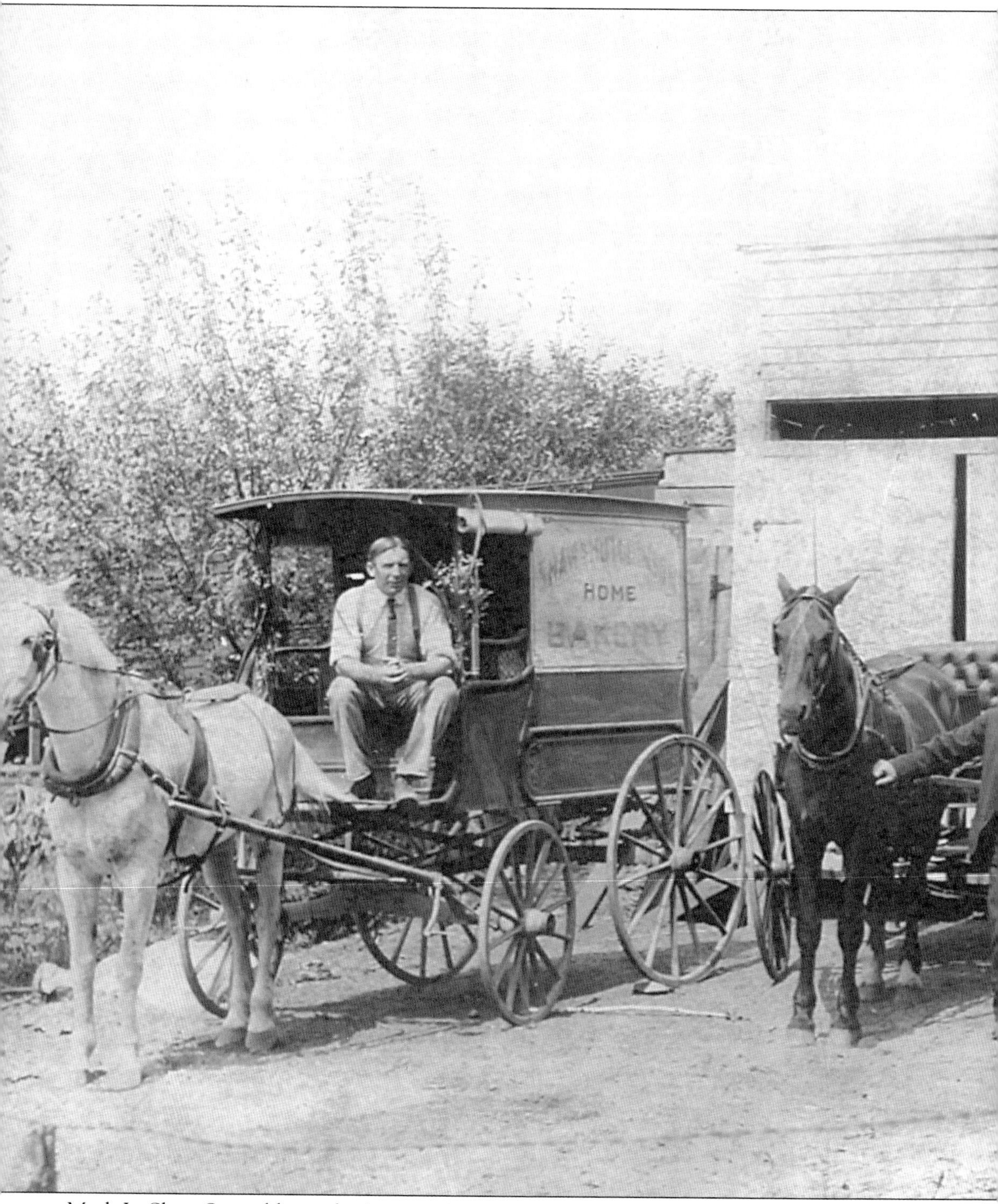

Mark L. Shaw Sr. and his wife, Annie, of Nova Scotia, were married on November 27, 1889, after which they ran the Shaw-Hutchinson Bakery seen here. They had three children: Mark L. Shaw Jr., Albert, and Gladys. In 1908, they purchased a plot of land at 195 New Boston Road and built a house, barn, and milk house, establishing Shaw Dairy Farm. In 1912, their son Mark

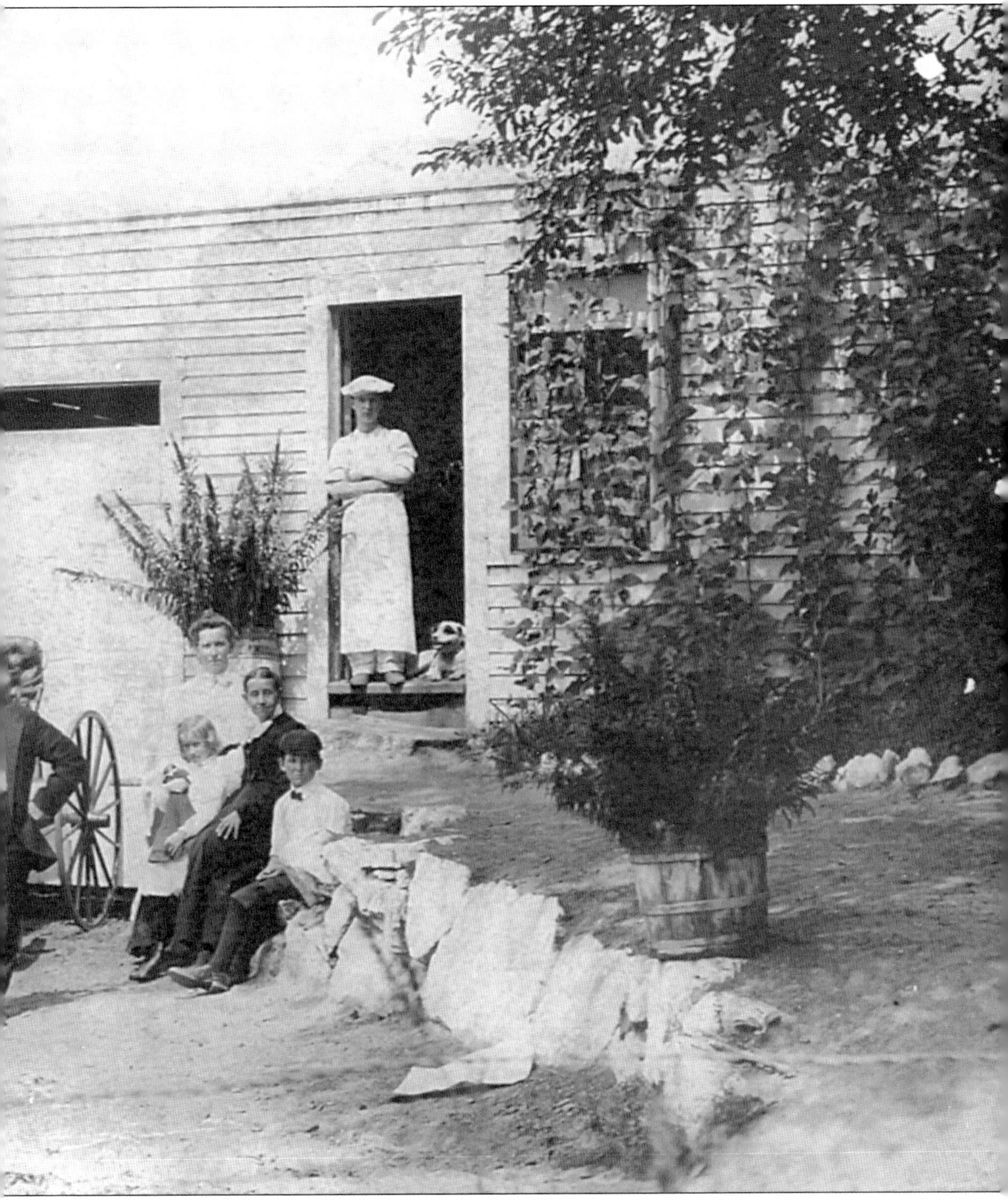

Jr. began working at the Oliver J. Coburn Farm delivering milk. The Coburn farm was located where the Dracut Historical Society is today. When the Coburn farm went out of business, Shaw Jr. had the opportunity to retain the home delivery customers he had served while working for Coburn. (Courtesy Warren Shaw.)

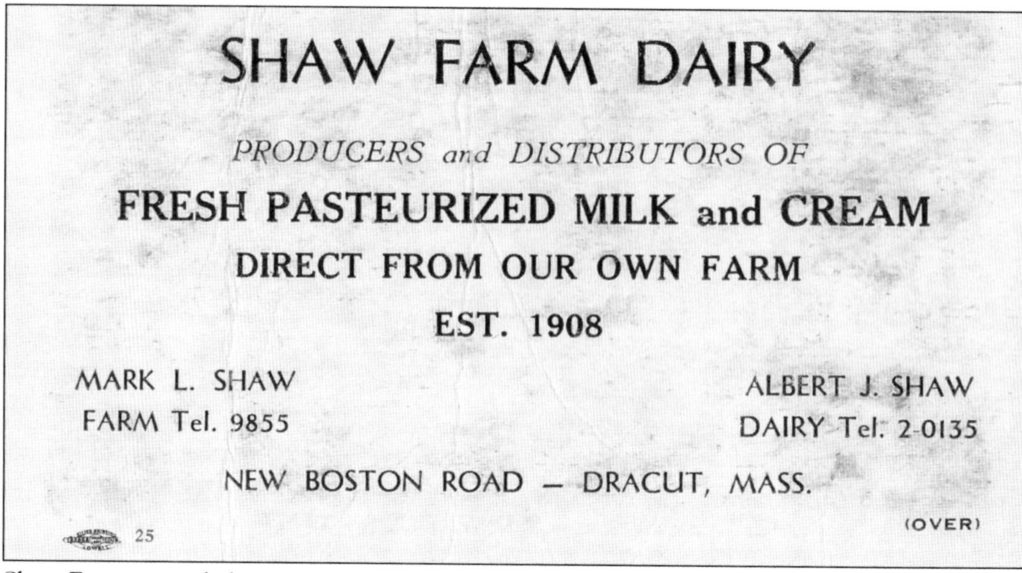

Shaw Farm expanded its operations in 1917 when Mark L. Shaw Jr. had a bottling facility built after enlarging the farm's customer base with the closing of the Coburn farm. Shaw delivered milk to his customers with his trusted horse, Prince, until 1927, when the horse was retired and home delivery was done by truck.

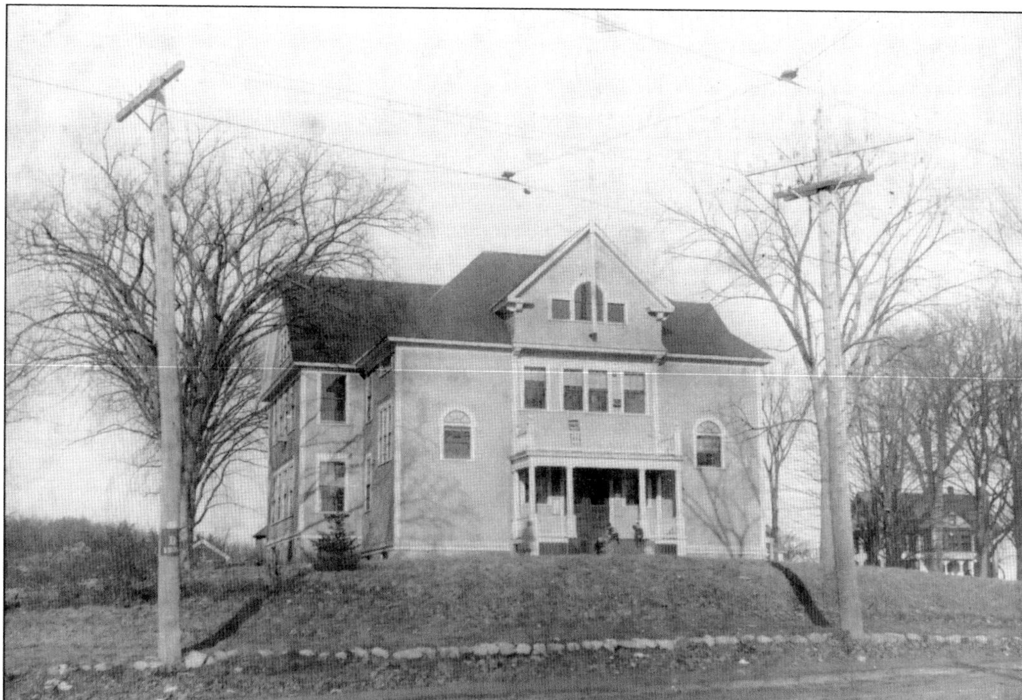

The Collinsville Grammar School was built in 1891. It received honorable mention at the 1893 world's fair in Chicago for being "an ideal country school and grounds." It was closed in 1981, but is still used by the school department for the district's central administration. It is now known as the Arthur Eldridge Administration Building, after the long-serving school committee board member.

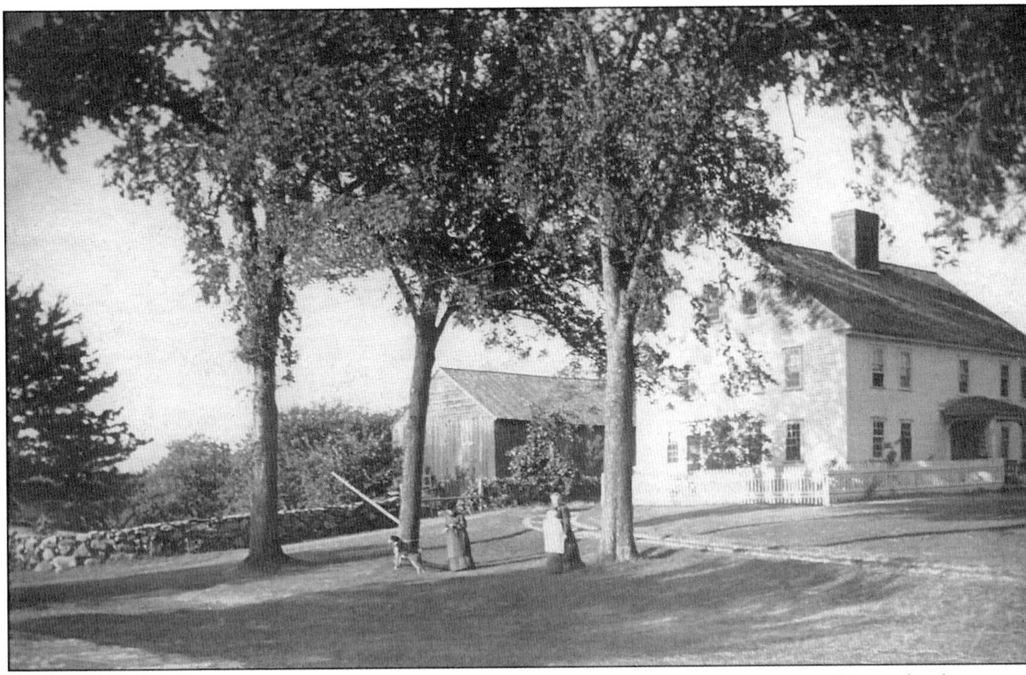

The Abbott House was located about a quarter mile north of Hovey Square. It was built around 1757 by John Bowers. Daniel Abbott bought the home around 1792. The property remained in the Abbott family until 1916, when Daniel Abbott's granddaughter Lucelia Abbott Willoughby passed away. This photograph was taken in 1912.

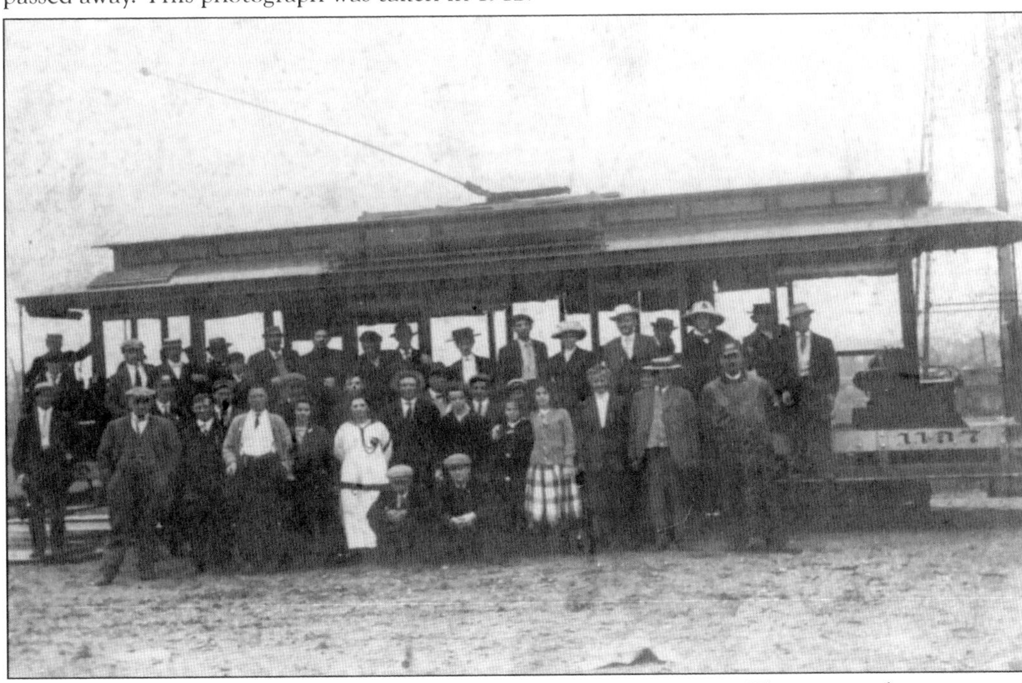

In 1906, Daniel Fox headed a deep-fishing expedition to Swampscott. The trip was by an open-air trolley, the first of which was built in 1889. Fox lived on Marsh Hill Road, and his family was one of the first to settle in Dracut.

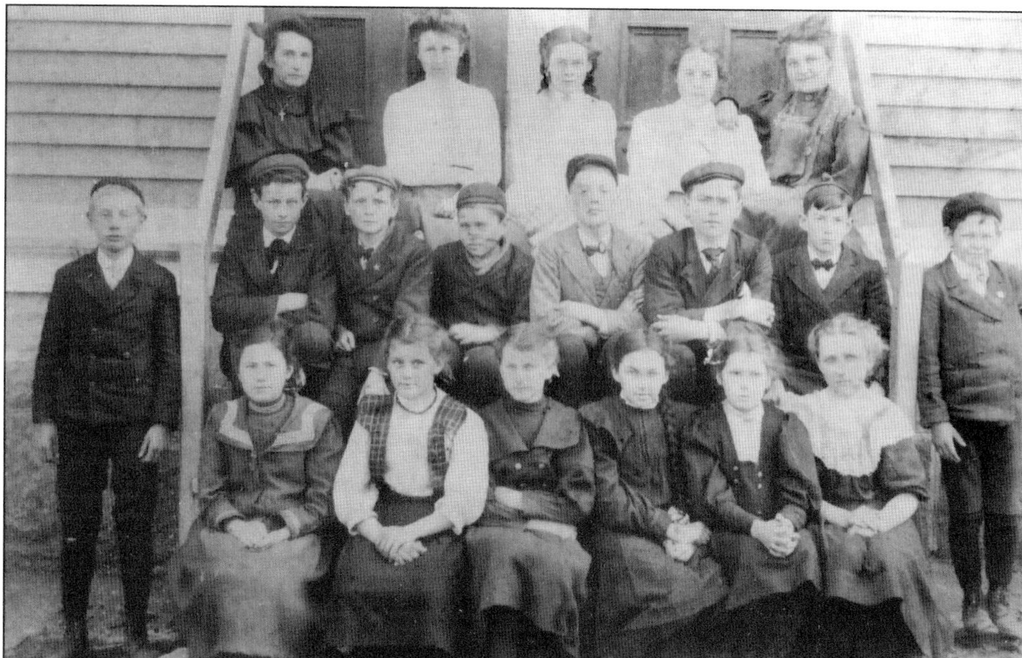

A Collinsville School class poses on the steps in the 1890s. In 1874, when Pawtuckerville was annexed to Lowell, Collinsville became school district two, and it was eventually named district three. The original Collinsville School was built on land from the George Brown farm, originally the Augustus Coburn Farm.

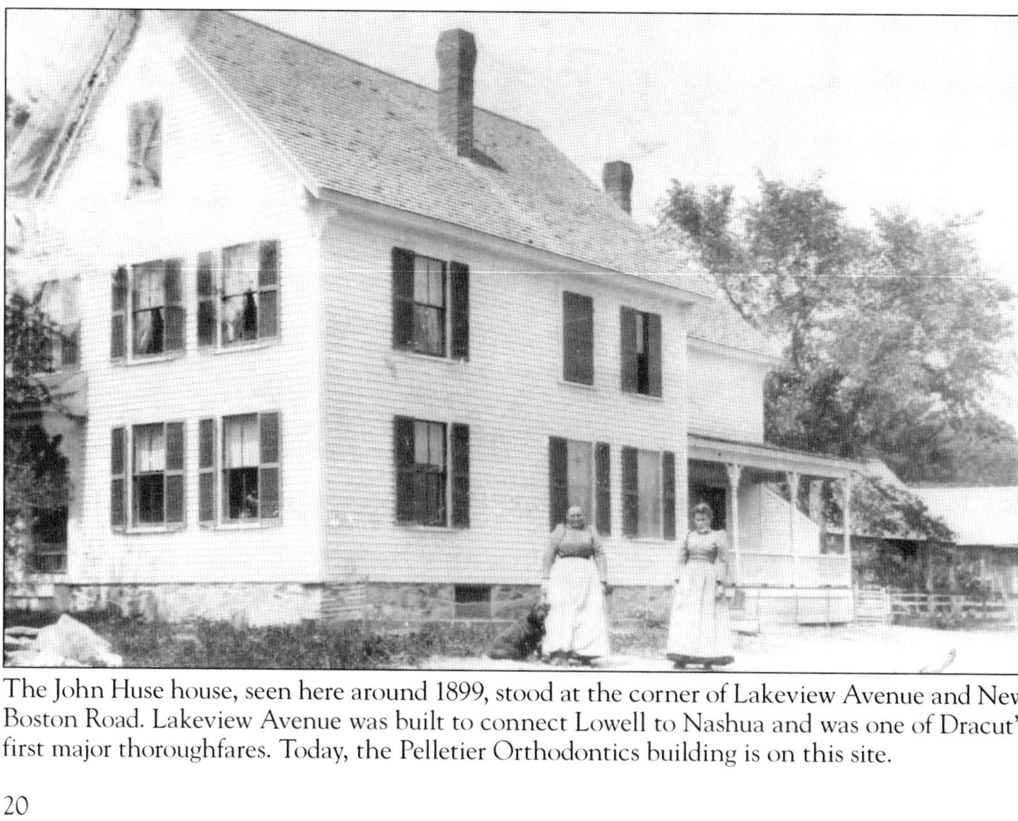

The John Huse house, seen here around 1899, stood at the corner of Lakeview Avenue and New Boston Road. Lakeview Avenue was built to connect Lowell to Nashua and was one of Dracut's first major thoroughfares. Today, the Pelletier Orthodontics building is on this site.

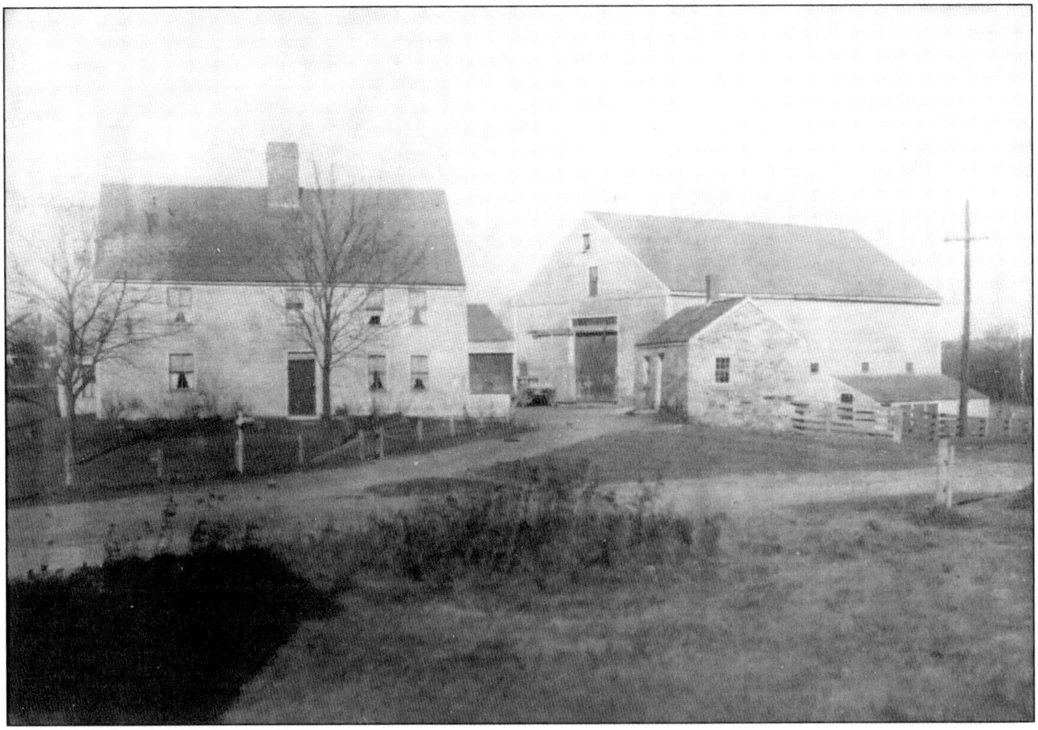

This photograph shows the town farm, which included the town jail—the small stone building. The town farm was used for orphans, indigent, or ill town residents. It was located at the end of Arlington Avenue. One of the more notable Dracut residents to live at the town farm was Sarah Lew, the daughter-in-law of Barzillai Lew, who was listed as a resident of the town farm on the 1860 census. She died on December 30, 1863, at the age of 103.

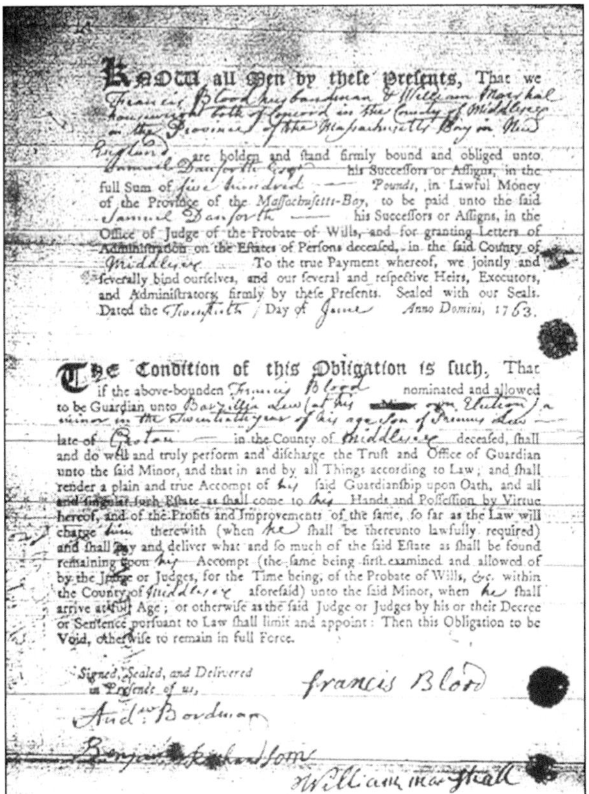

KNOW all Men by these Presents, That we Francis Blood husbandman & William Marshal housewright both of Concord in the County of Middlesex in the Province of the Massachusetts Bay in New England are holden and stand firmly bound and obliged unto Samuel Danforth Esqr his Successors or Assigns, in the full Sum of five hundred Pounds, in Lawful Money of the Province of the Massachusetts-Bay, to be paid unto the said Samuel Danforth his Successors or Assigns, in the Office of Judge of the Probate of Wills, and for granting Letters of Administration on the Estates of Persons deceased, in the said County of Middlesex To the true Payment whereof, we jointly and severally bind ourselves, and our several and respective Heirs, Executors, and Administrators, firmly by these Presents. Sealed with our Seals. Dated the Twentieth Day of June Anno Domini, 1763.

THE Condition of this Obligation is such, That if the above-bounden Francis Blood nominated and allowed to be Guardian unto Barzillai Lew (at his own Election) a minor in the twentieth year of his age son of Primus Lew late of Groton in the County of Middlesex deceased, shall and do well and truly perform and discharge the Trust and Office of Guardian unto the said Minor, and that in and by all Things according to Law; and shall render a plain and true Accompt of his said Guardianship upon Oath, and all and singular such Estate as shall come to his Hands and Possession by Virtue hereof, and of the Profits and Improvements of the same, so far as the Law will charge him therewith (when he shall be thereunto lawfully required) and shall pay and deliver what and so much of the said Estate as shall be found remaining upon his Accompt (the same being first examined and allowed of by the Judge or Judges, for the Time being, of the Probate of Wills, &c. within the County of Middlesex aforesaid) unto the said Minor, when he shall arrive at full Age; or otherwise as the said Judge or Judges by his or their Decree or Sentence pursuant to Law shall limit and appoint: Then this Obligation to be Void, otherwise to remain in full Force.

Signed, Sealed, and Delivered in Presence of us,

Andw Bordman

Benjamin Richardson

Francis Blood

William Marshall

Barzillai Lew was born on November 11, 1743, in Groton. His parents both passed away before he was 18, and this guardianship paper placed him in the care of Francis Blood. After serving in the Revolutionary War, he settled in Dracut. The Lew's farm was located on what was referred to as Zeal Road and is now Totman Road. He is buried in Claypit Cemetery.

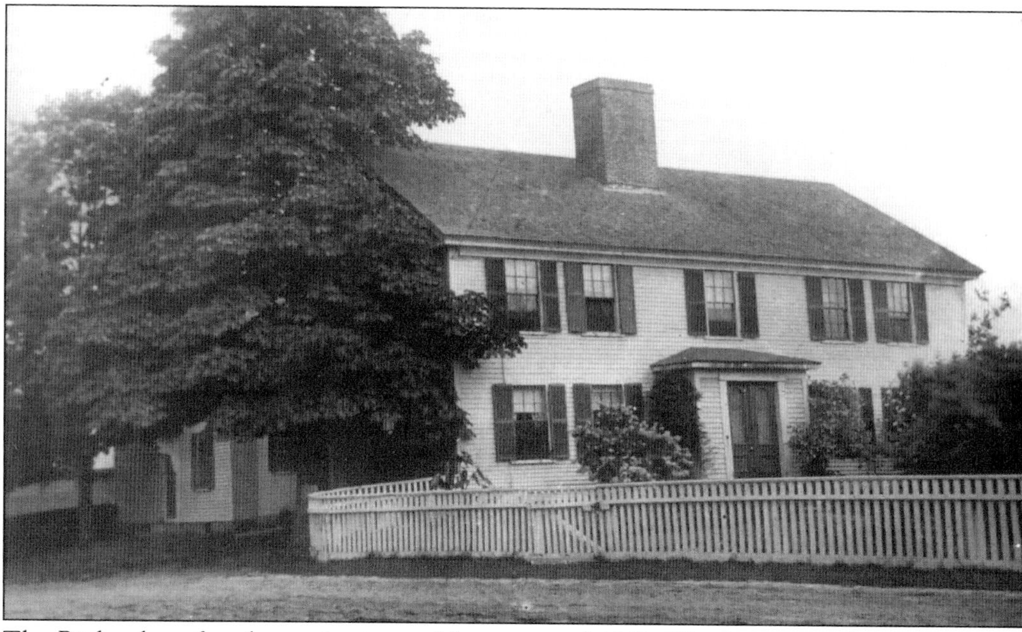

The Richardson farmhouse is pictured here around 1883. The house was built in 1736 by Abraham Varnum and was bought by Justus Richardson in 1841. The Richardsons enlarged their farm by purchasing the Oliver Coburn Farm, today the Dracut Historical Society. In 1945, they rented land along Lakeview Avenue for the Richardson Airport, now the Dr. Christos Daoulas Education Complex.

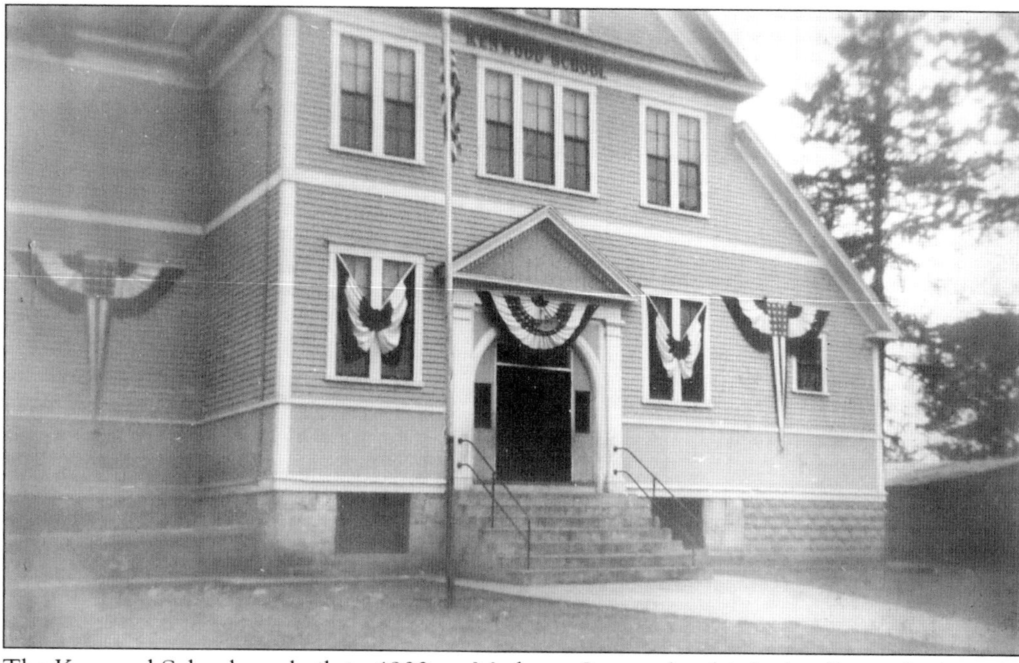

The Kenwood School was built in 1900 on Methuen Street, the third schoolhouse built in the Kenwood area. It was used as a school until 1974, when the Joseph Campbell School was built. The Kenwood School building was used as the offices for the special education department until it was closed in 1981.

Young Raymond Brown, his grandmother, and the dog are seen here outside their home on Pleasant Street in about 1910. (Courtesy Eleanor Duda.)

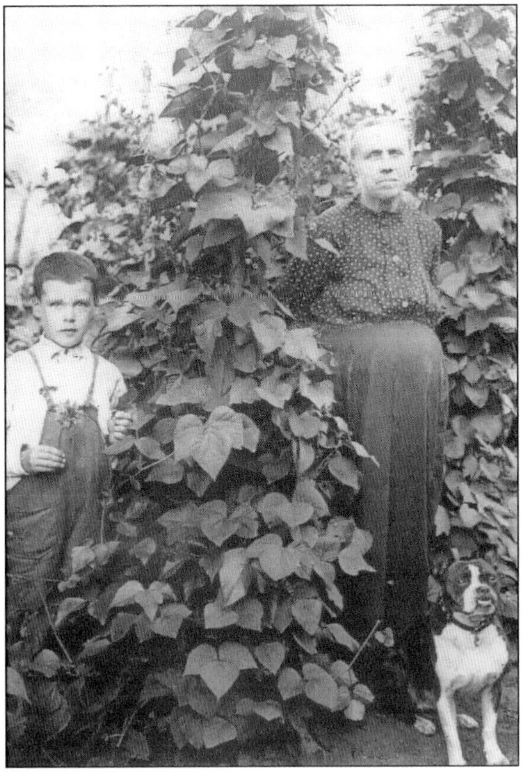

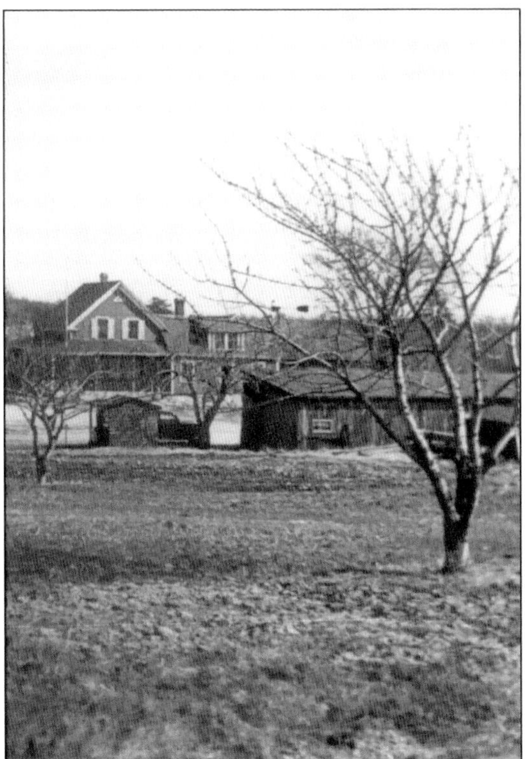

The Chrystinia farm was located in East Dracut. It was located across from where the Centerville Sportsman Club on Wheeler Road is today. The CSC Building was once a schoolhouse and was used by East Dracut students until 1902. Students from East Dracut were then sent to Dracut Center School. The farm was owned by the grandparents of Eleanor Duda, who was born in Dracut in 1933 and is no relation to the author. (Courtesy Eleanor Duda.)

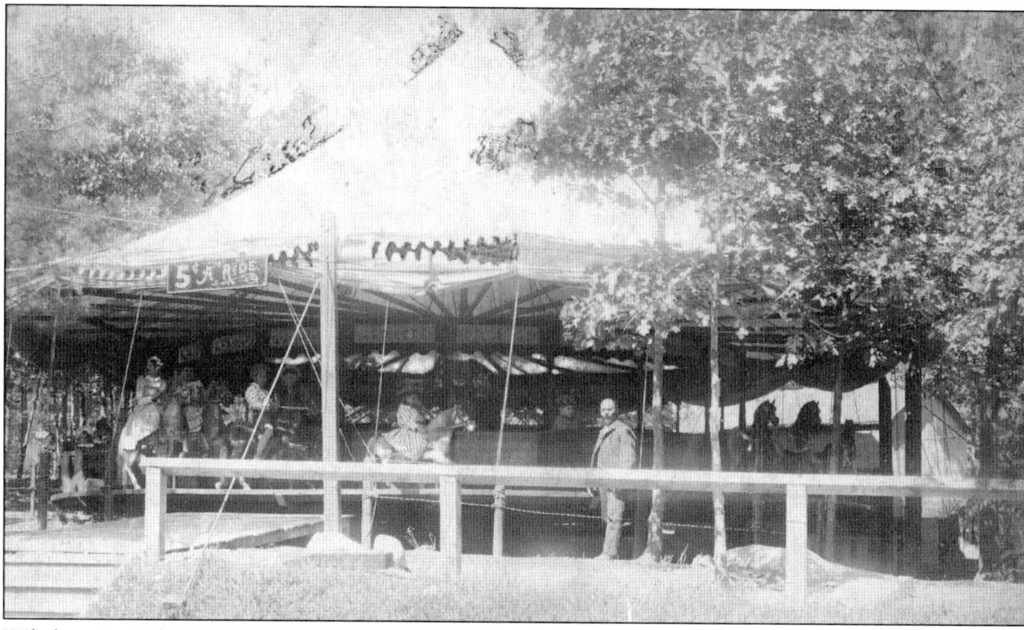

While not working on their farms or in the mills, Dracut residents had the opportunity to spend their weekends and other free time on Lake Mascuppic at Lakeview Park. The recreational spot was established in 1889 by the Lowell and Suburban Trolley Company. One of the main attractions at Lakeview was the merry-go-round, shown here in 1889. The "Flying Horses" were operated by Louis Bopp and were brought to Lakeview from Germany for the park's opening.

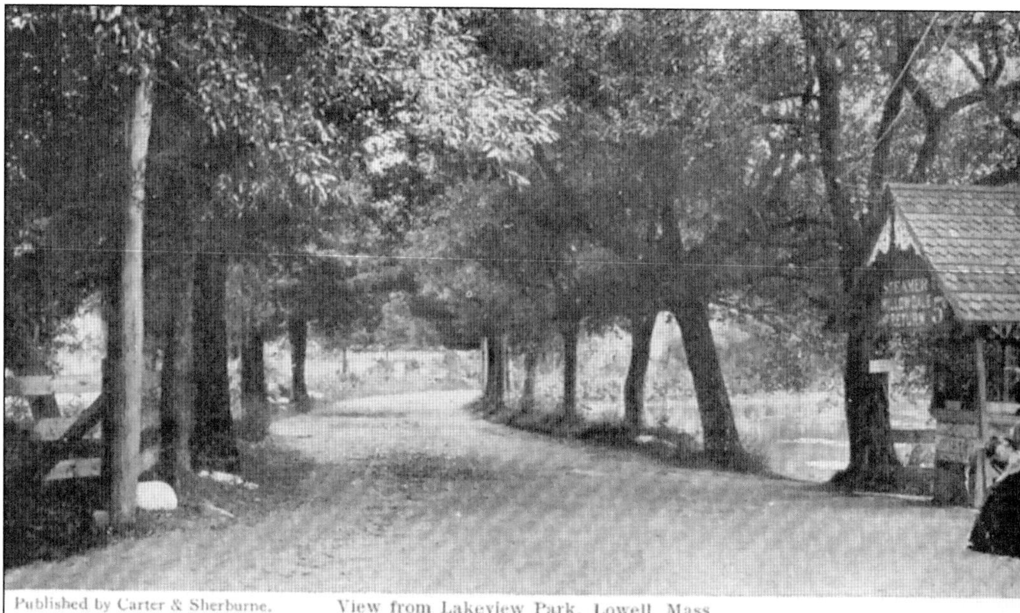

This postcard shows the picturesque entrance to Lakeview. On the right is the pier, from which passengers could take a ride on the Willow Dale Steamer around Lake Mascuppic for only 5¢. Willow Dale Park was established before Lakeview Park was built in 1899. (Courtesy Paul Dumont family.)

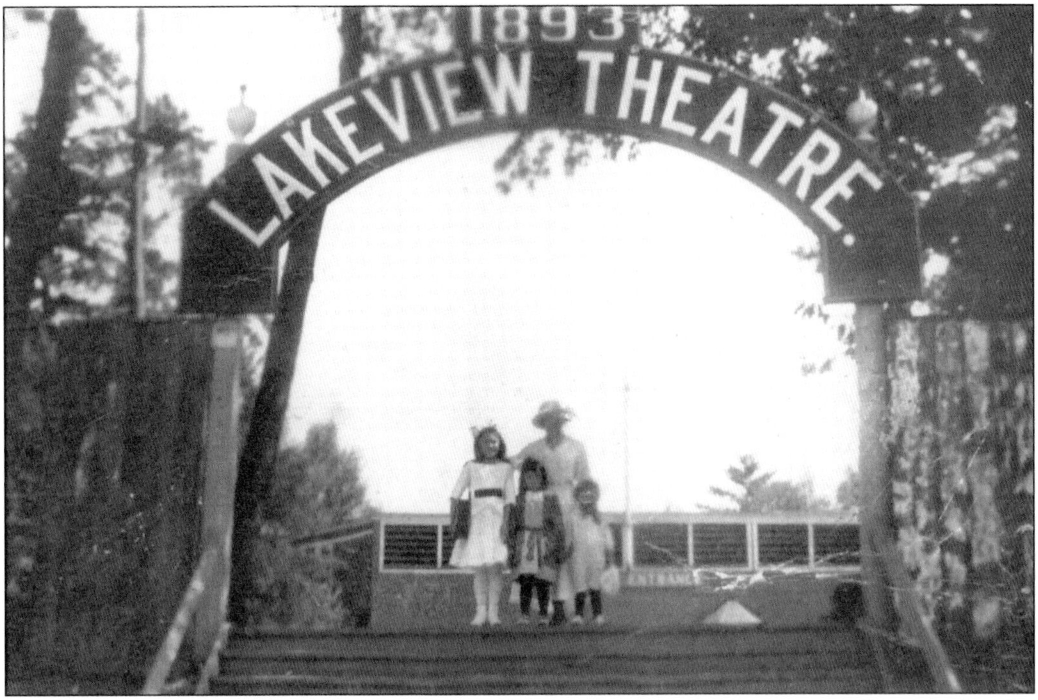

One of the many attractions at Lakeview was a summer theater. Here, in July 1919, Cecilia Gamache and her three children, from left to right, Loretta, Edna, and Arthur, pose on the steps. For a time, visitors to Lakeview who wanted to attend a Catholic Mass had to attend services at St. Mary's of the Assumption in Collinsville. But in 1918, the theater at Lakeview started being used for services.

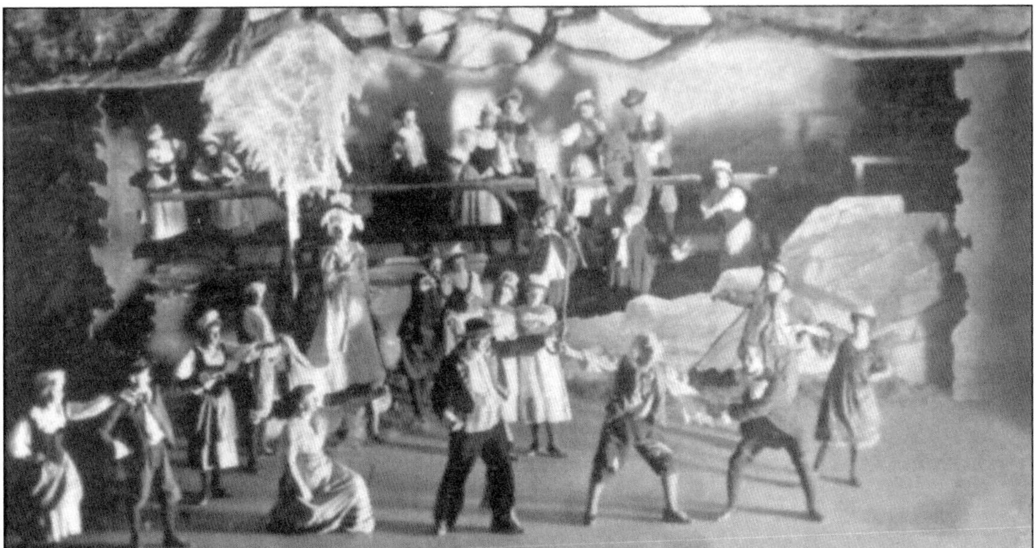

The Lakeview Theatre opened on July 1, 1893, and closed on August 24, 1912. The building was used for Masses beginning in 1918, to save visitors a trip to St. Mary's in Collinsville. It was razed in 1938. In 1931, the decision was made to build a church near the lake. First called St. Mary's by the Lake, it is now St. Mary Magdalen.

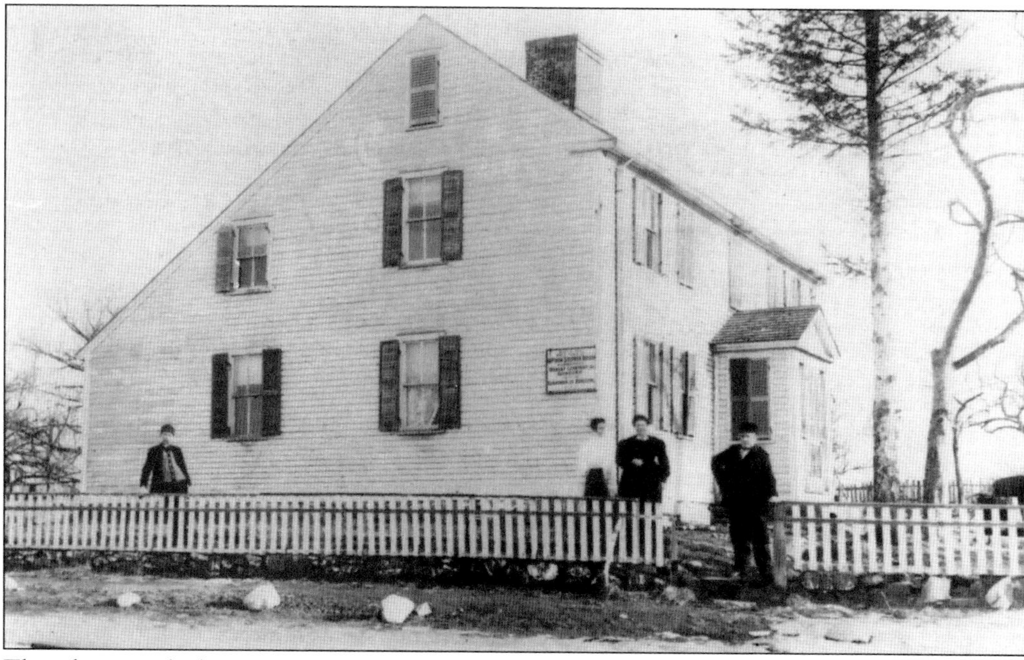

This photograph shows 533 Pleasant Street around 1910. The house belonged to Capt. Stephen Russell, who served in the American Revolution. At 2:00 p.m. on April 19, 1775, he heard the signal from Tewksbury and led a group of 87 minutemen down to Lexington and Concord. This house was built around 1680 and is still standing on Pleasant Street. (Courtesy of Eleanor Duda.)

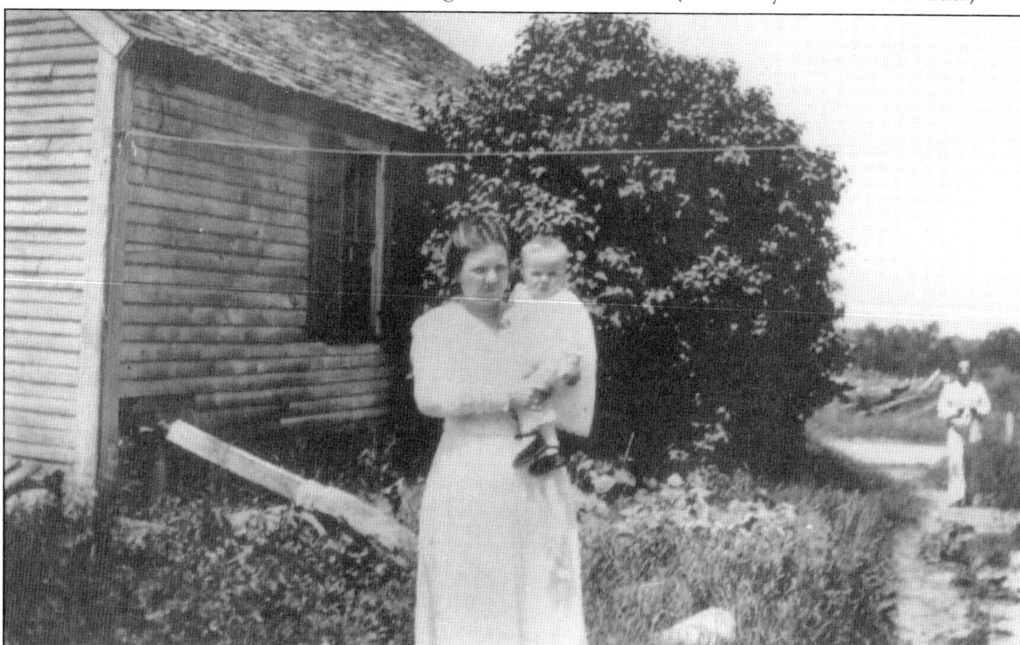

Martha (Chrystinia) Brown holds her baby daughter Eleanor Brown behind the Capt. Stephen Russell House at 533 Pleasant Street. Captain Russell was born in this 17th-century house, and in 1940, it was purchased by Mr. and Mrs. George Dockett, who did much restoration work on the home. (Courtesy Eleanor Duda.)

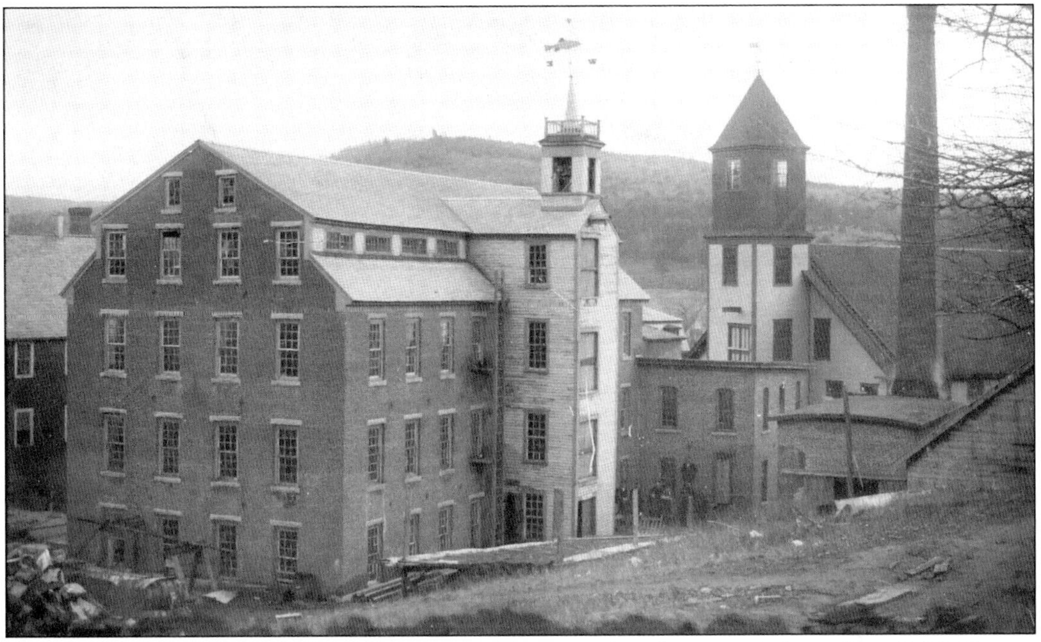

The Collinsville Mills along Beaver Brook are shown in this photograph from about 1898. Cotton mills were on this site as early as 1850. The property was owned by John Pierceson of Boston but was managed by his agent, George Lawson, and was commonly known as Lawson's Mill. Lawson operated it until it was sold in 1863.

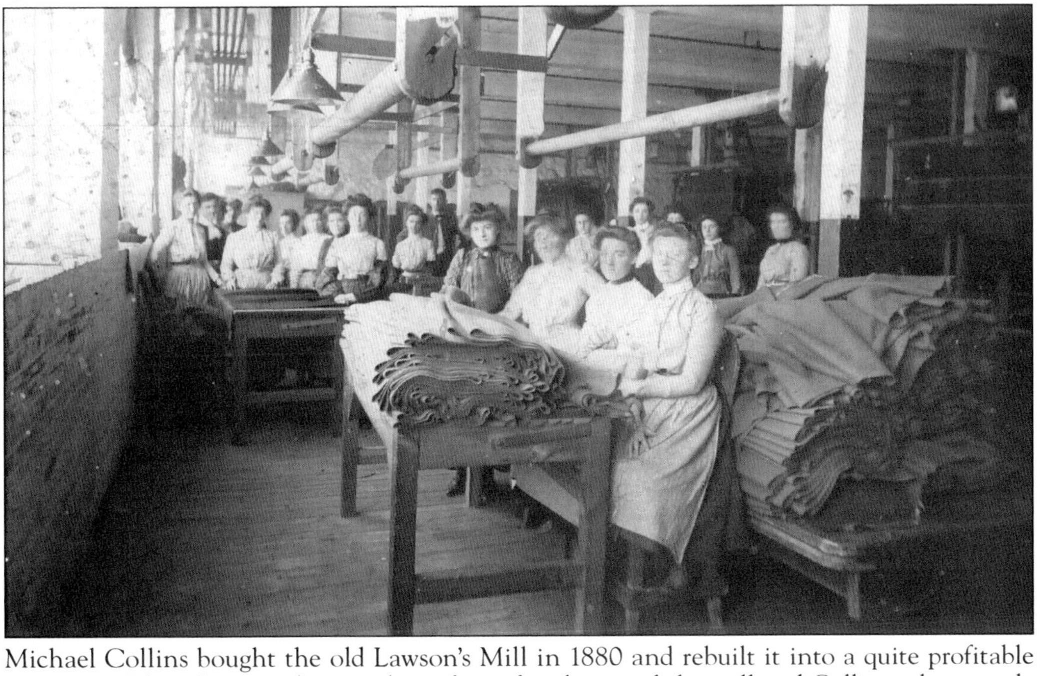

Michael Collins bought the old Lawson's Mill in 1880 and rebuilt it into a quite profitable enterprise. This photograph was taken after a fire destroyed the mill and Collins subsequently sold it to the American Woolen Company. It then became known as the Beaver Brook Mill and was in operation until after World War II. The area in Dracut known as Collinsville is named for Michael Collins.

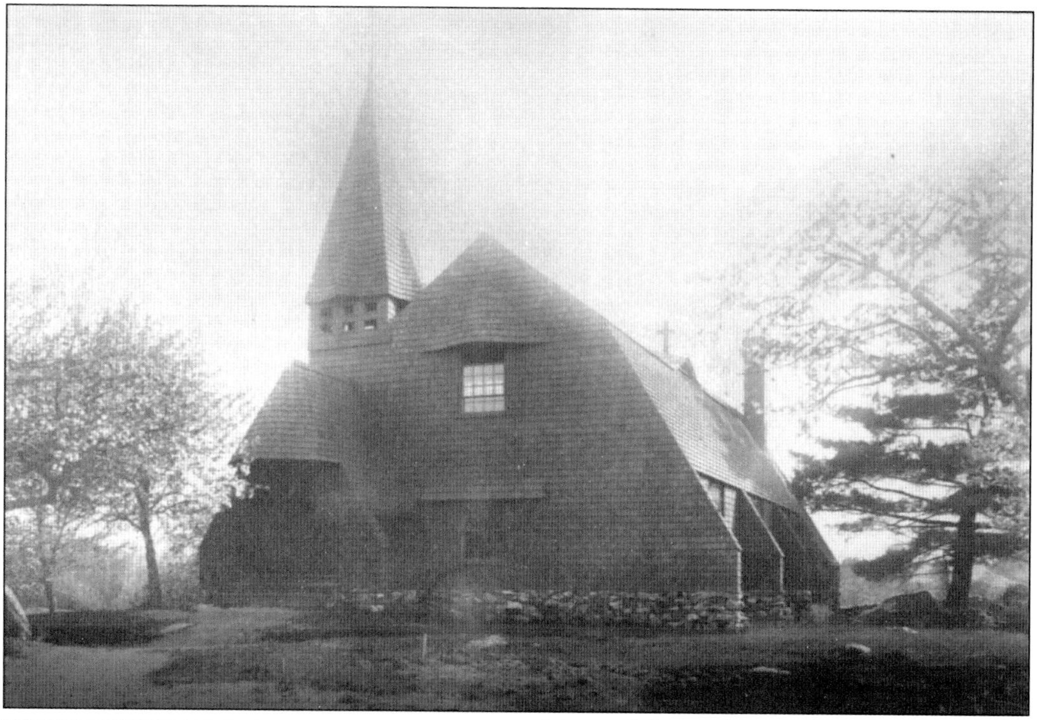

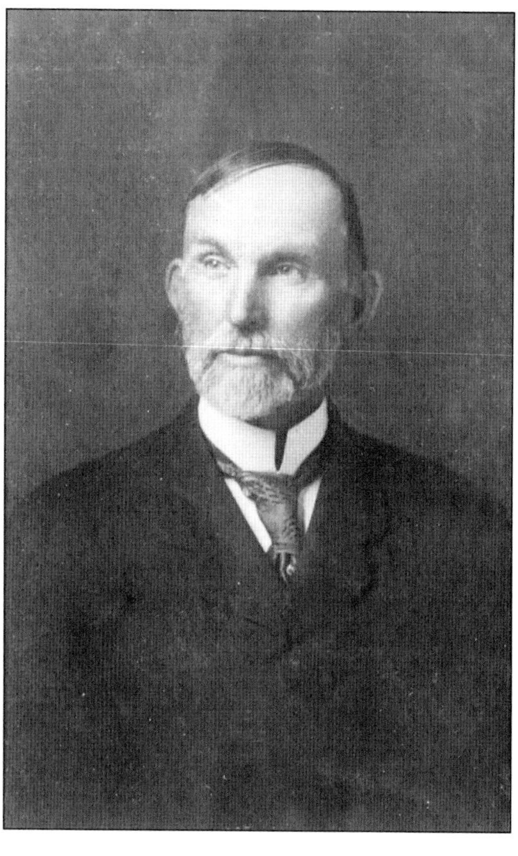

Many of the workers at the Collins Mills were Irish Catholic. Collins constructed a small building for the worshippers at his own expense of $2,000, and priests from St. Michael's in Lowell celebrated Mass there until August 15, 1901, when the church was officially dedicated and named St. Mary's of the Assumption. In 2001, it merged with St. Marguerite D'Youville Parish.

Other religious denominations were in need of a place of worship in Collinsville, so George B. Brown donated land for the Collinsville Union Mission in 1896. Brown lived at the corner of Lakeview Avenue and Mammoth Road. Today, there is a gas station there and that corner is referred to as Brown's Lane.

The Union Mission was established in 1896 when George Brown donated the land for it, and the first service was held on November 15, 1896. Worshippers were predominantly Methodist but all denominations were welcome.

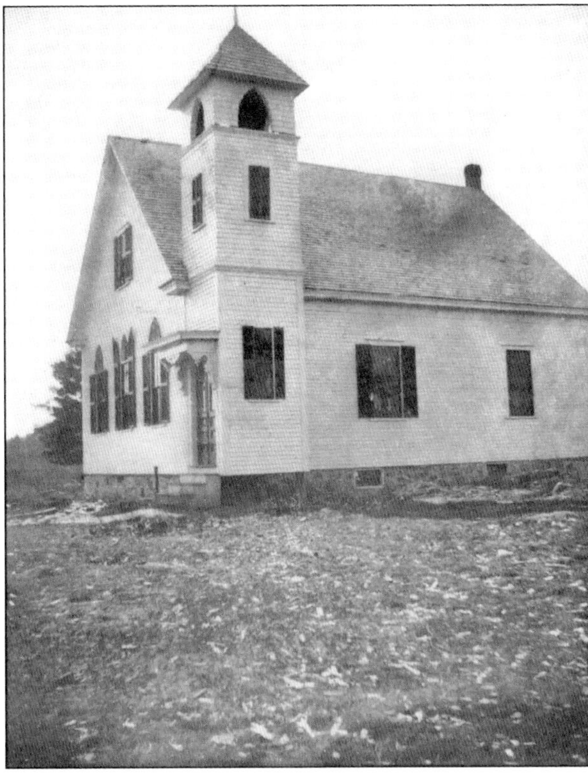

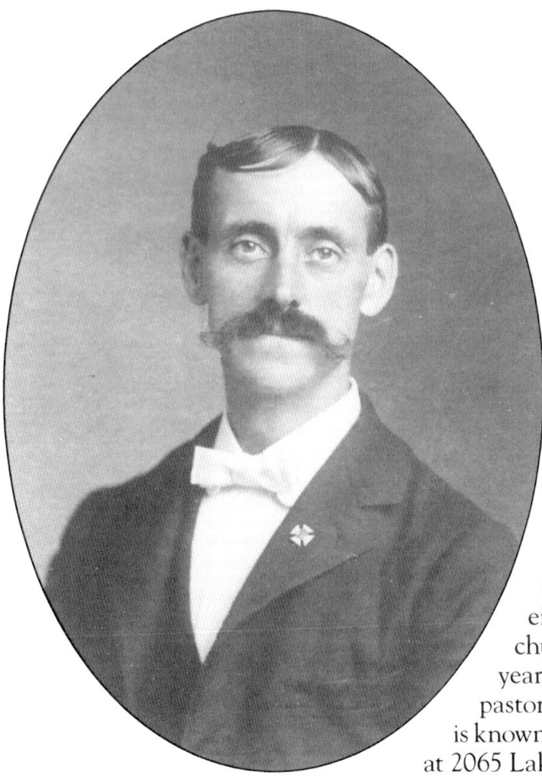

Rev. Samuel Worth, of Lowell, served as the minister at the Collinsville Union Mission for eight years; six of which without a salary. The church was enlarged in 1919, and in 1936, the same year that Reverend Worth was named permanent pastor, fire damaged the building. Today, the church is known as the Collinsville Bible Church and is located at 2065 Lakeview Avenue.

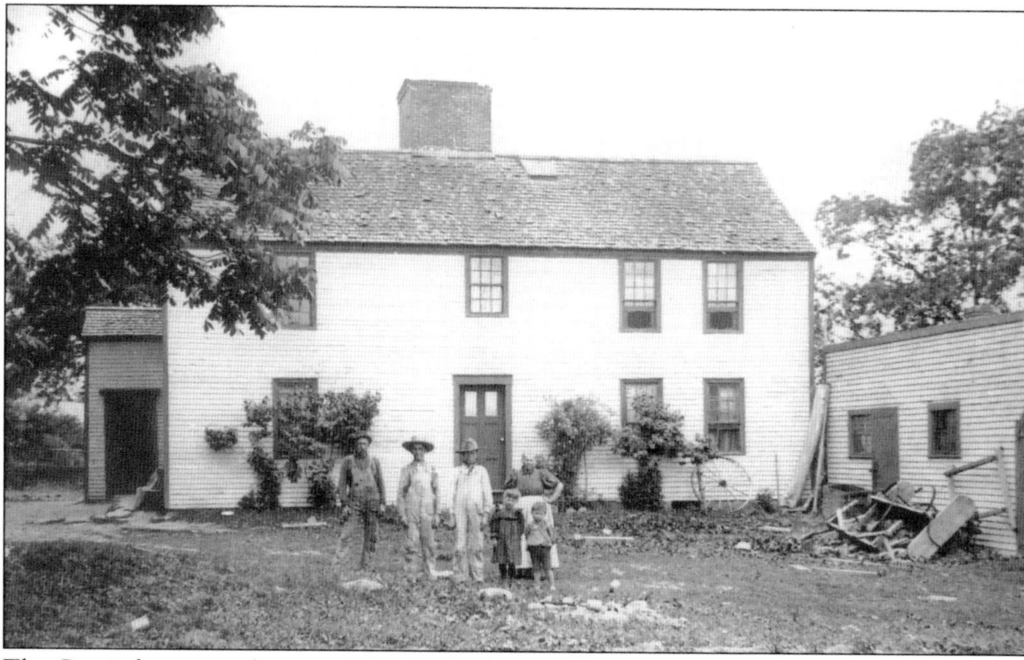

The Curtis farm, seen here in 1900, was built by Ephraim Curtis on Broadway Avenue across from Fox Avenue in 1737. After the French and Indian War, the Curtis home was one of many in Dracut to take in displaced Acadians from Canada. The town reimbursed families who took in the Acadian refugees. This house was torn down in 1930.

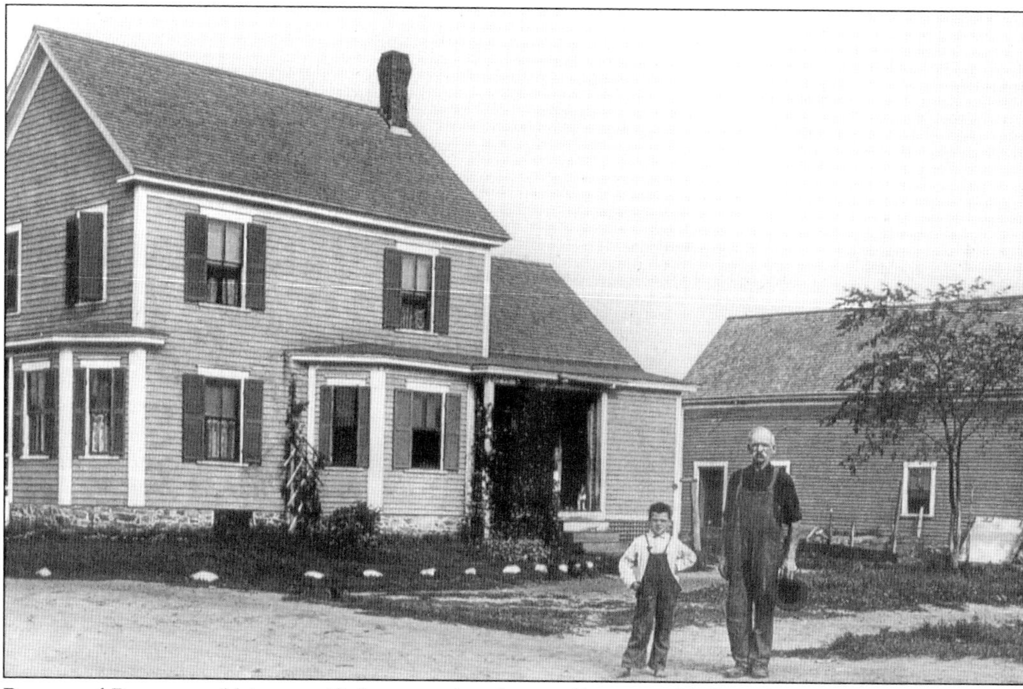

Raymond Brown and his grandfather stand in front of his grandfather's home on Pleasant Street around 1910. The house is still there on the corner of Pleasant and Huron Streets. (Courtesy Eleanor Duda.)

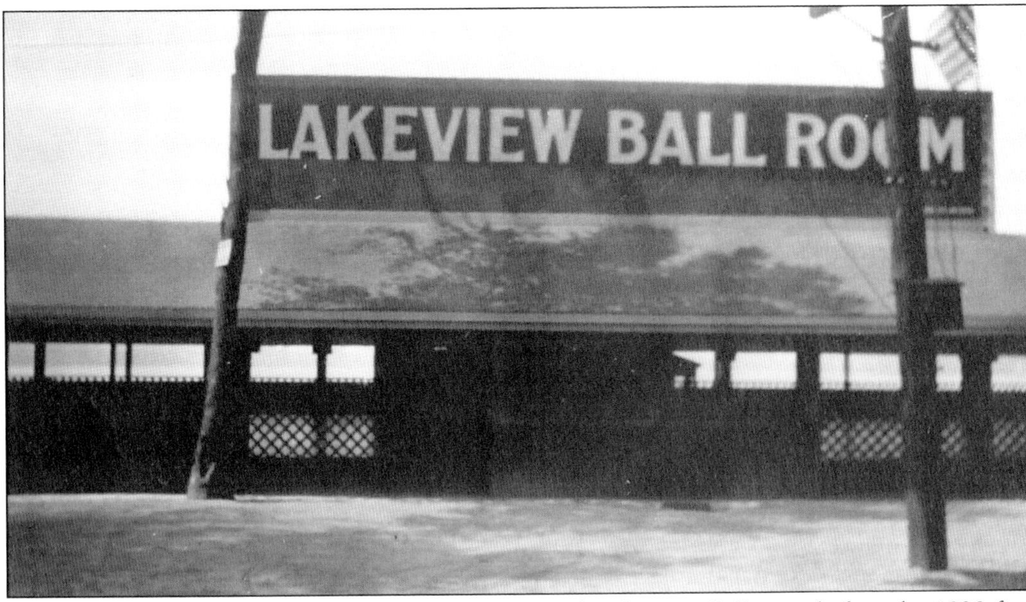

This photograph shows the entrance to the original Lakeview Ballroom before the 1928 fire. The park was opened from April to Labor Day each year and had so many visitors that trolley cars left Kearney Square in Lowell every five minutes. The fare was only 5¢. (Courtesy Paul Dumont family.)

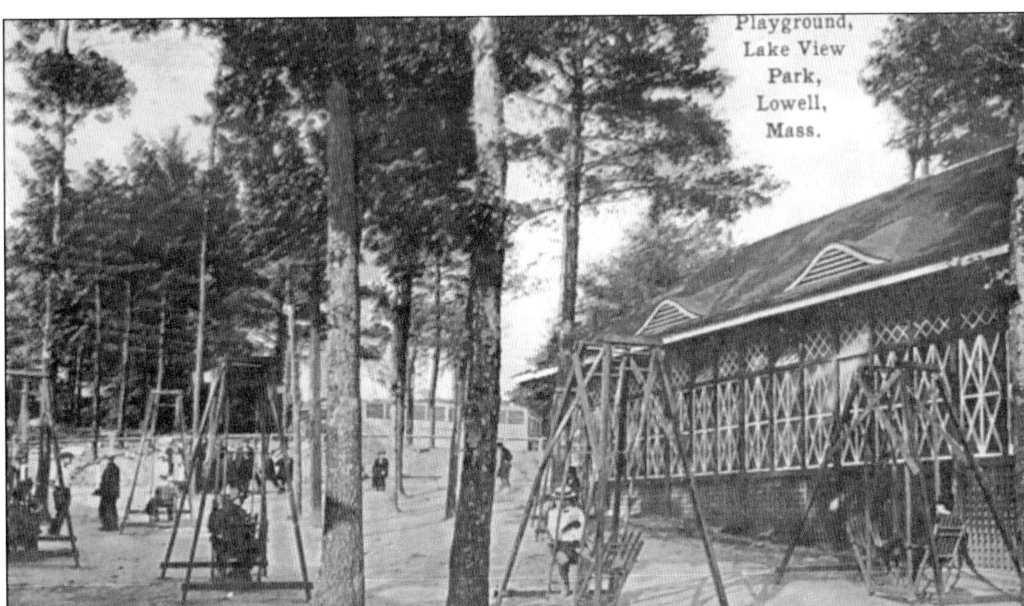

Park visitors enjoy the outdoor swings near the pavilion in this postcard. It was not uncommon for postcards to list Lakeview as a Lowell attraction, since Lowell was better known than Dracut and because the trolley service to Lakeview originated in Lowell. (Courtesy Paul Dumont family.)

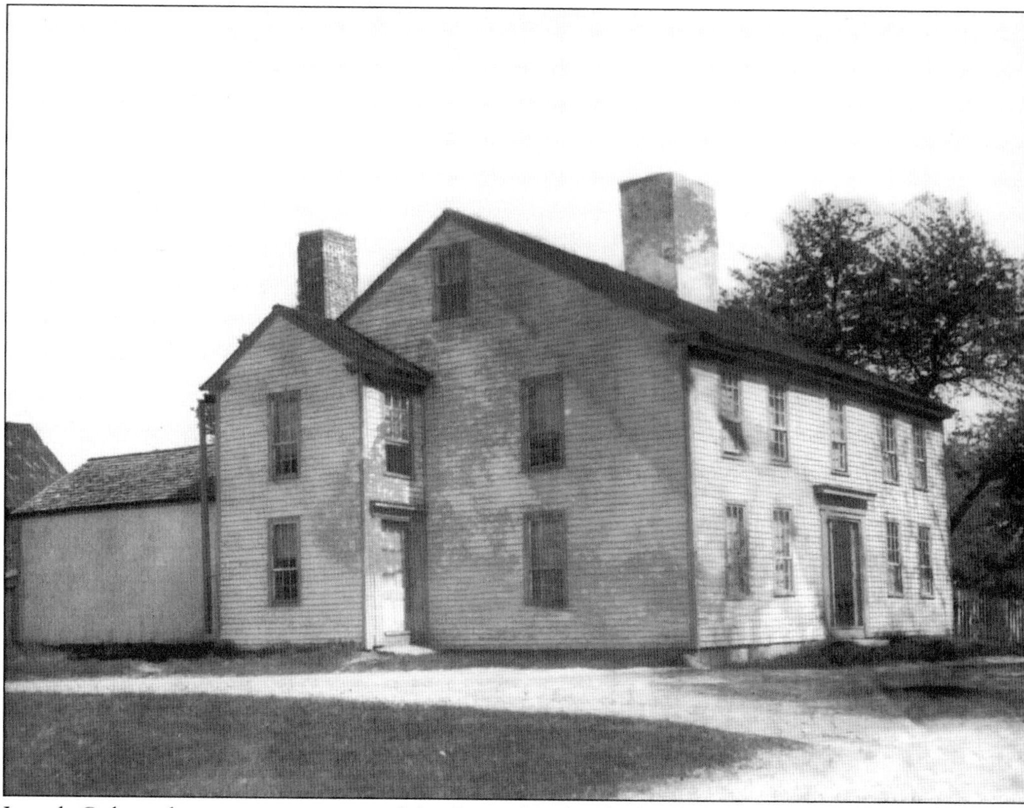

Joseph Coburn began construction of this home but he died before construction was completed. Thomas Hovey purchased it in 1759 and finished it. For years, the house served as a tavern at the busy crossroads in Dracut that became known as Hovey Square. The house was located across from the current Hannaford's supermarket.

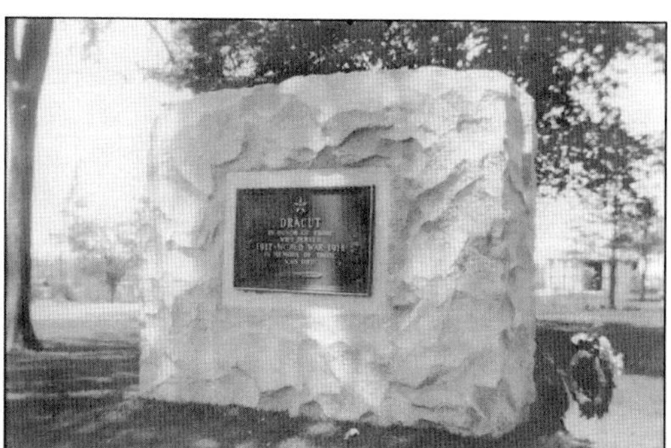

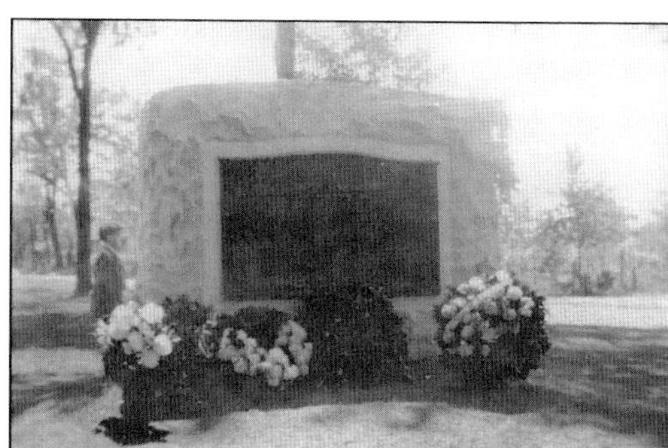

The monument that graces the center of Hovey Square was dedicated in 1925 and honors the Dracut men who served in World War I. The land was donated to the town by George Hovey Jr., who later moved to Chicago. He was a descendant of Thomas Hovey, whose family lived in the home for 150 years.

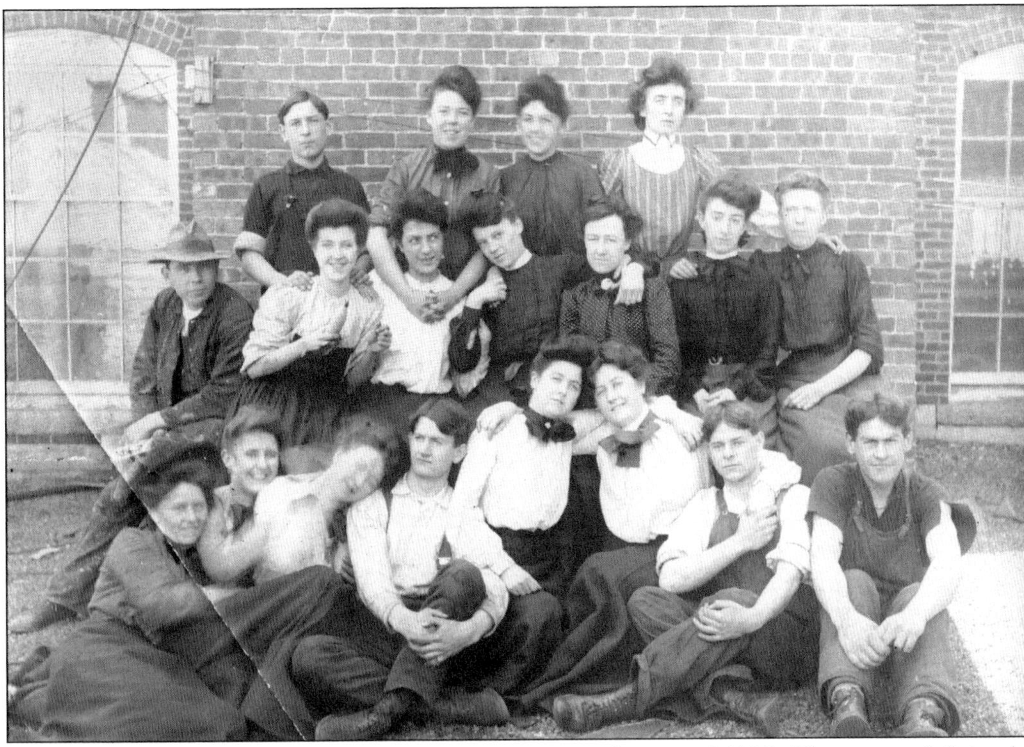

Collinsville mill workers pose for a group picture outside around 1900. The man at left in the middle row, with the hat, is Herbert R. Fish, who married the third girl from the right in the center row wearing a polka dot dress, Mary Agnes Bromley.

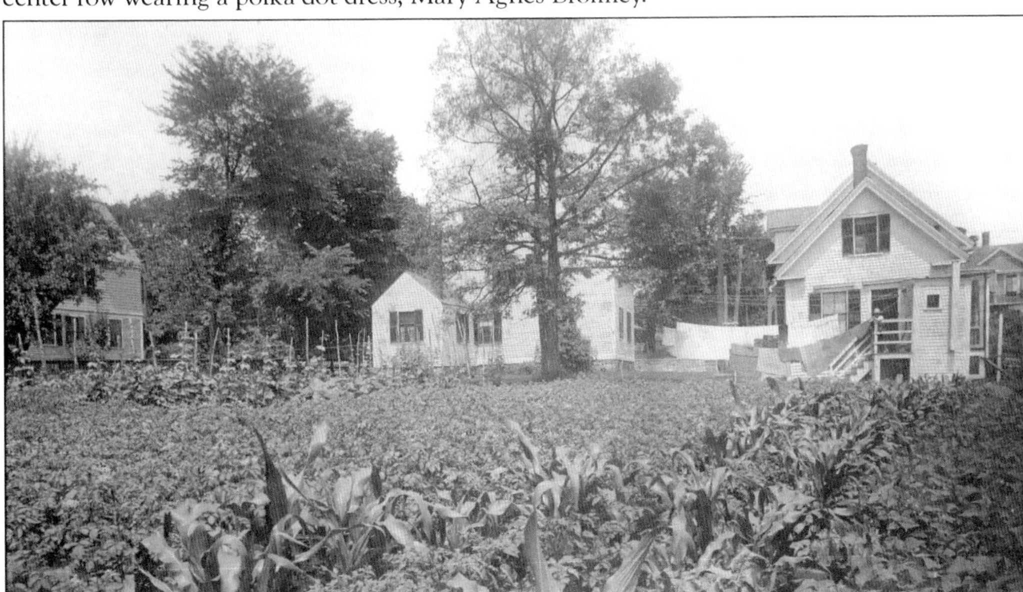

Michael Collins built several homes along Mill Street for the mill workers, some of which are seen here in this 1917 photograph. Many of the homes still remain today. In addition to homes, he also built St. Mary of the Assumption Catholic Church, since many of the mill workers were Irish Catholic. Collins was also named the town's first postmaster.

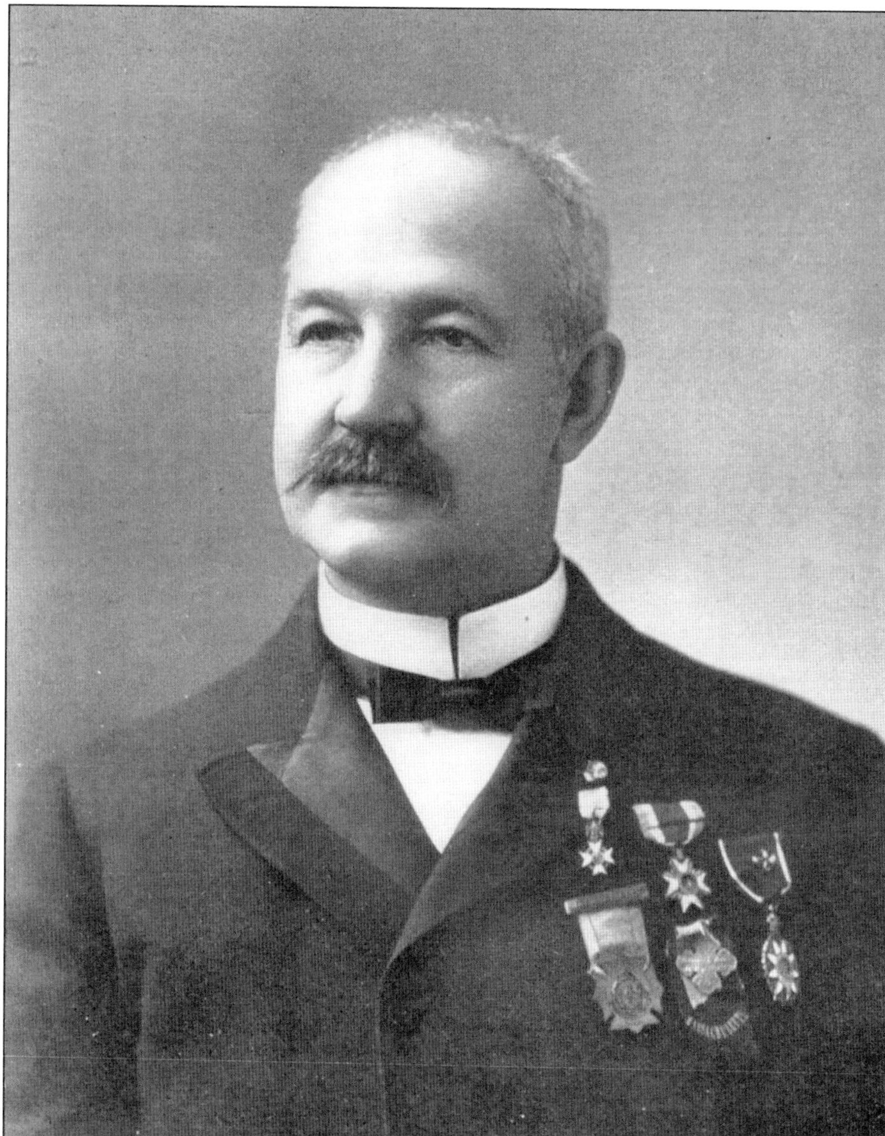

MOSES GREELEY PARKER, M.D.

President Massachusetts Society, S. A. R.

Moses Greeley Parker is one of Dracut's most famous residents. He was a descendant of Deacon Thomas Parker, Dracut's first minister, who arrived in America in 1635. M.G. Parker was born in 1842 and graduated from Phillips Academy in Andover and then Harvard Medical School in 1864. Upon graduation, he enlisted in the Army to fight for the Union, serving as an assistant surgeon in the 2nd US Colored Cavalry. He was honorably discharged and established his own medical practice in Lowell in 1866. During his career, he served as a trustee of Lowell General Hospital, served as president of the Middlesex North District Medical Society, and even became interested in the telephone industry, serving as a member of the executive committee of the New England Telephone and Telegraph Company. In 1892, Parker became an active member in the Sons of the American Revolution. He died in 1917 and is buried in Lowell Cemetery.

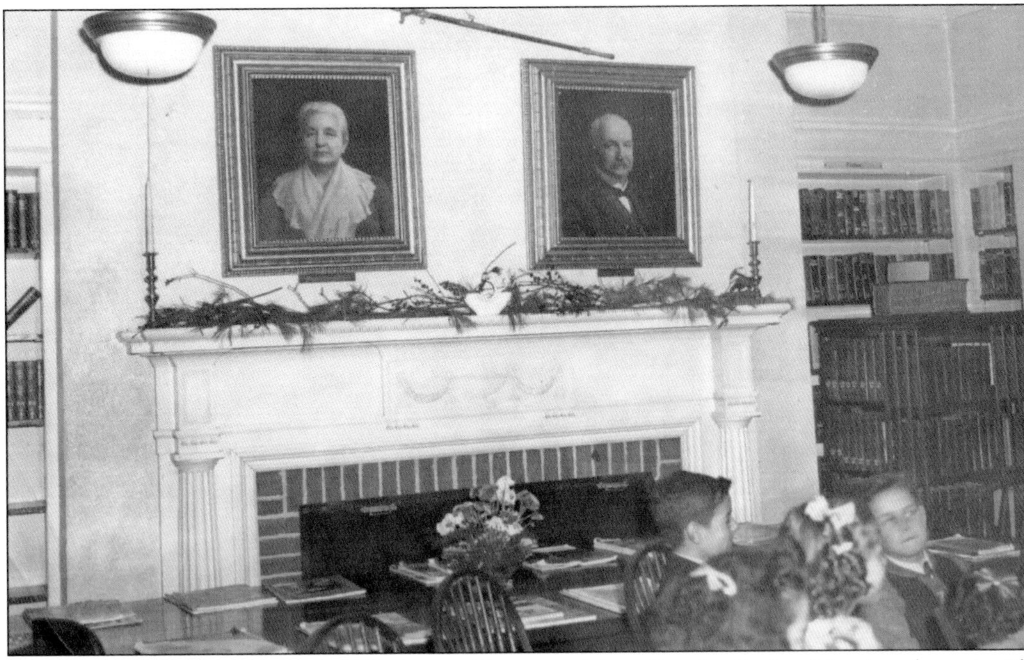

These portraits of Moses Greeley Parker and his sister Mary Greeley Parker Morrison hang inside the library named in his honor on Arlington Street. For 30 years, the Dracut Historical Society was housed in the library's basement until it moved into its current location on Lakeview Avenue in 1964. The library was expanded in 2004 and the current library director is Robert Randyshaw.

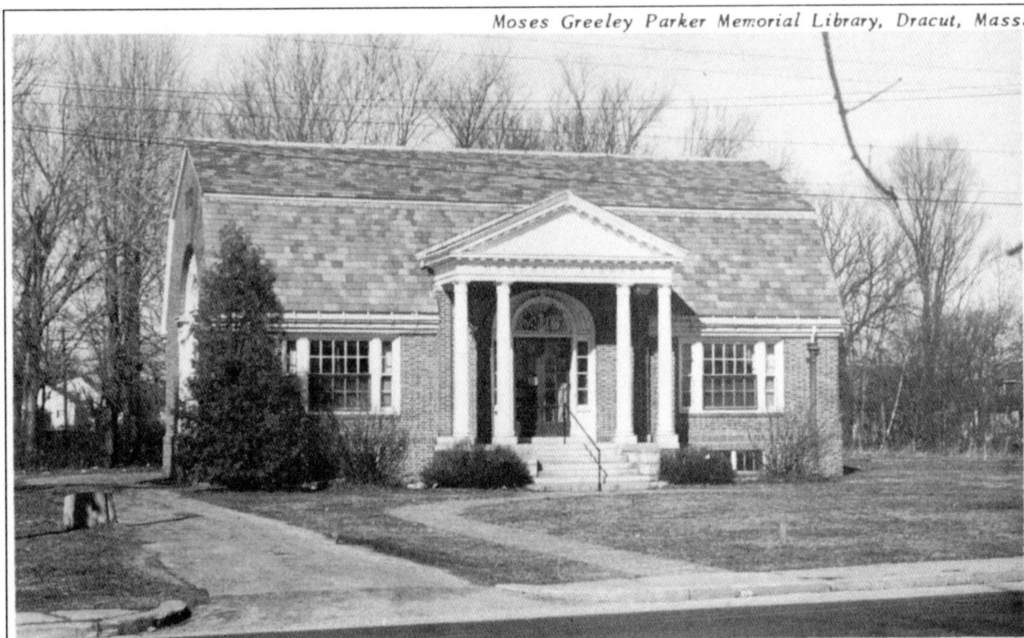

The town's library, shown in this postcard, was first established by town meeting in 1900 and was housed on the second floor of the town hall. In 1923, with the $10,000 that M.G. Parker donated just prior to his death in 1917, a new permanent home was built for the town's library. (Courtesy Paul Dumont family.)

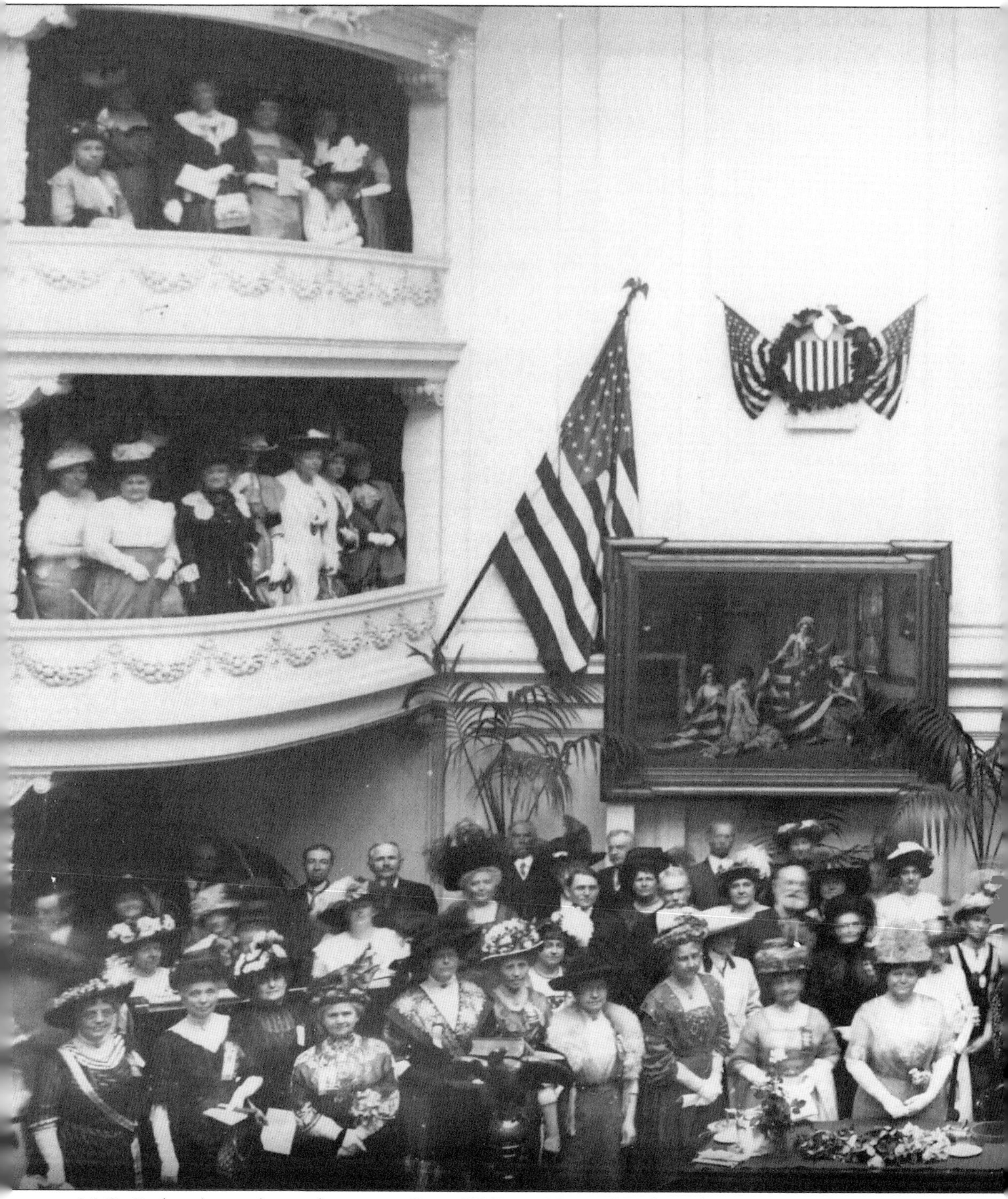

M.G. Parker (center) stands next to Pres. William Howard Taft at the 1912 Daughters of the American Revolution Congress. In addition to his impressive military, medical, and philanthropic efforts, Parker was very much interested in innovative technology. He became fascinated with Alexander Graham Bell's newly invented telephone and is credited with developing the telephone

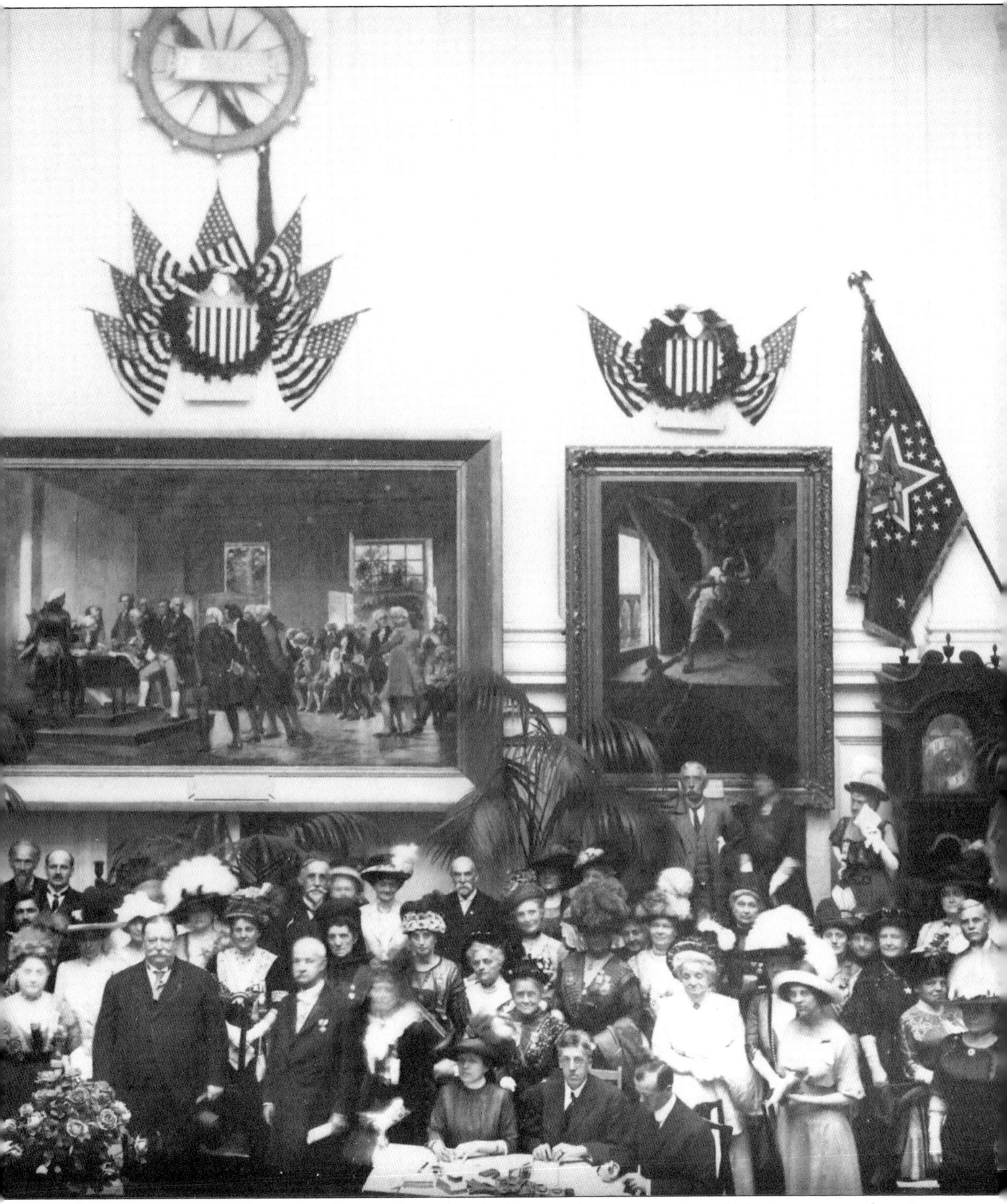

directory system still used today, with each telephone subscriber assigned their own number. In addition, Parker is credited with being the first to photograph the tubercular bacillus, the bacteria that causes tuberculosis.

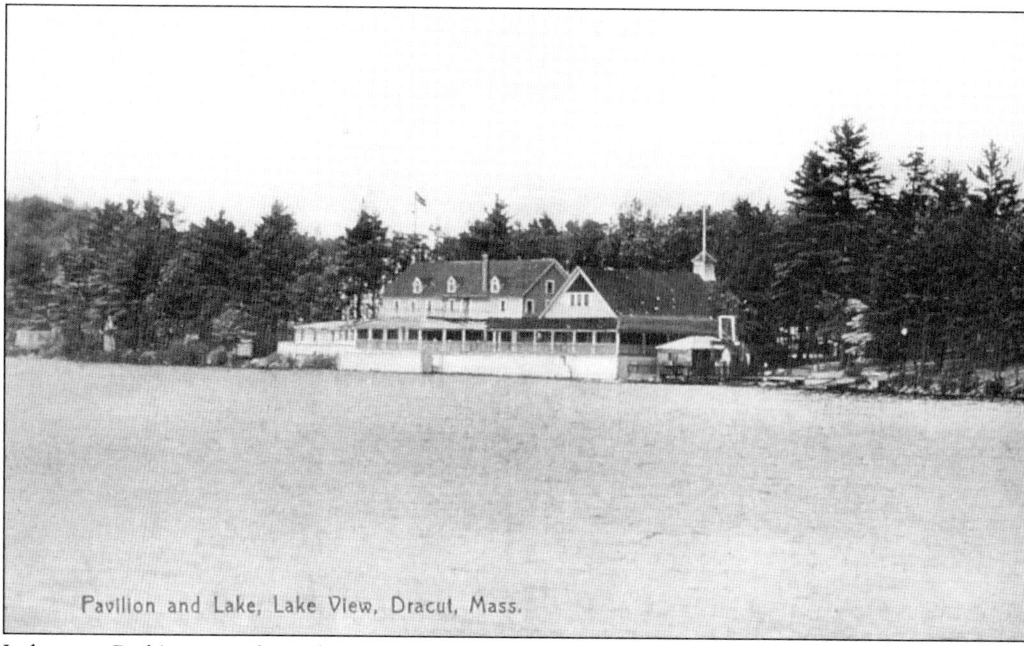

Lakeview Park's original pavilion and dance hall is pictured here in this postcard from around 1912. There were many activities at Lakeview for adults and children, such as the Willow Dale Steamer or canoe rentals for 10¢ an hour. (Courtesy of William Dumont family.)

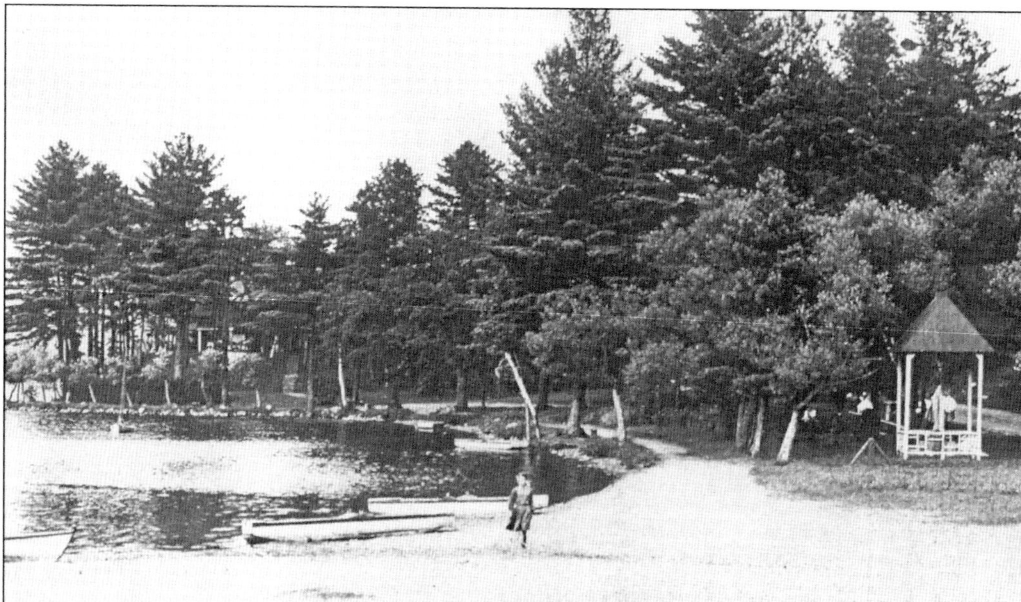

This postcard shows the General Jackson Monument along the shores of Lake Mascuppic. There were several of these, as well as ship figureheads of the Greek god Neptune and Chief Mascuppic. As visitors cruised along the lake on the Willow Dale Steamer, they would stop here to picnic and view this odd collection. (Courtesy Paul Dumont family.)

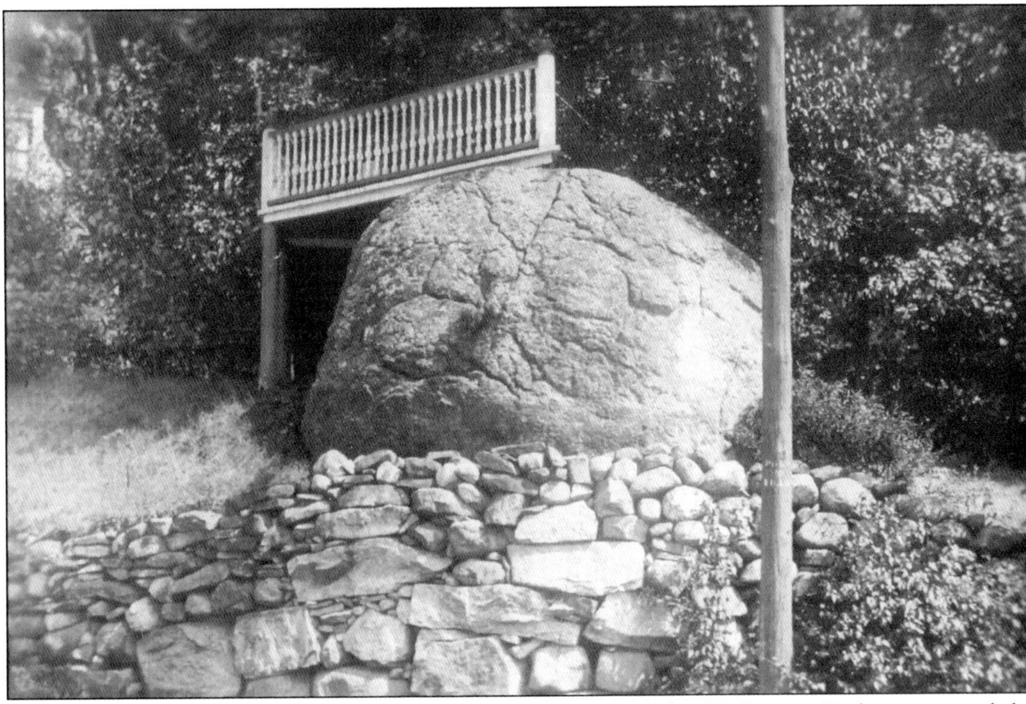

This unique rock formation at Lake Mascuppic on the grounds of Lakeview Park was named the "Pray-Table Rock." The word Mascuppic is believed to be an Algonquin word meaning "place of the large rocks." Lake Mascuppic, whose many coves were once filled with water lilies, is also referred to as Tyng's Pond after colonial settler Jonathan Tyng. Long before Lakeview Park was established in 1889, Willow Dale Park was established on the shores of Lake Mascuppic by Jonathan Bowers in 1867. Admission to the 140-acre Willow Dale Park was 5¢.

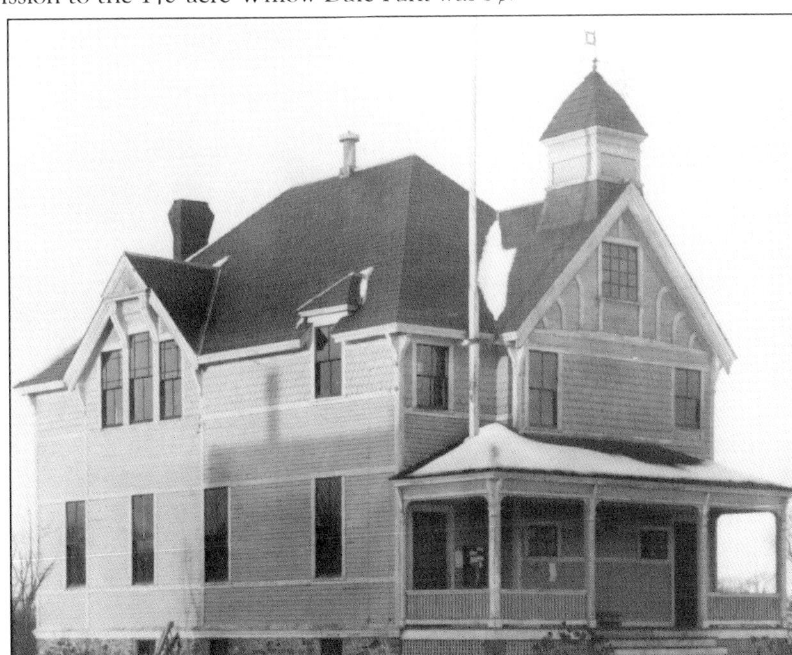

The Dracut Center School was built on Arlington Street in 1883 and is still in use as the town hall today. The building has been used for town offices since 1889, when a new Dracut Center School was built on Spring Park Avenue that today is Town Hall Annex. (Courtesy Lenny Proposki.)

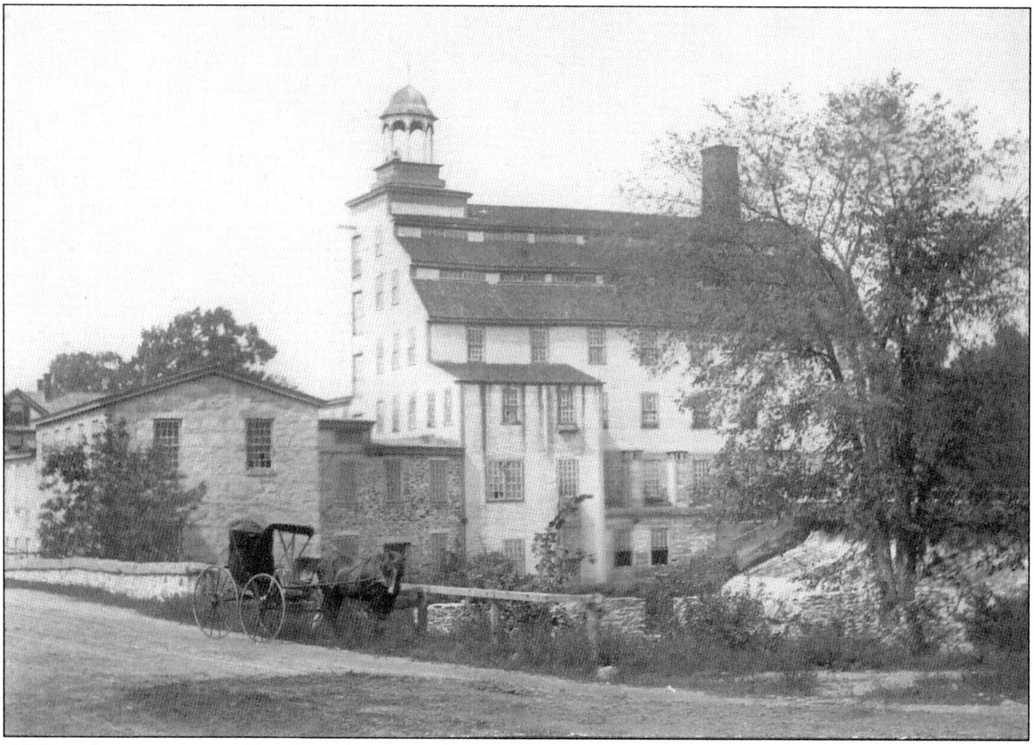

Although unrecognizable, this photograph is in fact Lakeview Avenue at the Beaver Brook Mills. At the time of the photograph, it was still the site of Collinsville Mills. The mill burned down in 1899 but was replaced by Michael Collins.

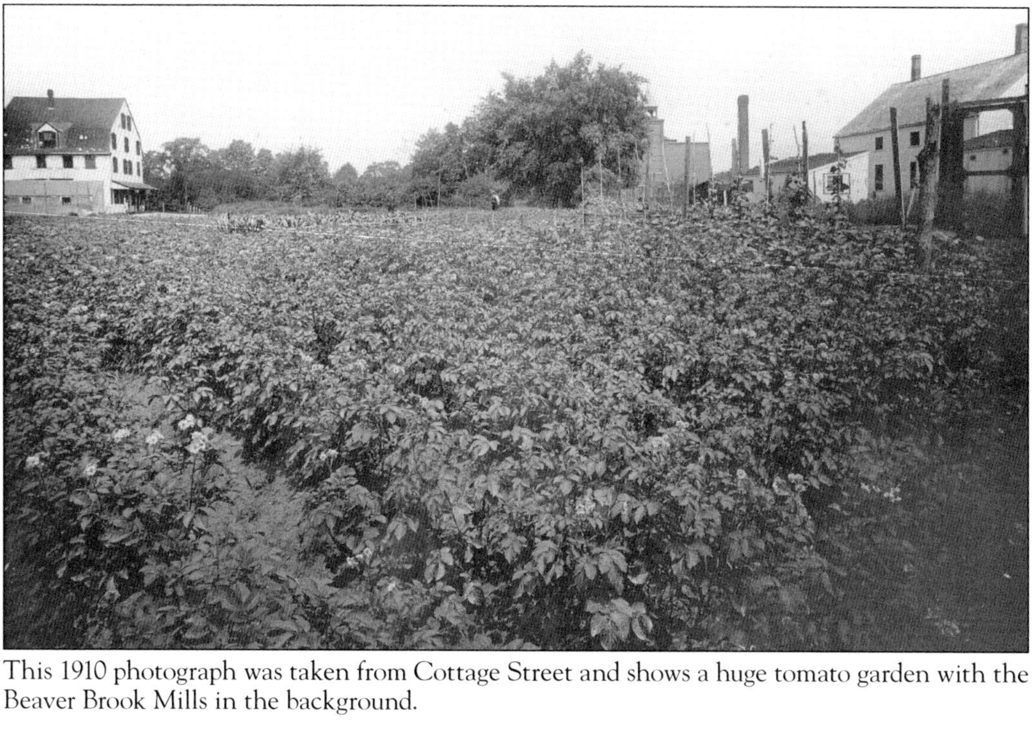

This 1910 photograph was taken from Cottage Street and shows a huge tomato garden with the Beaver Brook Mills in the background.

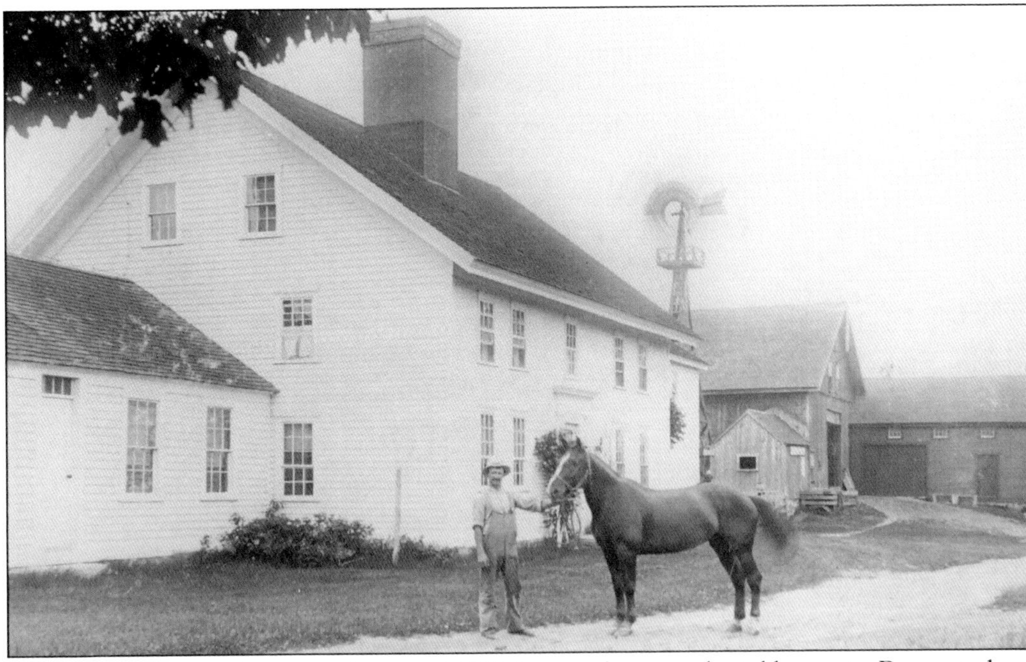

The Ezekial Cheever house, built around 1775, is one of many colonial homes in Dracut to have burned to the ground. The home was located on Arlington Street across from Cheever Street.

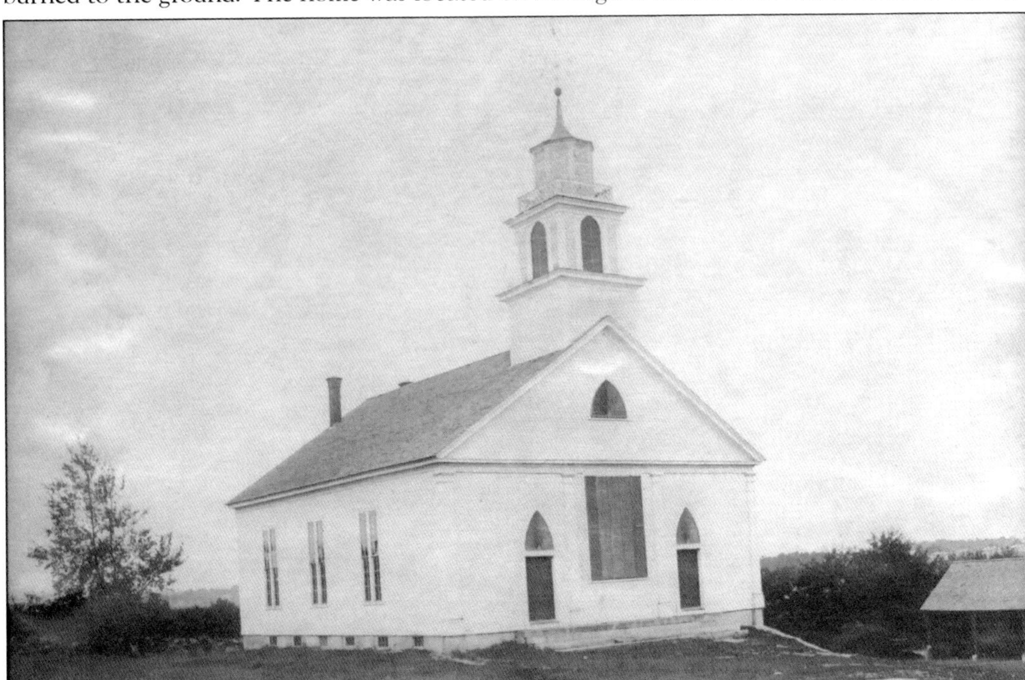

Hillside Church was built in 1834 on Pleasant Street heading toward the Navy Yard District. The church was first named First Evangelical Church and was damaged by fire in 1905. On May 12, 1969, the Hillside Church and the Central Congregational Church were united and renamed Christ Church United and services were held at the Old Yellow Meeting House. In 1973, the Hillside church building was destroyed by fire.

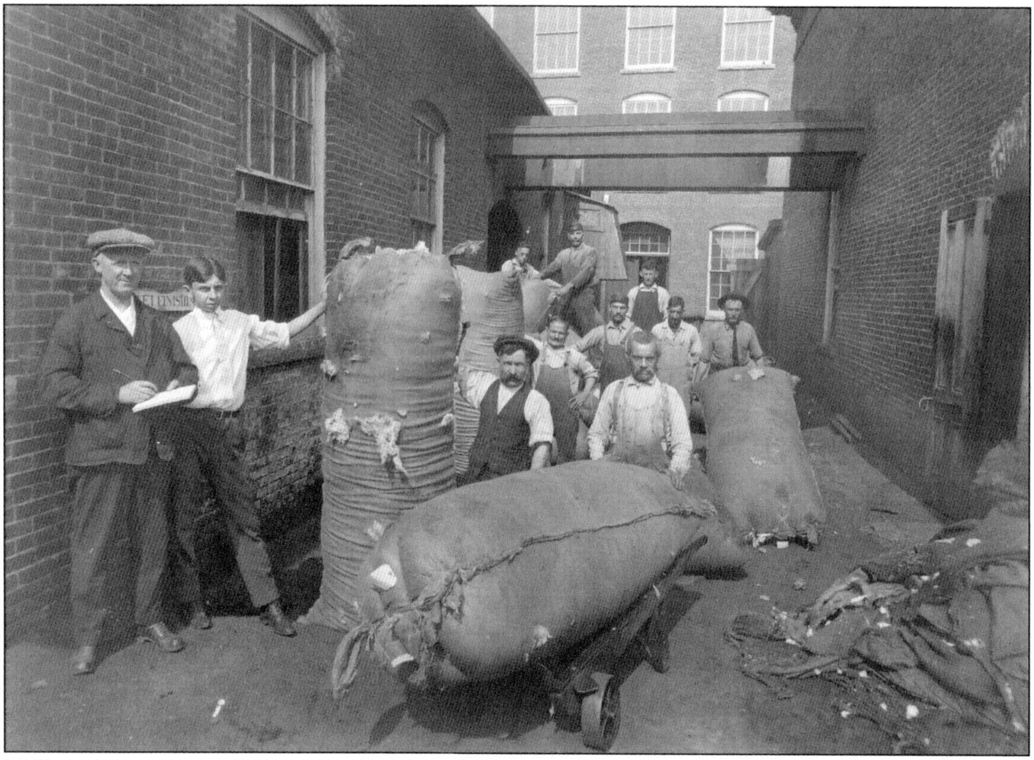

Mill workers move a shipment of wool at the Beaver Brook Mills in this photograph. The only canal system in Dracut was built by Michael Collins to harness the waterpower of Beaver Brook for his mill. After the mill burned in 1899, he rebuilt the mill using brick and by 1893, it was six stories high.

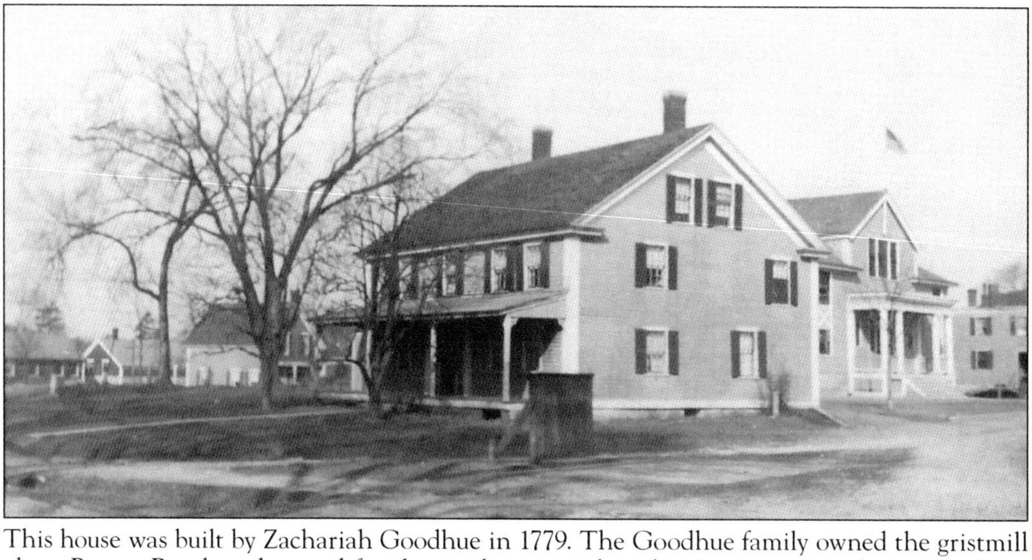

This house was built by Zachariah Goodhue in 1779. The Goodhue family owned the gristmill along Beaver Brook and several family members served in the American Revolution. In 1906, when the Parker Avenue School needed additional space, a two-room schoolhouse was built behind the Goodhue home. It remained a schoolhouse until 1981 and is now the Goodhue Professional Building.

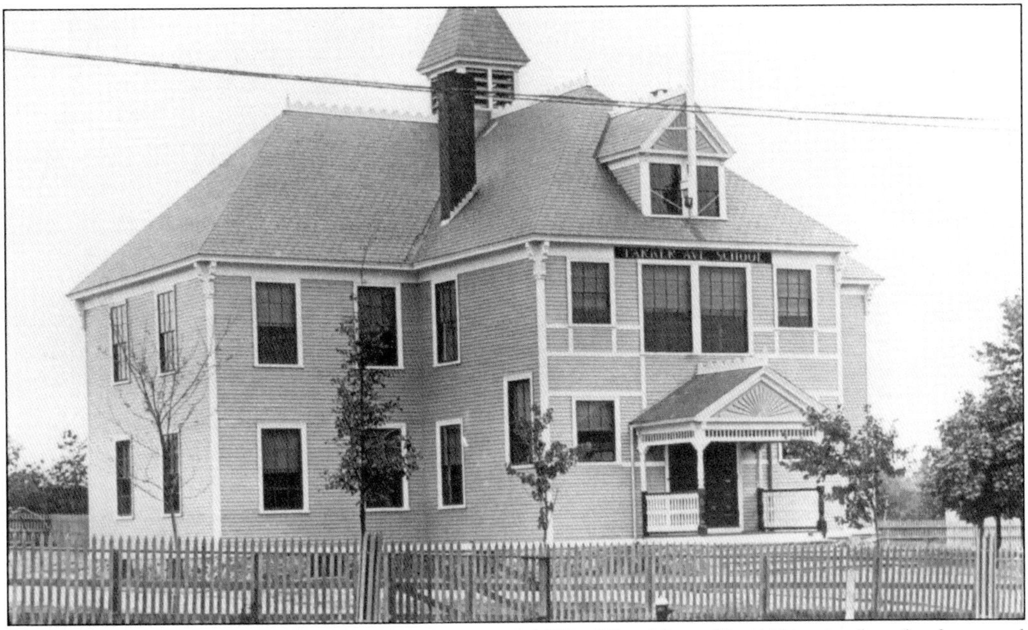

The Parker Avenue School is seen here around 1880. The Navy Yard District has had several schoolhouses. In 1874, after part of Dracut was annexed to Lowell—what is known today as Pawtucketville—a new schoolhouse was built just north of the Navy Yard District on Parker Avenue. In 1924, a new Parker Avenue School was built to replace the one seen here and is still in use today.

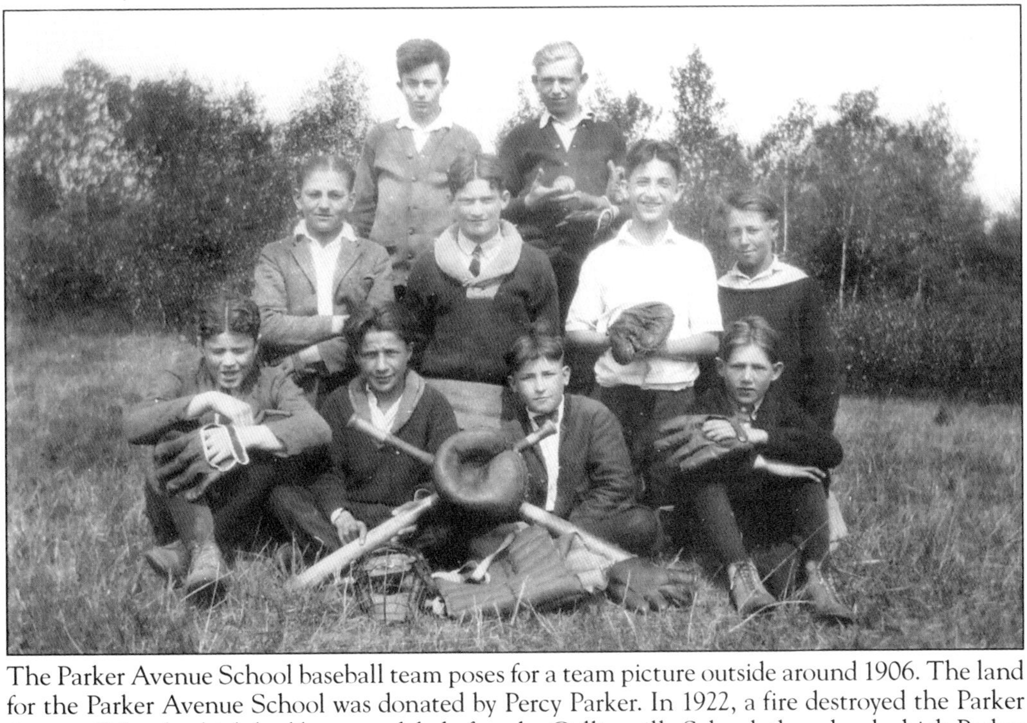

The Parker Avenue School baseball team poses for a team picture outside around 1906. The land for the Parker Avenue School was donated by Percy Parker. In 1922, a fire destroyed the Parker Avenue School, which had been modeled after the Collinsville School, the school which Parker students attended while a new Parker Avenue School was built.

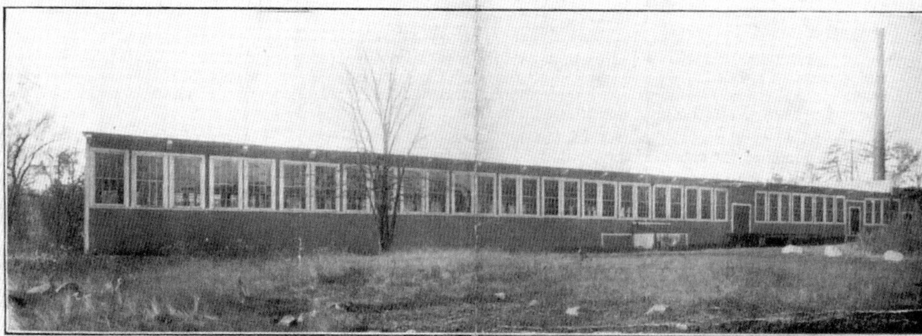

The Whiteley Bleachery, Inc.

ABOUT 22.76 ACRES, MANUFACTURING BUILDINGS,
WATER RIGHTS, REMAINING MACHINERY,
RESIDENCE AND BARN

Situated in Dracut, Mass., 2 Miles from the Center of Lowell

PLEDGED TO BE SOLD TO THE
HIGHEST BONAFIDE BIDDER AT

PUBLIC AUCTION

In Accordance With Terms and Conditions of Sale, in Separate Parcels, and
As a Unit in One Lot, on the Premises

LAKEVIEW AVENUE, DRACUT, MASS.

ON

Friday, November 19, 1926, Commencing at 2.30 P.M.

WALTER E. GUYETTE & CO., AUCTIONEERS

82 DEVONSHIRE STREET, BOSTON, MASS.
Telephone CONGRESS 2963

53 CENTRAL STREET, LOWELL, MASS.
Telephone 6996 and 6997

There were other industries in town besides dairy farms and Collins's mills. At the other end of Lakeview Avenue on Beaver Brook, Moses Goodhue established a gristmill in the Navy Yard District that he subsequently sold to his sons, Moses Jr. and Aaron. They continued the gristmill and also carded wool. The Goodhue brothers sold the property in 1839 to Samuel Griffin and Darius Young. A paper mill was established at that time. The property was sold in 1870 to the Lowell Wadding and Paper Company. The M.L. Bassett Company bought the business in 1877 and expanded the profitable mill until a flood ruined the mill on February 27, 1900. By the time the company rebuilt, they had lost their business to neighboring paper mills in Lowell.

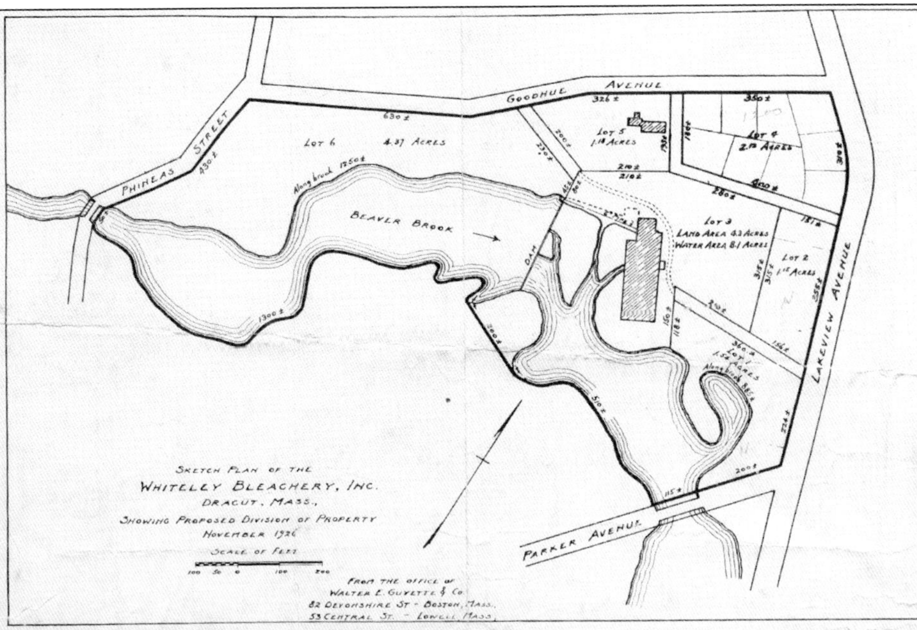

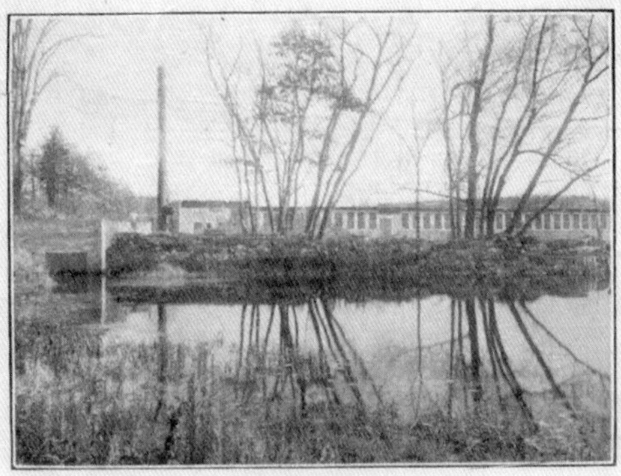

Beaver Brook and Dam

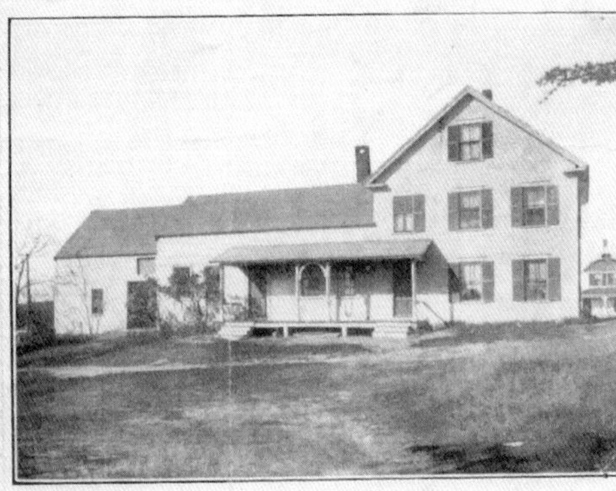

The Residence and Barn

The paper company buildings were left vacant until a fire on July 4, 1911, destroyed them. Since that time, the Whitely Bleachery moved into the property and operated until 1925. Industry had been established in Navy Yard District dating back to 1739, when James Varnum sold water rights and land along the west bank of Beaver Brook to Ephraim Hildreth. Hildreth already owned 1,300 acres on the western side of Beaver Brook, which he had acquired back in 1709. Hildreth then sold several acres to Goodhue, and by 1739, Goodhue and Hildreth had established a mill along Beaver Brook, for which they built two dams.

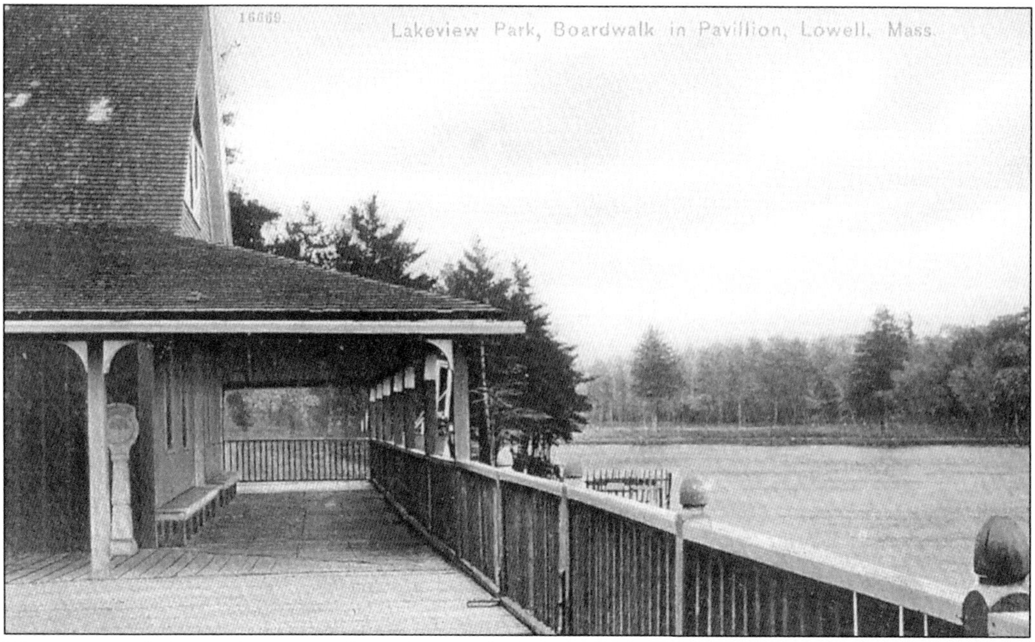

This postcard shows the original pavilion at Lakeview Park. The Willow Dale Steamer was not the only ship visitors could take for a ride around Lake Mascuppic; there was also the *Kitty B*, which sank off Willow Dale Point. Another favorite past time at Lakeview was eating famous Willow Dale chips. (Courtesy Paul Dumont family.)

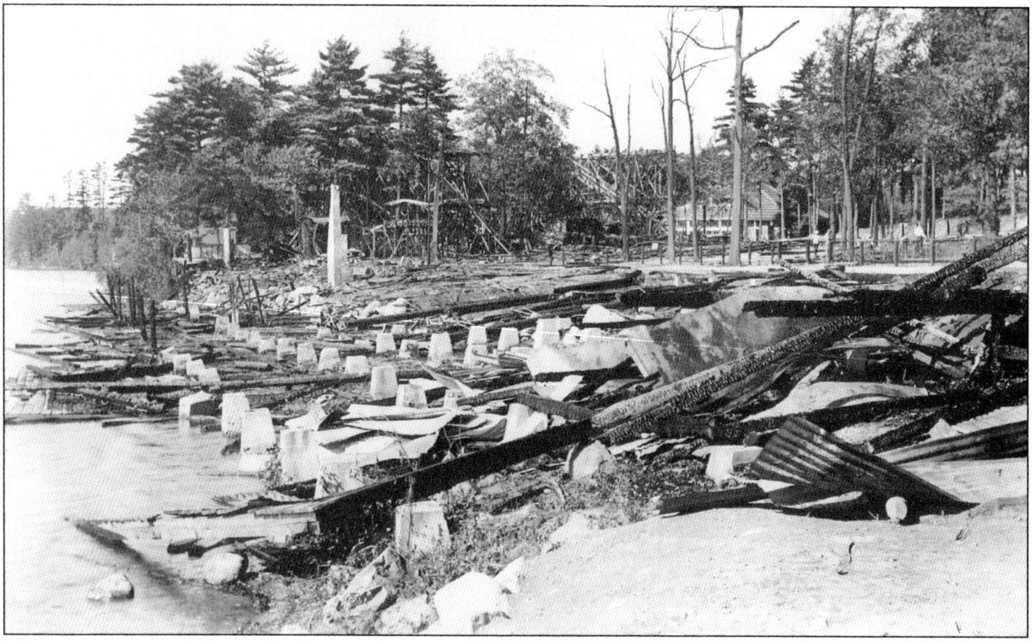

The pavilion and dance hall were destroyed by a fire in 1927. However, owner Harry Kittredge did not allow the fire to ruin Lakeview. He rebuilt the pavilion into a much grander dance hall. The new Lakeview Ballroom was built to accommodate 4,000 dancers, with almost 12,000 square feet of dance floor. Construction was done by John A. Miller of Illinois. (Courtesy Paul Dumont family.)

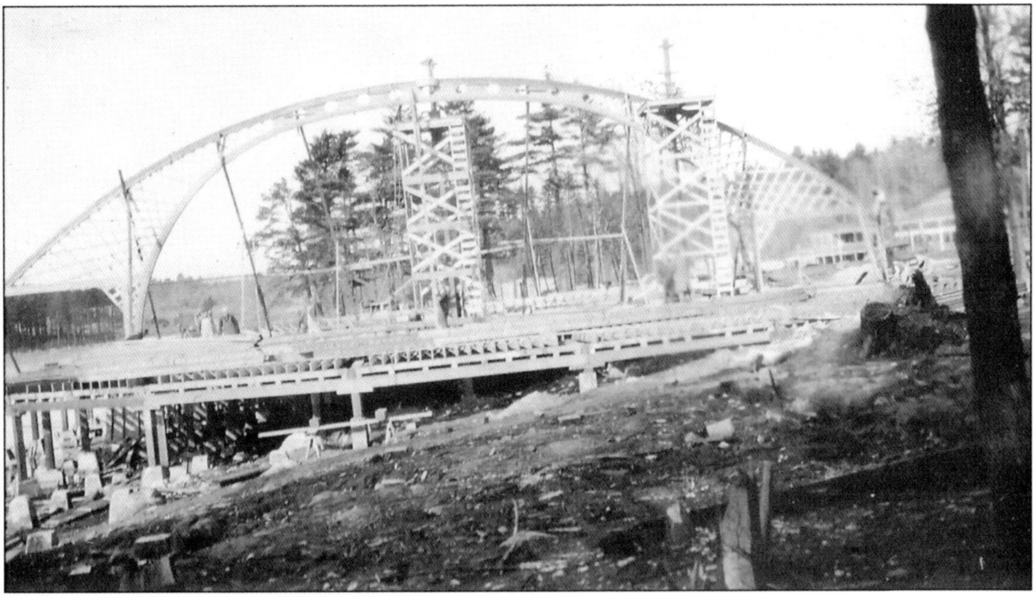

The September 1927 fire also destroyed the arcade, rifle range, and roller coaster. The damage was estimated at $100,000. The construction of the new dance hall was engineered so that the dance floor would be built under a large dome truss, eliminating the need for pillars inside. (Courtesy Paul Dumont family.)

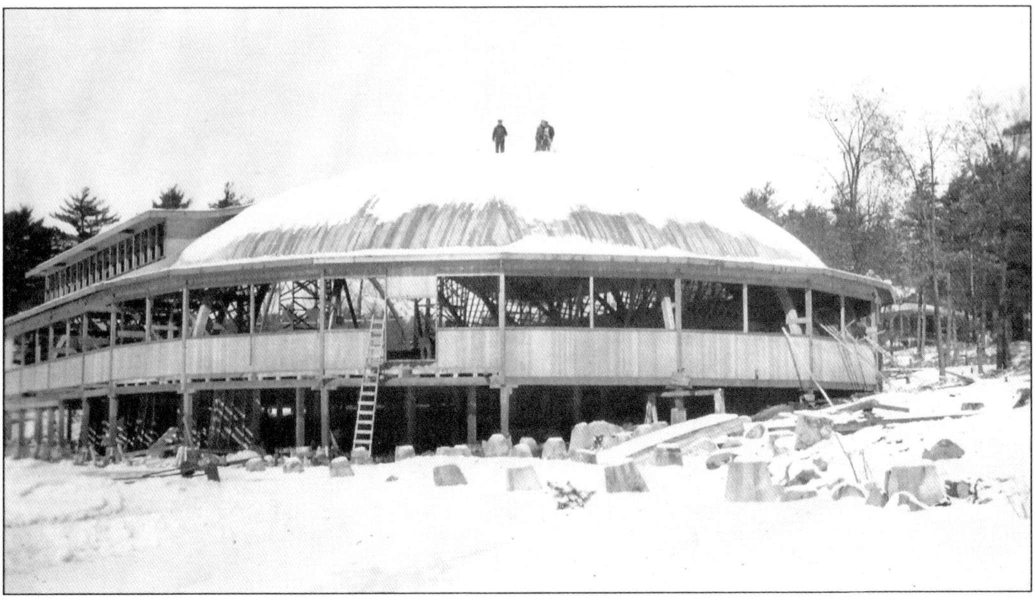

Construction on the new ballroom continued throughout the winter of 1927–1928. In the foreground are the charred remains from the old dance hall and pavilion. The design for the new ballroom also called for an extended boardwalk and a new roller coaster to be built all around the ballroom. (Courtesy Paul Dumont family.)

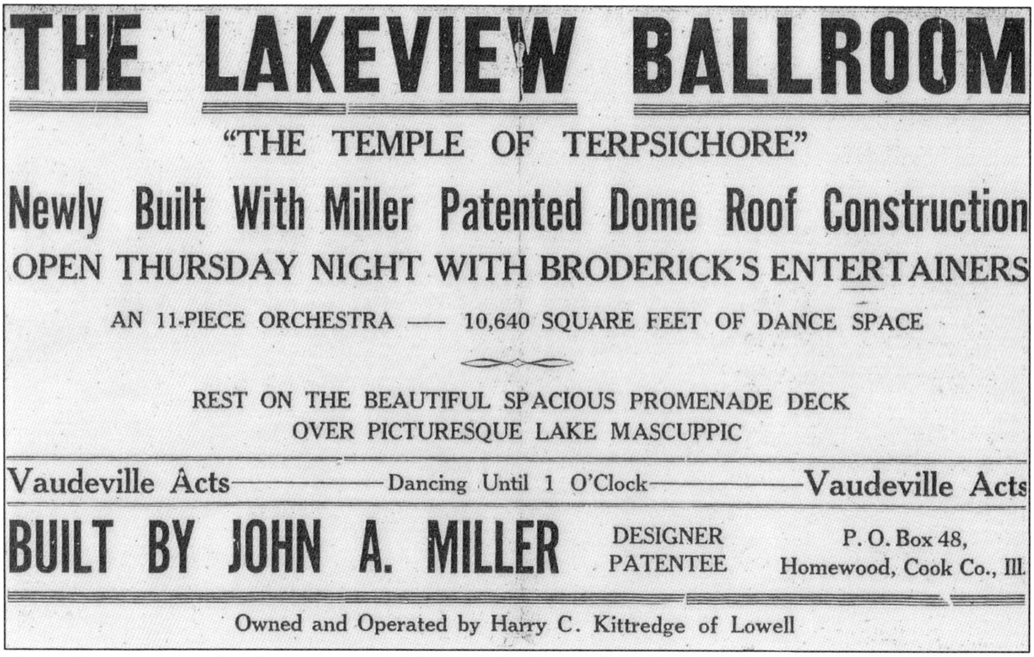

THE LAKEVIEW BALLROOM

"THE TEMPLE OF TERPSICHORE"

Newly Built With Miller Patented Dome Roof Construction

OPEN THURSDAY NIGHT WITH BRODERICK'S ENTERTAINERS

AN 11-PIECE ORCHESTRA — 10,640 SQUARE FEET OF DANCE SPACE

REST ON THE BEAUTIFUL SPACIOUS PROMENADE DECK
OVER PICTURESQUE LAKE MASCUPPIC

Vaudeville Acts——Dancing Until 1 O'Clock——Vaudeville Acts

BUILT BY JOHN A. MILLER DESIGNER PATENTEE P. O. Box 48, Homewood, Cook Co., Ill.

Owned and Operated by Harry C. Kittredge of Lowell

This advertisement for the opening of the new ballroom billed it as "The Temple of Terpsichore," or the "Temple of Dance," in reference to its design, modeled after the Mormon Tabernacle in Salt Lake City. (Courtesy Paul Dumont family.)

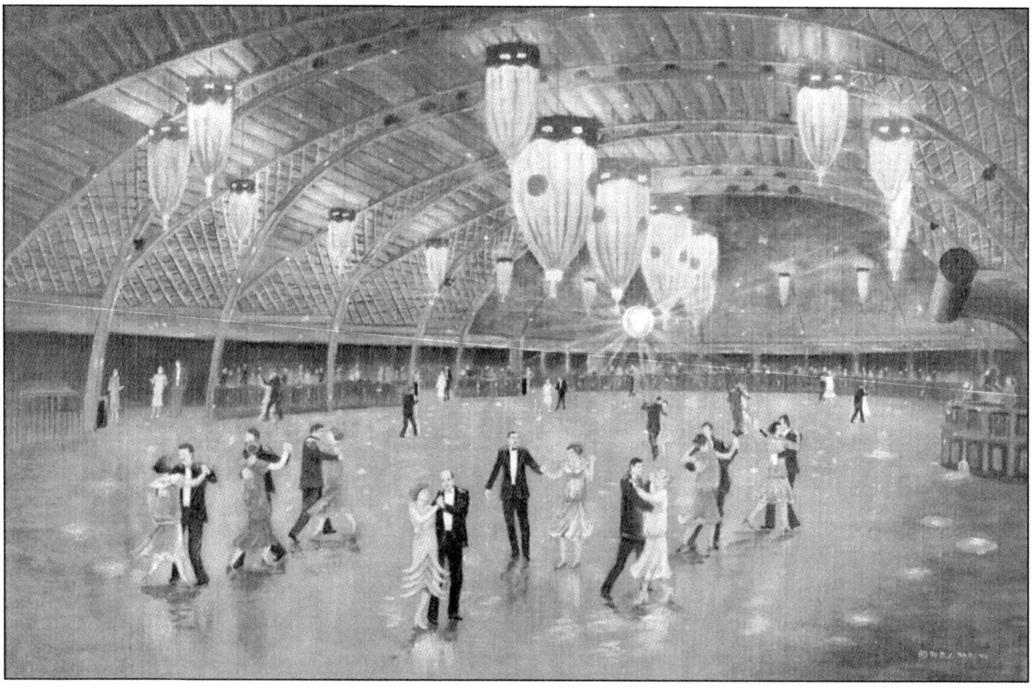

This artist's rendering of the completed Lakeview Ballroom in 1928 celebrated the new building on postcards. It had many modern features, including a new lighting and public address system. The acoustics were also very good and the ballroom was very well received for its grand opening on Thursday, May 10, 1928. (Courtesy Paul Dumont family.)

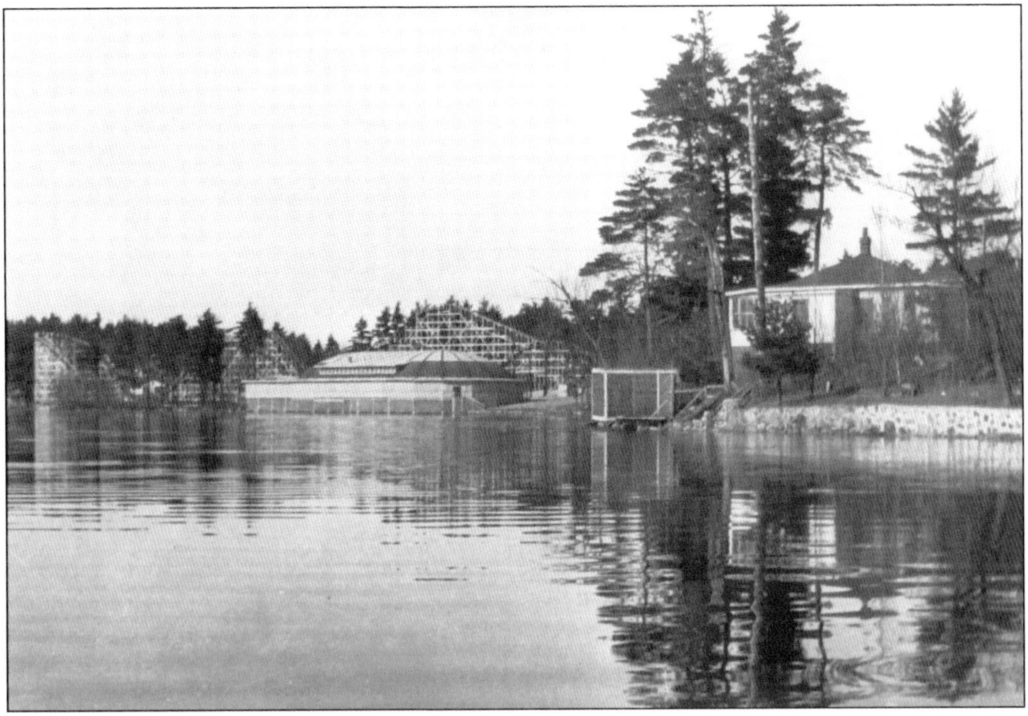

This photograph from across Lake Mascuppic shows the new ballroom with the Deep Dip roller coaster surrounding it. The Deep Dip included a 70-foot plunge for the 12-person passenger cars. There was over 2,000 feet of track. (Courtesy Paul Dumont family.)

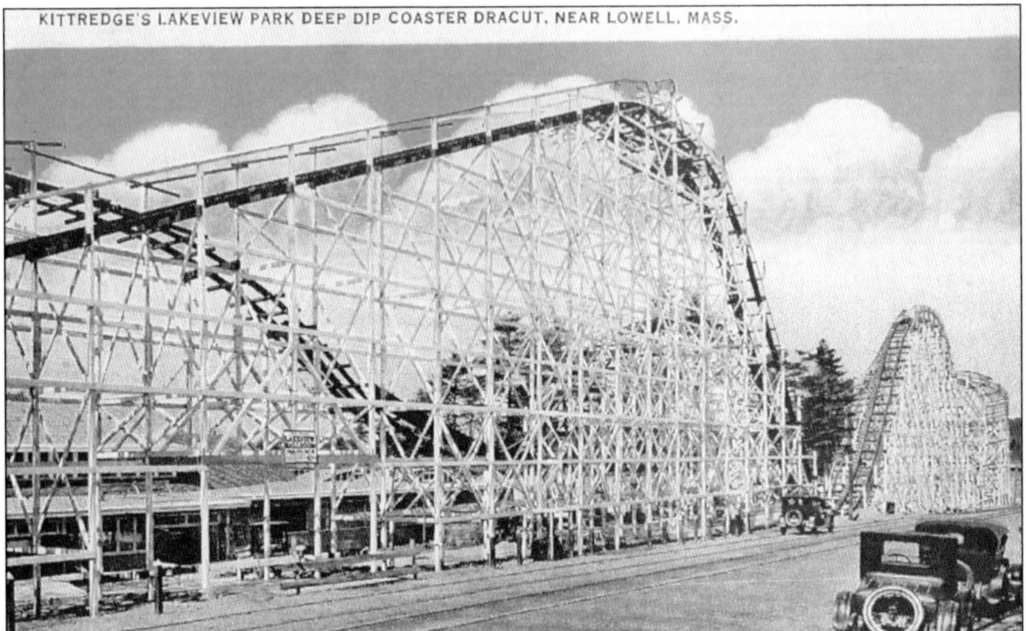

This 1928 postcard shows the Deep Dip roller coaster from the entrance of Lakeview Park. The waiting platform to board the roller coaster was 50 feet long. If visitors were not daring enough to ride the Deep Dip, the "Flying Horses" were still in operation. (Courtesy Paul Dumont family.)

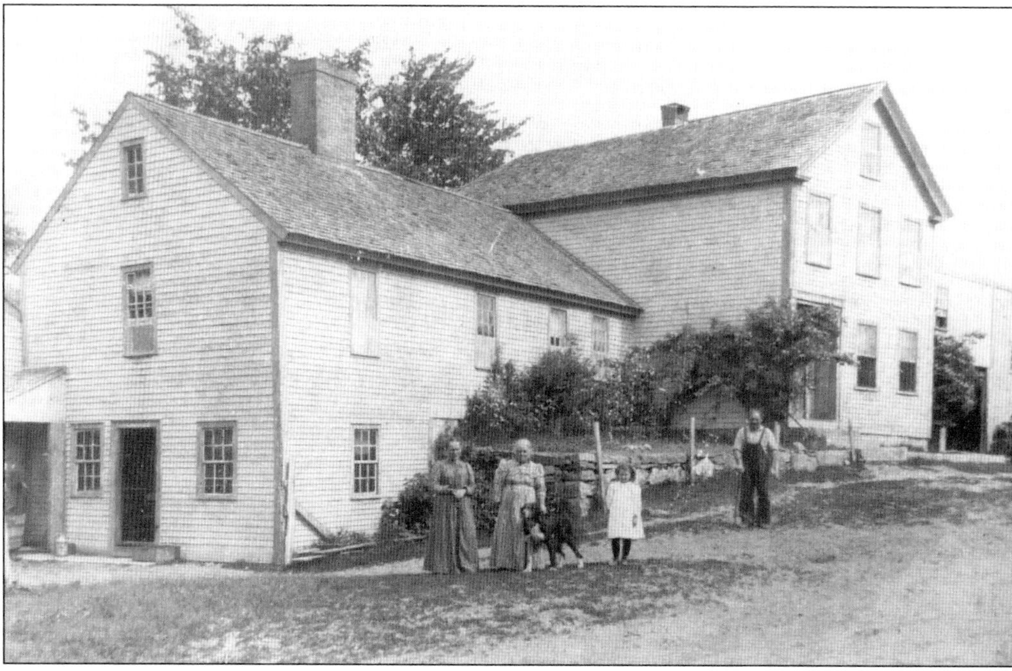

The Richardson family stood in front of their house on Mammoth Road in the early 1900s. They are, from left to right, Lucinda Richardson; Emma Richardson, wife of Charles Richardson, who is not pictured; Florence Richardson, daughter of Emma and Charles; and Silas Richardson, brother of Charles.

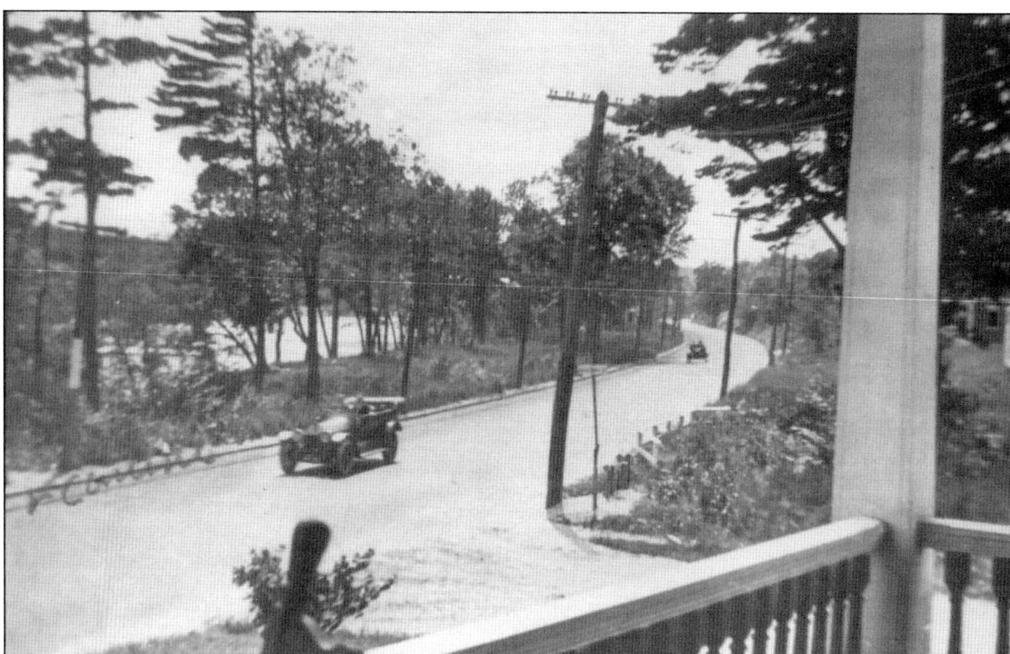

This photograph from a front porch looking over Route 110 along the Merrimack River was taken around 1910. This section of Dracut, known as Kenwood, once featured a ski lift, as well as Belle Grove, located on the Merrimack. (Courtesy Eleanor Duda.)

Broderick's Entertainers of Lowell played the opening evening of the new Lakeview Ballroom, which stayed open until 1:00 a.m. The big bands of Glenn Miller and Guy Lombardo also played at the Lakeview Ballroom. In the center of the new dance floor was a revolving crystal ball that beautifully illuminated the dance floor.

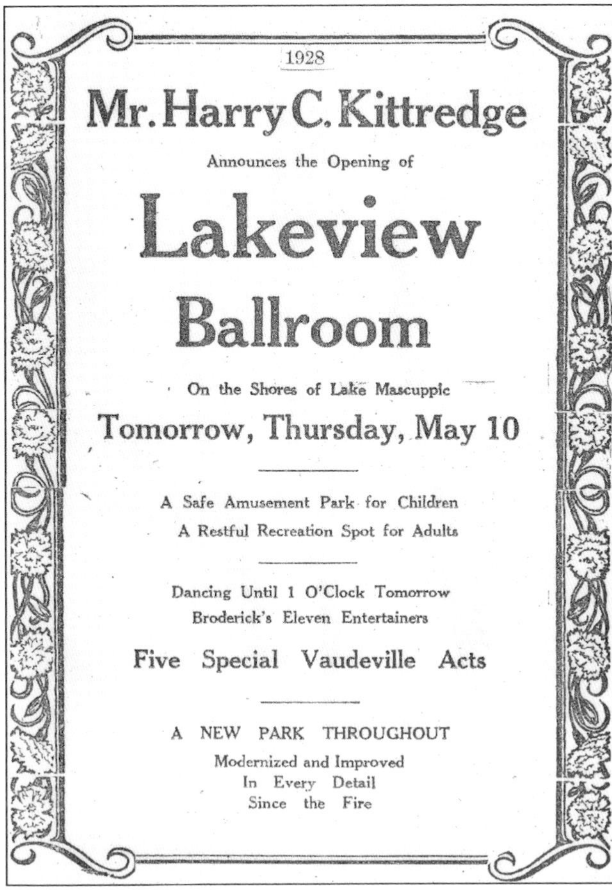

1928

Mr. Harry C. Kittredge

Announces the Opening of

Lakeview

Ballroom

On the Shores of Lake Mascuppic

Tomorrow, Thursday, May 10

A Safe Amusement Park for Children
A Restful Recreation Spot for Adults

Dancing Until 1 O'Clock Tomorrow
Broderick's Eleven Entertainers

Five Special Vaudeville Acts

A NEW PARK THROUGHOUT
Modernized and Improved
In Every Detail
Since the Fire

This postcard from around 1928 shows the entrance to the new ballroom. For many years, Matthew Urquart was the superintendent of Lakeview Park. His daughter Polly was well known throughout Dracut as the owner of Polly's Variety at the corner of Lakeview Avenue and Mammoth Road. The corner is now a park and was named "Polly's Corner" in her honor. (Courtesy Paul Dumont family.)

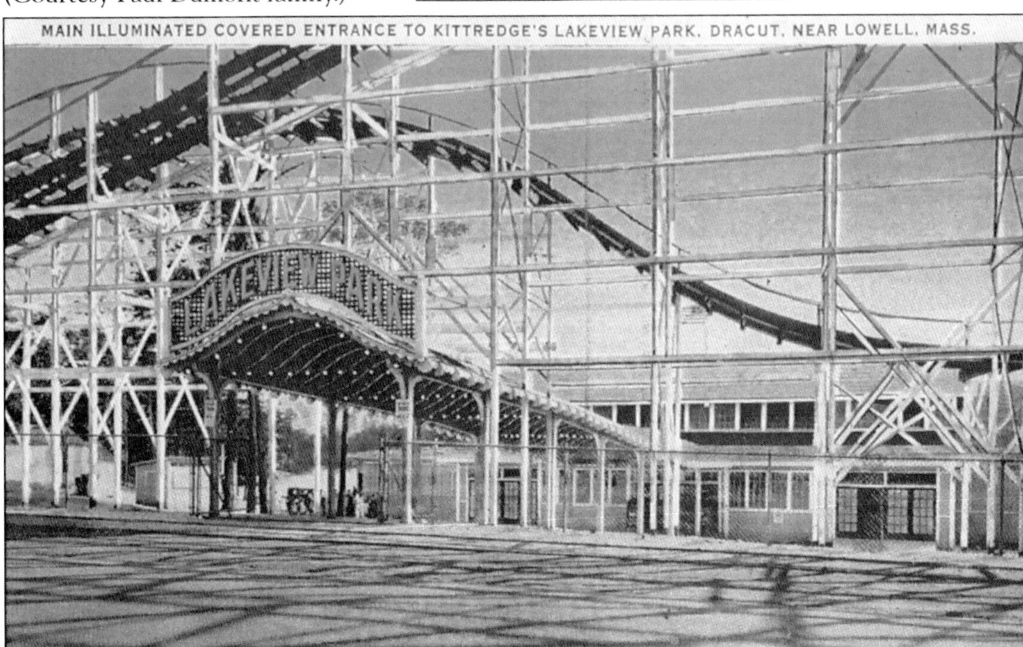

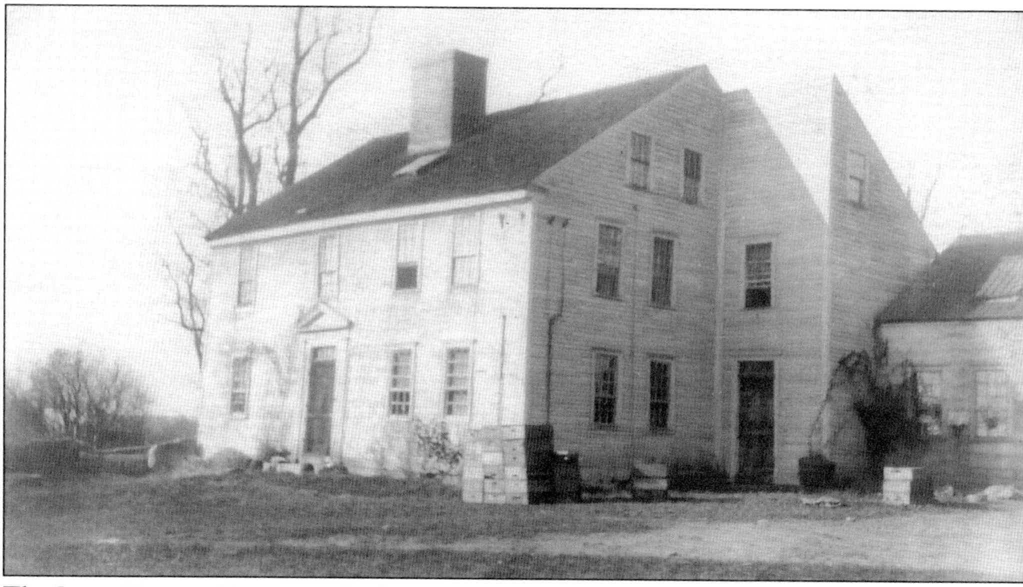

The Jonas Varnum House was built in 1781 on Varnum Road between Long Pond Road and Charles Street. Jonas Varnum was a veteran of the Battle of Bunker Hill. The home remained in the Varnum family until the 1940s. Unfortunately, like so many of Dracut's 18th-century homes, it was razed in 1953.

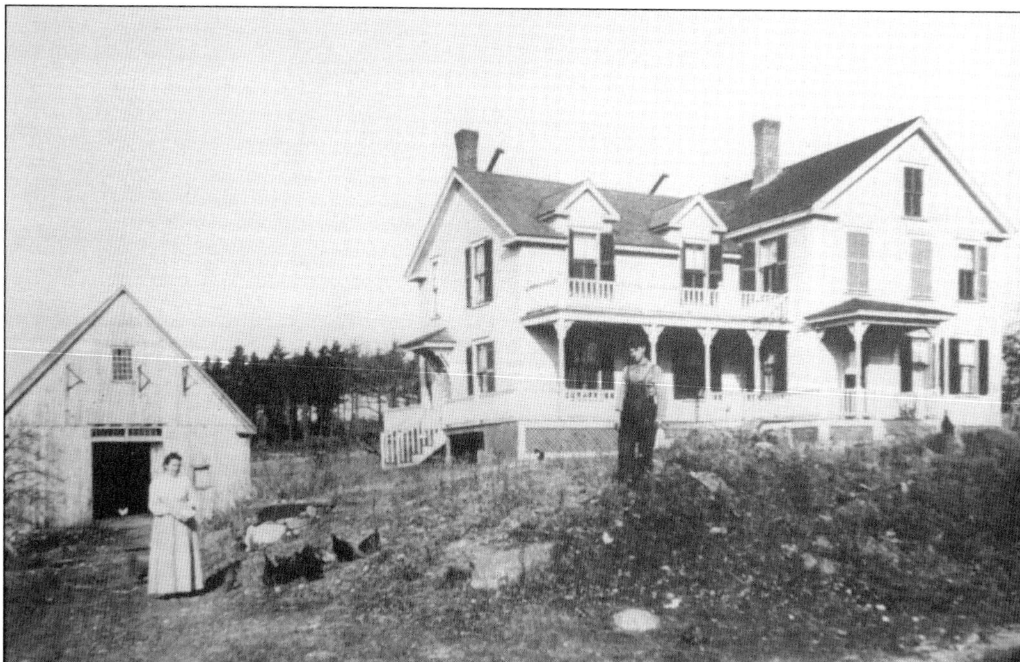

This has been a popular spot in Dracut for over a century. Previously the Black North Inn, today it is known as the Village Inn Restaurant. The dirt road in the foreground is Broadway Avenue. Local legend has it that the Village Inn is haunted. (Courtesy Lenny Proposki.)

Two

Growth and Expansion
1930–1960

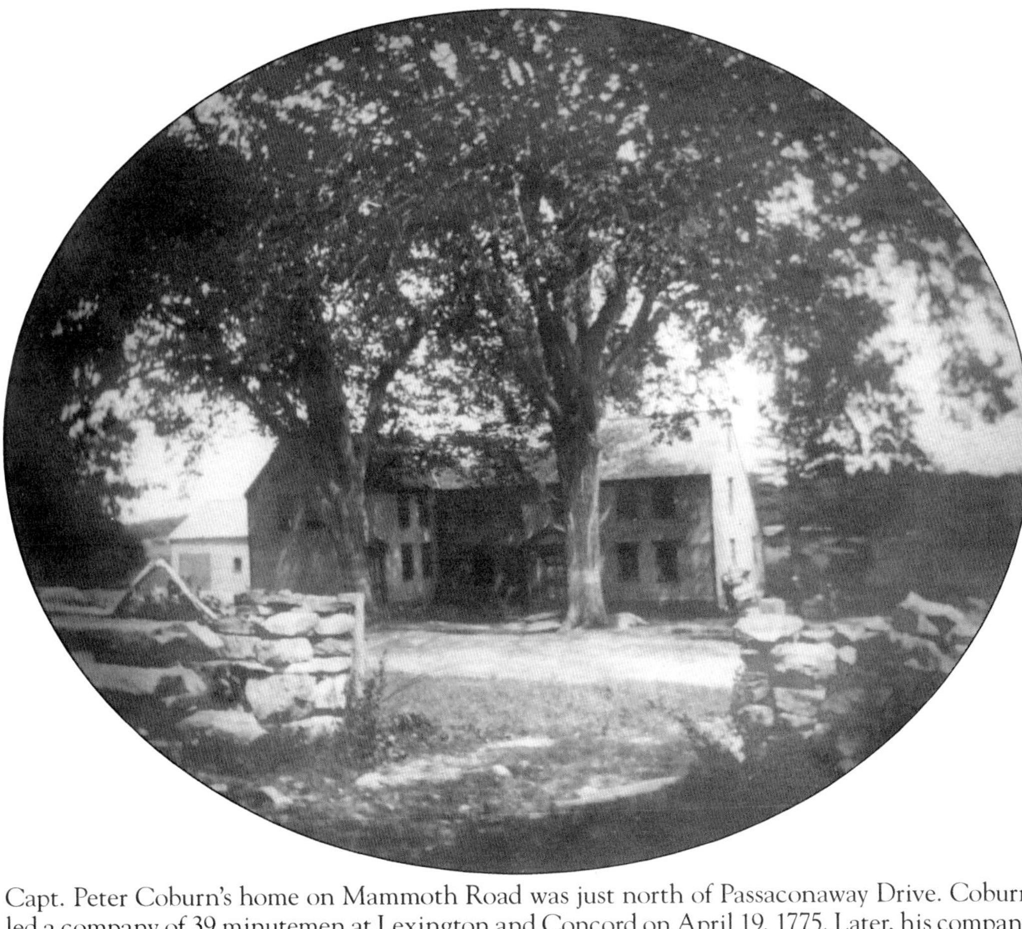

Capt. Peter Coburn's home on Mammoth Road was just north of Passaconaway Drive. Coburn led a company of 39 minutemen at Lexington and Concord on April 19, 1775. Later, his company also served in the siege of Boston and at Bunker Hill. The Coburn home burned in 1930.

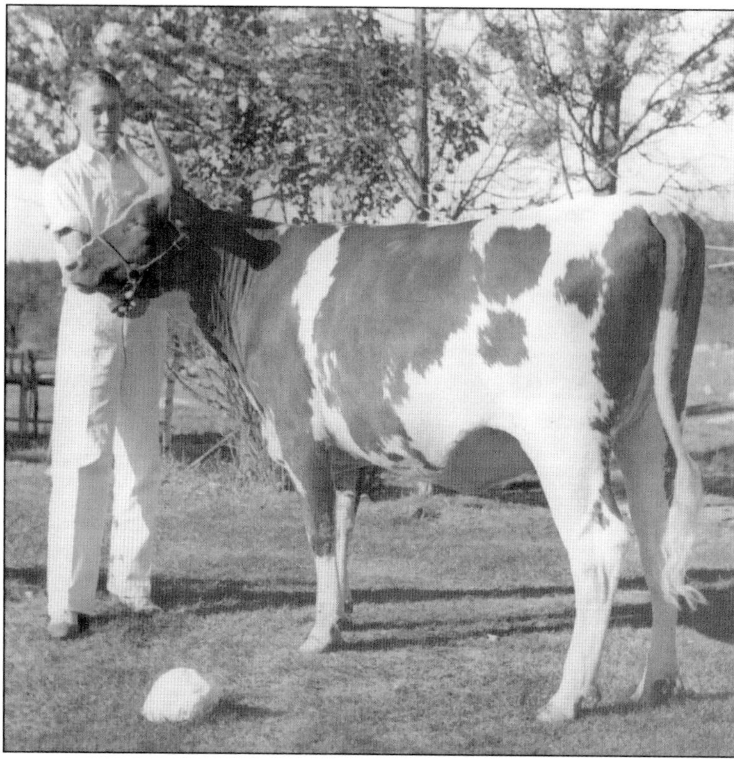

Willard Hibbard Jr. bred and raised an Ayshire heifer at his family farm off of Nashua and Davis Roads. In 1940, his heifer was named grand champion in the 4-H class at the Topsfield fair and champion at the Acton fair. The Middlesex County Farm Bureau Association praised him in their monthly newsletter, "That's a record to be proud of for a youngster who has never shown before." The Hibbard Farm was established by Willard Hibbard Sr. in the 1920s. (Both images courtesy Willard Hibbard Jr.)

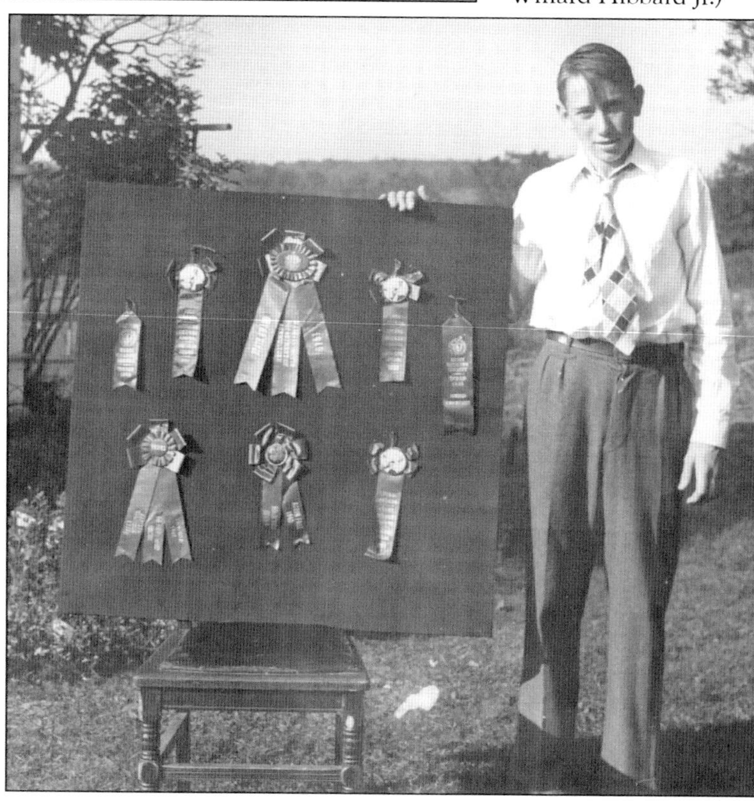

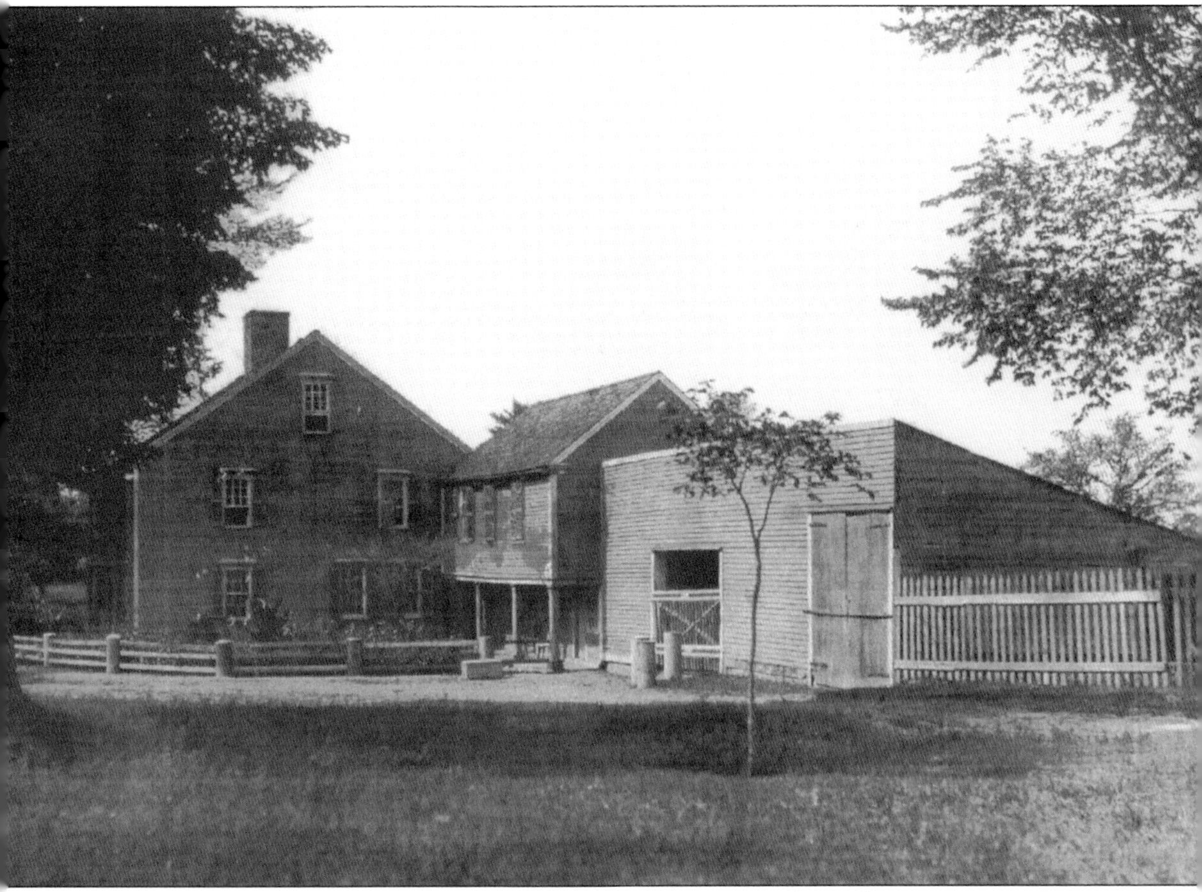

No history of Dracut would be complete without mentioning Joseph Bradley Varnum. His home, which burned in 1930, was located on the corner of Methuen Street and Parker Avenue. J.B. Varnum was a descendant of Samuel Varnum, Dracut's first permanent settler, and was born in the family home in 1751. With the outbreak of the Revolutionary War, J.B. Varnum served under Capt. Stephen Russell, whose home still stands on Pleasant Street, at the Battle of Lexington and Concord. Later, he his company were at Saratoga when British general Burgoyne surrendered. After the Revolution, he was called upon to help put down Shay's Rebellion by the governor of Massachusetts in 1786. After his military career, J.B. Varnum had an impressive political career, holding the offices of state senator, US senator, US congressman, Speaker of the House of Representatives, and justice of the court of common pleas. Varnum died on March 4, 1811, and is buried in the Varnum Cemetery.

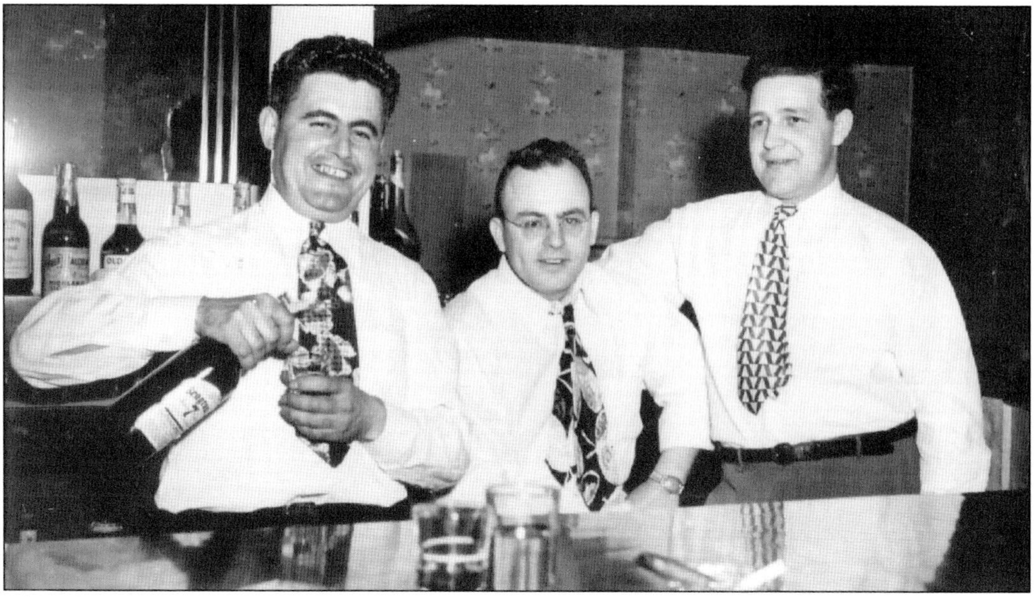

This photograph from around the mid-1940s was taken inside the Dracut Inn, which was on Nashua Road where Allardvale had been. Thomas Grondine is pictured on the right with two unidentified men. Since the time of the Allardvale Farm and store, several things have stood on this location, including the Coq d'Or Restaurant and Ronnie's Steak House. Today, it is a housing development named Allard's Grove. (Courtesy Paul Dumont family.)

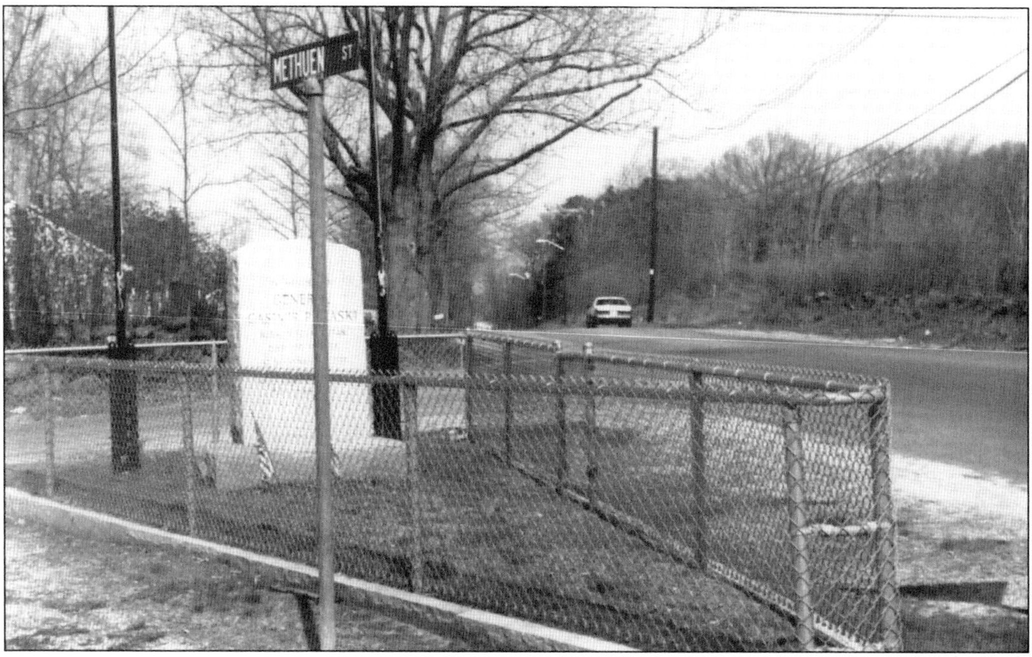

About 1933, a monument was erected to Casimir Pulaski by the Polish American residents of Dracut and Lowell. The monument is located at the junction of Arlington and Methuen Streets. Pulaski was from Poland, came to the colonies in 1777, and offered to help fight with the patriots and train the American cavalry. In 1778, he formed his own company of Polish soldiers and went to fight in the South.

John and Marie (Hebert) Elie owned the Golden Dairy and raised 10 children in Dracut: Ludgar, Leo, Yvette, Frederick, Raymond, Irene, Henry, Gerard, Theresa, and Arthur. Their youngest, Arthur, married Jeanette Perrault, and continued to run the dairy with his brothers. (Courtesy Paul and Bonnie Elie.)

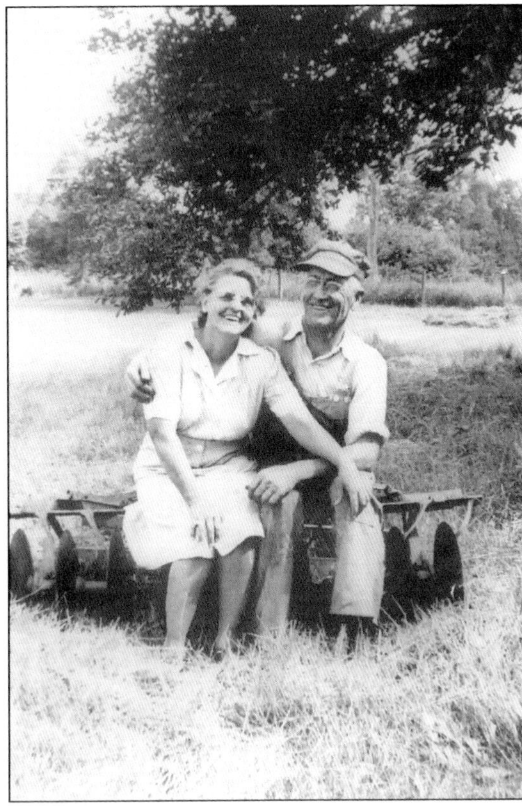

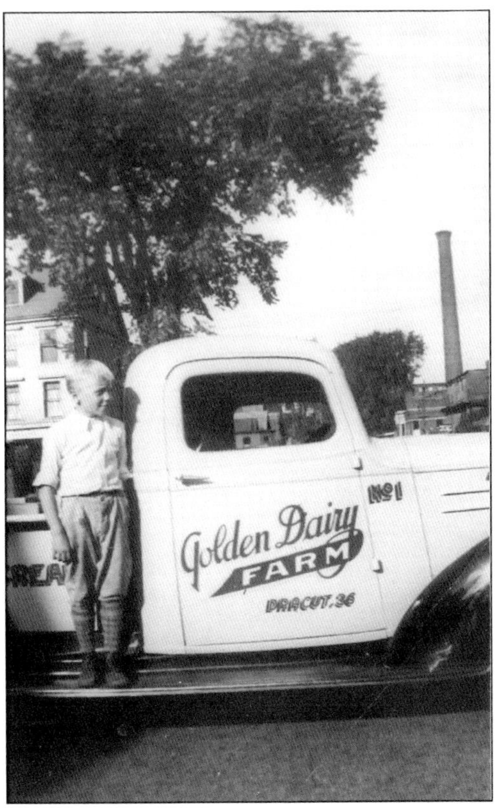

A little boy stands on the Golden Dairy truck on Lakeview Avenue. Arthur Elie, who ran the dairy for years, was killed in an automobile accident on the Aiken Street Bridge on January 26, 1963. After her husband's death, Jeannette sold the dairy. (Courtesy Paul and Bonnie Elie.)

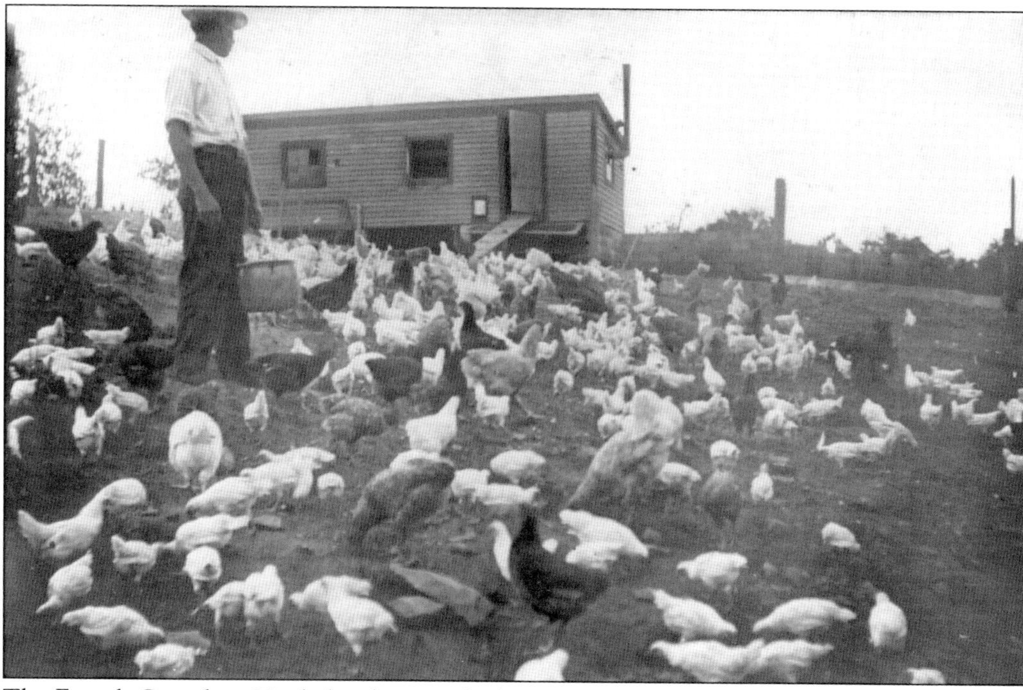

The French Canadian Houle brothers worked in the Lowell Mills and had a chicken farm on Arlington Avenue. In this photograph, Henry Houle Zoel feeds chickens on the farm around 1930. The Houle brothers also manufactured the first cement blocks ever used for commercial use in Dracut.

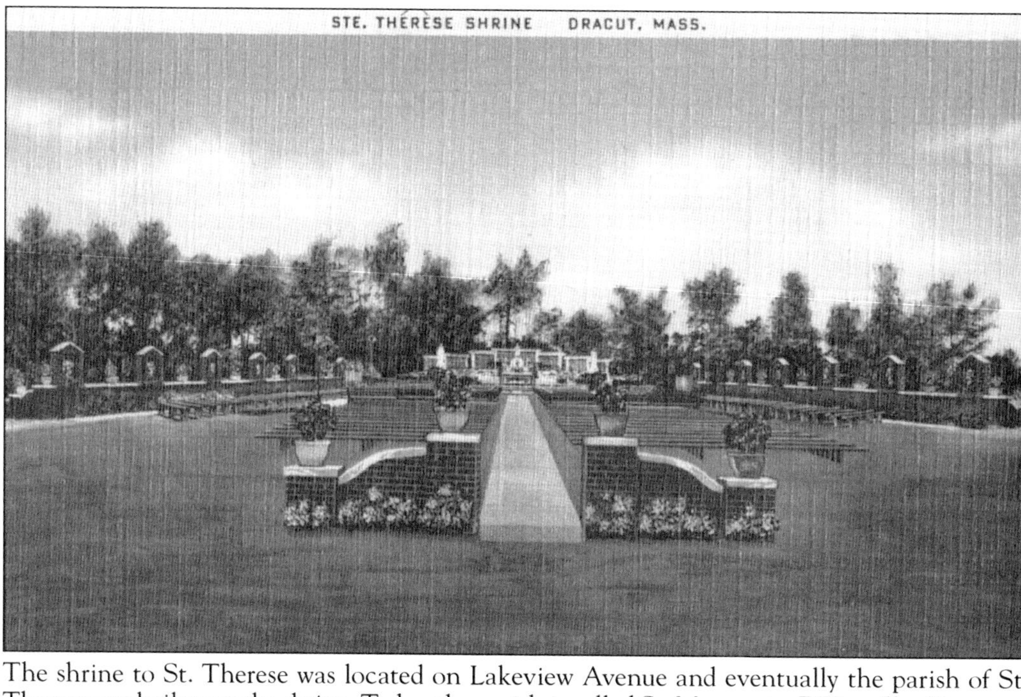

The shrine to St. Therese was located on Lakeview Avenue and eventually the parish of St. Therese was built near the shrine. Today, the parish is called St. Marguerite D'Youville. (Courtesy Paul Dumont family.)

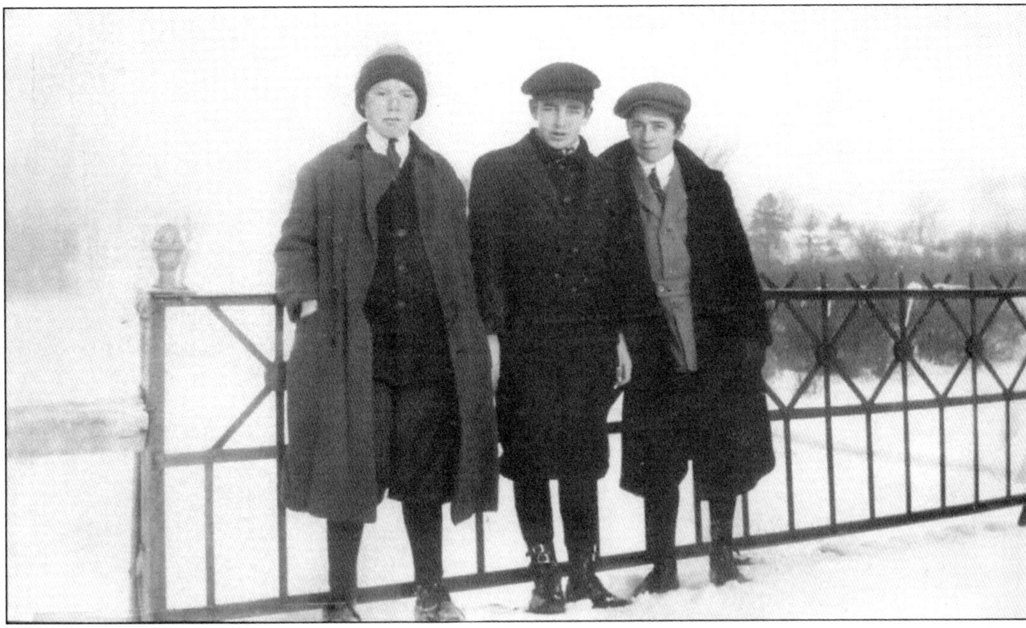

These young Dracut men are pictured on the old Parker Avenue Bridge in 1936 before the flood that year. It is difficult to decipher the names on the back of the photograph, but they appear to be, from left to right, as follows: Edward Taft, Lyle Smith, and Thomas Hoar.

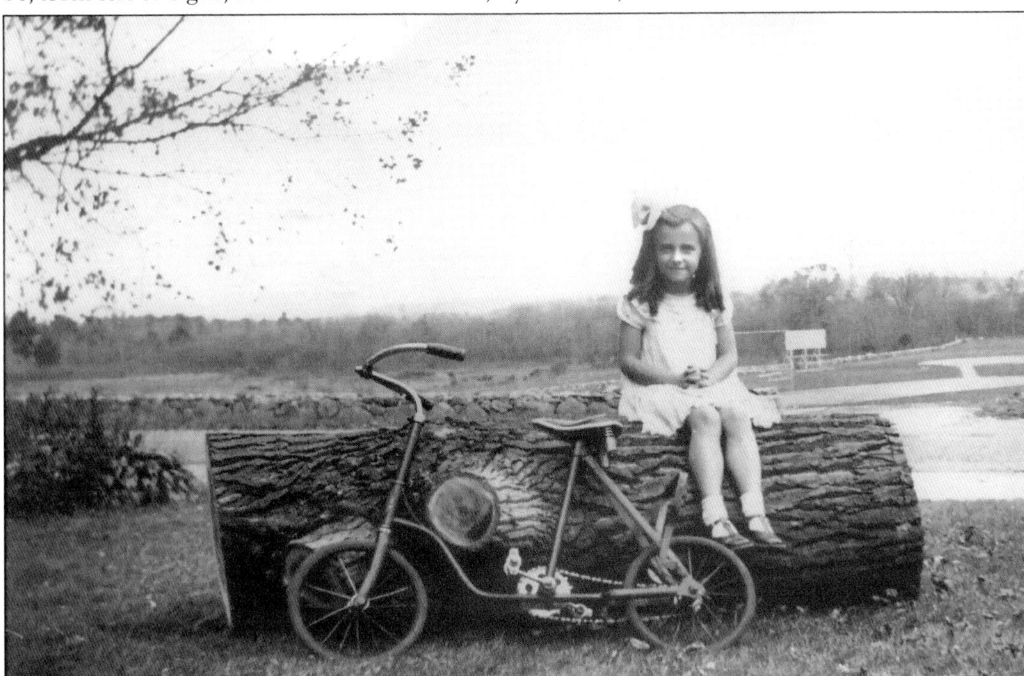

This young girl is sitting in front of the Thomas F. Carrick Field, which was built in the 1930s using Work Projects Administration funds. The park featured a brand new baseball diamond that was the first of its kind in Dracut. The official dedication ceremony for the field and a parade took place on May 28, 1938. The first baseball game played at Carrick field was between the Dracut Beavers and the Littleton Athletic Association. Dracut won the game 5-1.

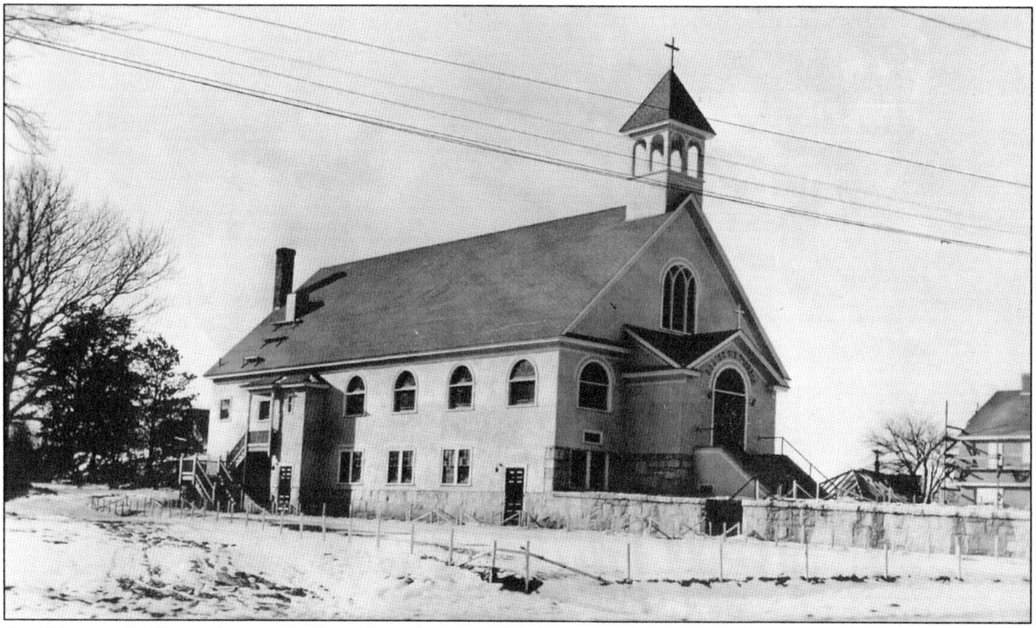

St. Therese's (French) Catholic Church on Lakeview Avenue was built in 1927 and burned on January 21, 1938, after a candle was knocked over on the altar. The parish merged in 2001 with St. Marguerite D'Youville. This photograph shows the church before the fire. (Courtesy Paul Dumont family.)

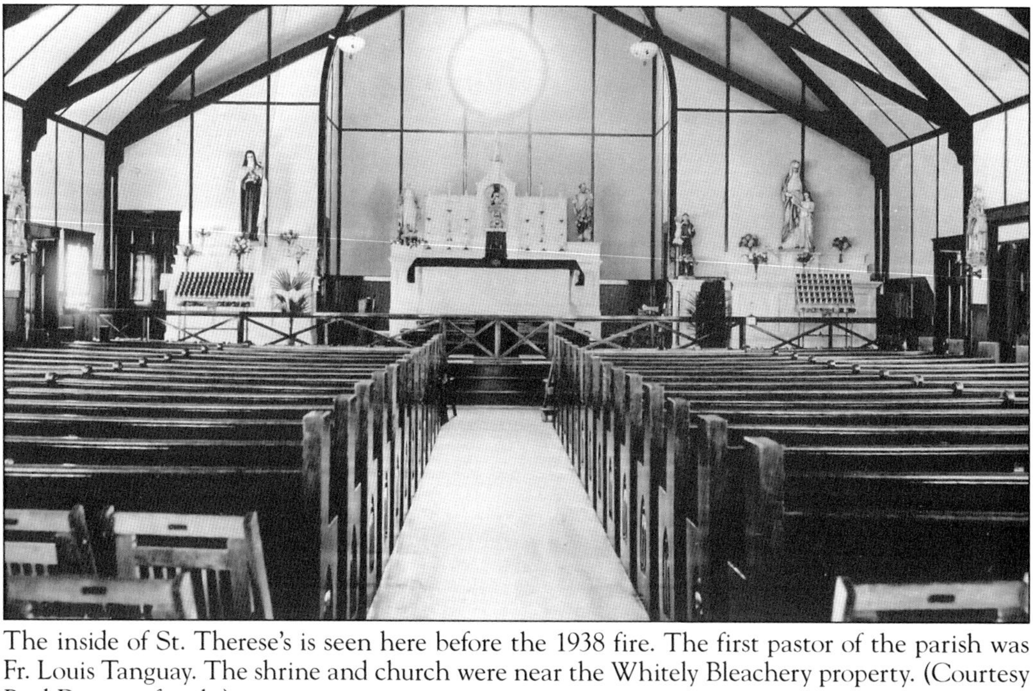

The inside of St. Therese's is seen here before the 1938 fire. The first pastor of the parish was Fr. Louis Tanguay. The shrine and church were near the Whitely Bleachery property. (Courtesy Paul Dumont family.)

Alice "Belle" Varnum-Isherwood (at right) lived on the Varnum estate on Methuen Street (Route 110) in the Kenwood district and created Belle Grove, a recreation area along the Merrimack River. Belle Grove was most popular between World War I and World War II.

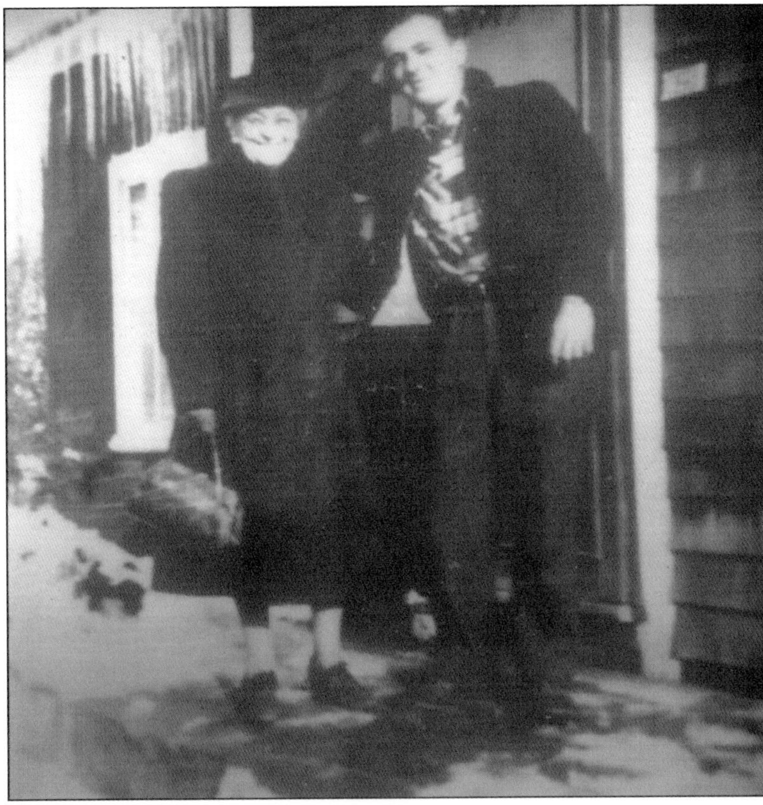

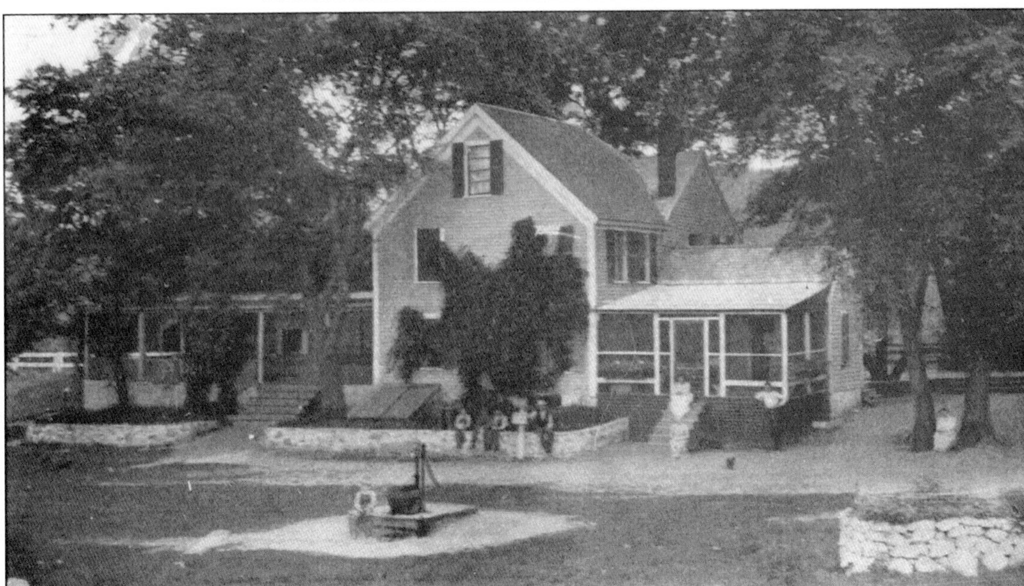

Belle Grove, Dracut, Mass.

The Red Rest Inn at Belle Grove, seen on this postcard, had to be razed in 1934 after a fire. Ernest Gunther, the fire chief, investigated the fire and determined that it began in the kitchen. Built before the boulevard along the river was created, the inn was only about 40 years old at the time of the fire. (Courtesy Paul Dumont family.)

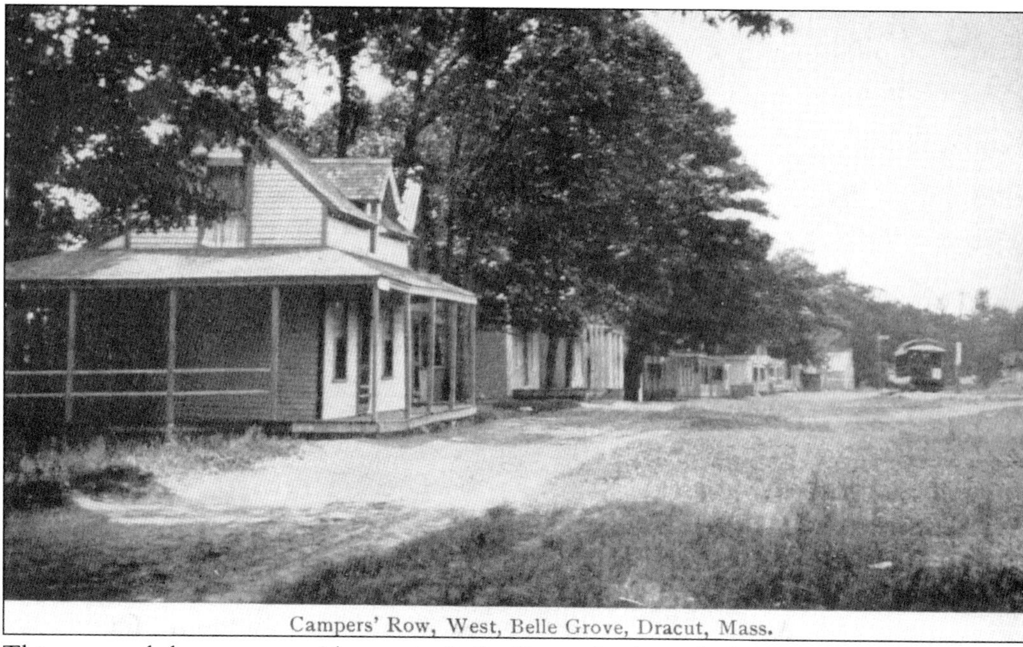

This postcard shows campers' homes in Belle Grove. In the right hand corner, a train brings campers to the popular recreation site. Visitors would also reach Belle Grove by boat. (Courtesy Paul Dumont family.)

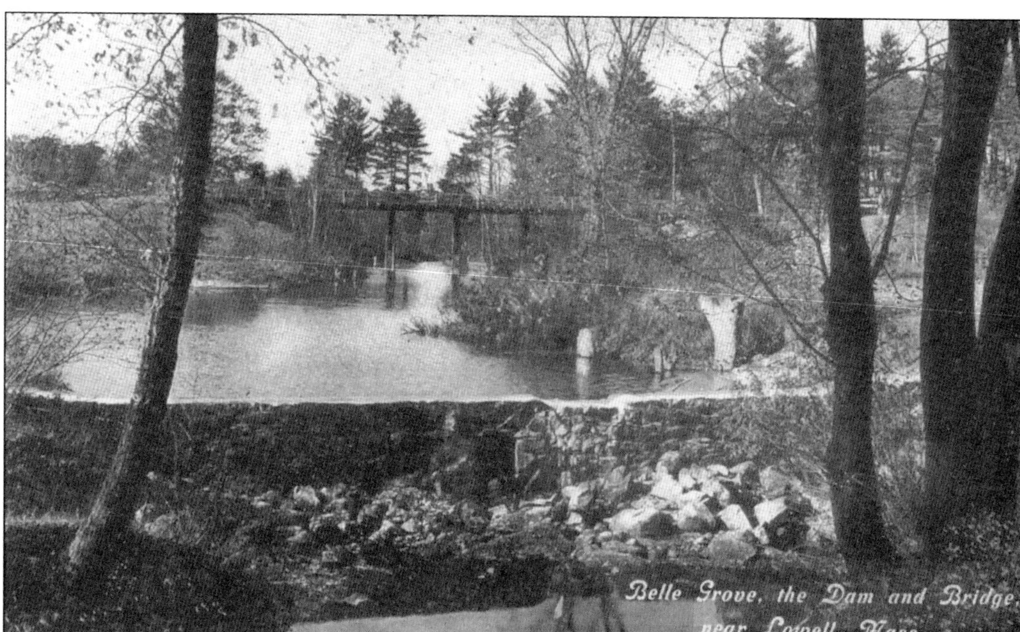

Belle Grove also offered picnic grounds, a dance hall, and swings for children. Belle Grove was finally shut down after the 1936 flood, but the Kenwood Improvement Association continued to use the area for picnics and other neighborhood activities. (Courtesy Paul Dumont family.)

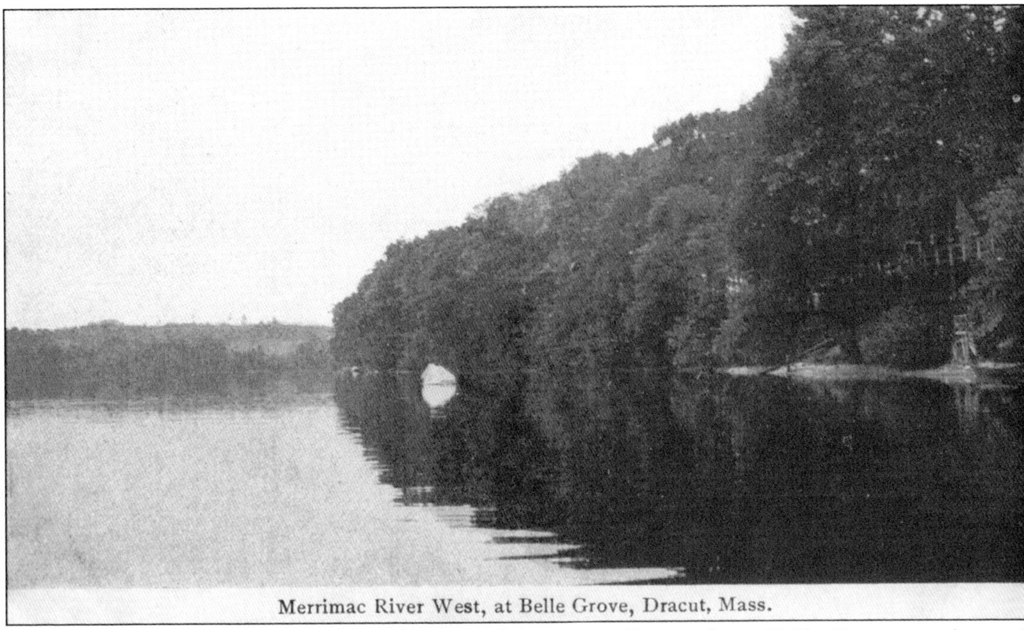

This postcard shows the shoreline along the Merrimack River where Belle Grove was located. Down the road from Belle Grove was Merrimack Park, which offered a small roller coaster, penny arcades, and boat rides along the river. Merrimack Park was ruined by the 1936 flood. (Courtesy Paul Dumont family.)

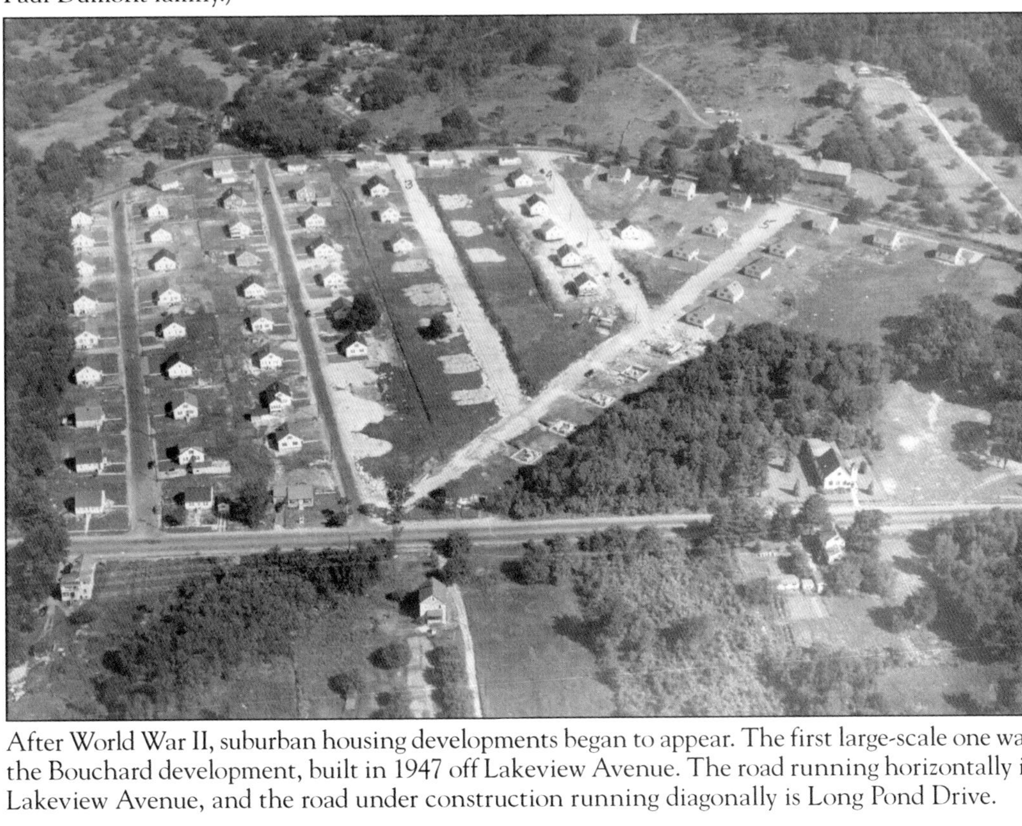

After World War II, suburban housing developments began to appear. The first large-scale one was the Bouchard development, built in 1947 off Lakeview Avenue. The road running horizontally is Lakeview Avenue, and the road under construction running diagonally is Long Pond Drive.

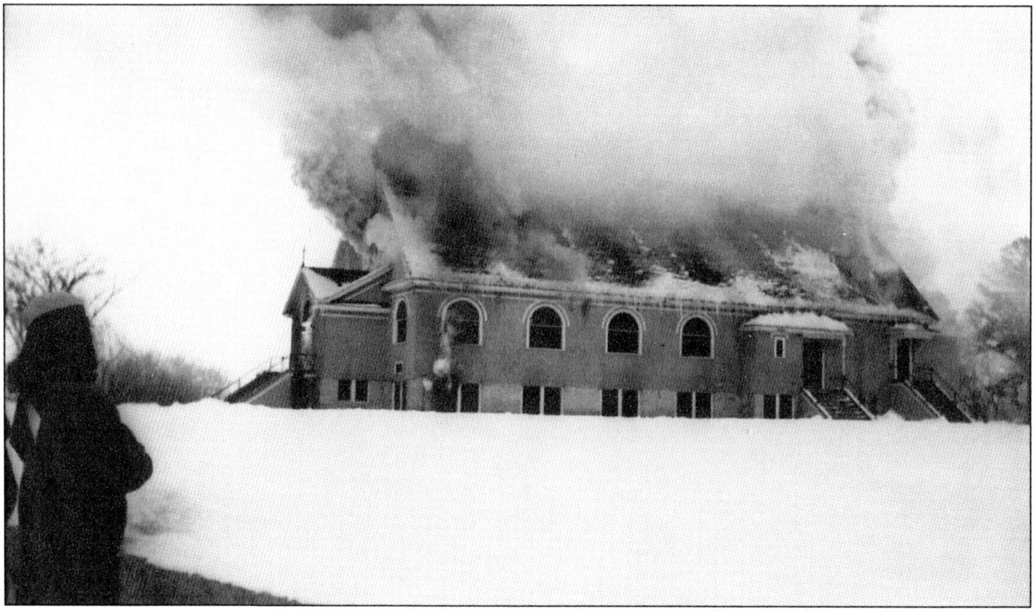

Tragedy struck St. Therese's Church on Lakeview Avenue in January 1938. A candle was knocked over and, very quickly, the building was engulfed in flames. The parish's second pastor, Fr. Francis Gauthier, had just retired when the fire destroyed the 10-year-old building. (Courtesy Paul Dumont family.)

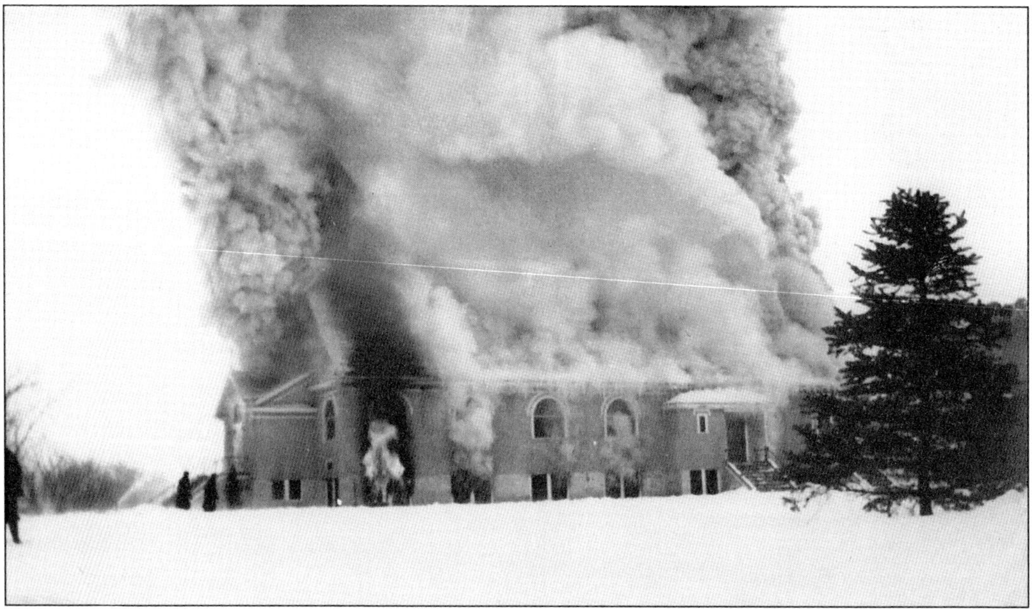

After the fire destroyed the church, it was rebuilt under Fr. Arthur Mercier. While the rebuilding took place, the Parker Avenue School was used for services. The new building was protected against future fires because it was made with brick obtained from the Lowell Technological Institute. (Courtesy Paul Dumont family.)

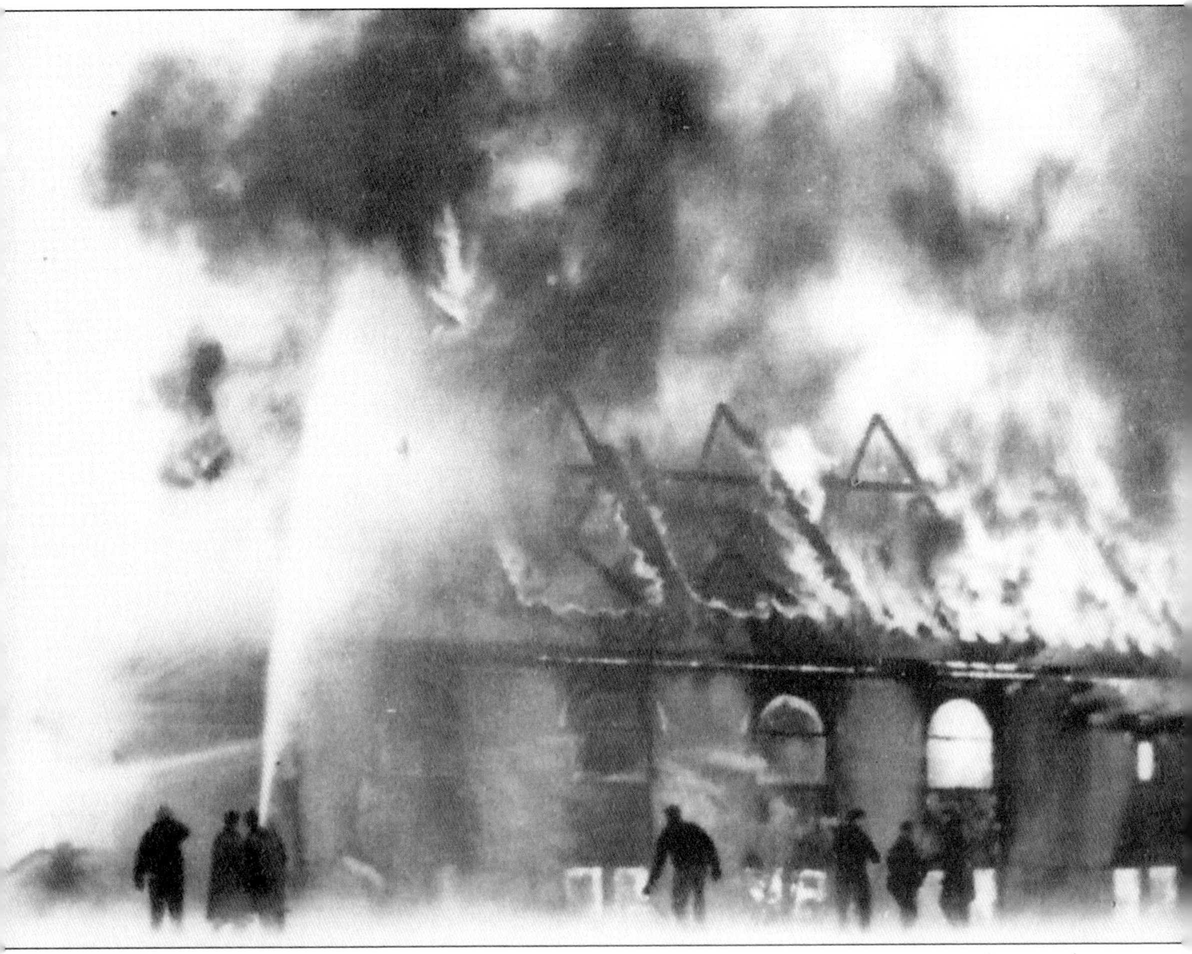

St. Therese's rebuilt after the 1938 fire and several changes were made to the church over the years. One significant change occurred in 1968, when Mass at St. Therese's was no longer said in French and all services switched to English. In 1975, a new convent was built for the nuns and the inside of the church received new pews. In 2001, a reconfiguration of parishes in the Archdiocese of Boston greatly affected St. Therese's when it was renamed St. Marguerite D'Youville Parish. St. Marguerite D'Youville was canonized by Pope John Paul II in 1990. She is known as the "Mother of Universal Charity" and was the first native-born Canadian to be elevated to sainthood. Her feast day is October 16. The current pastor of St. Marguerite D'Youville is Fr. Marc Bishop. (Courtesy Paul Dumont family.)

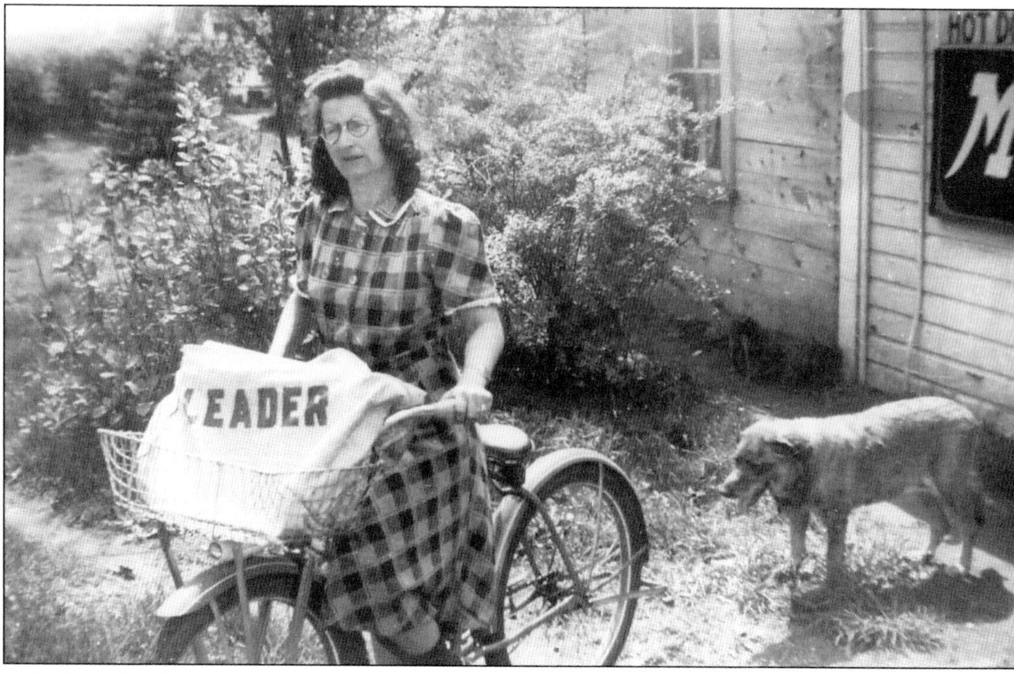

Polly Urquhardt was a regular fixture in Dracut for over 40 years. Her store, Polly's Variety, was at the corner of Lakeview Avenue and Mammoth Road. Today, the park at that corner, Polly's Corner, bears her name. She also delivered newspapers by bicycle.

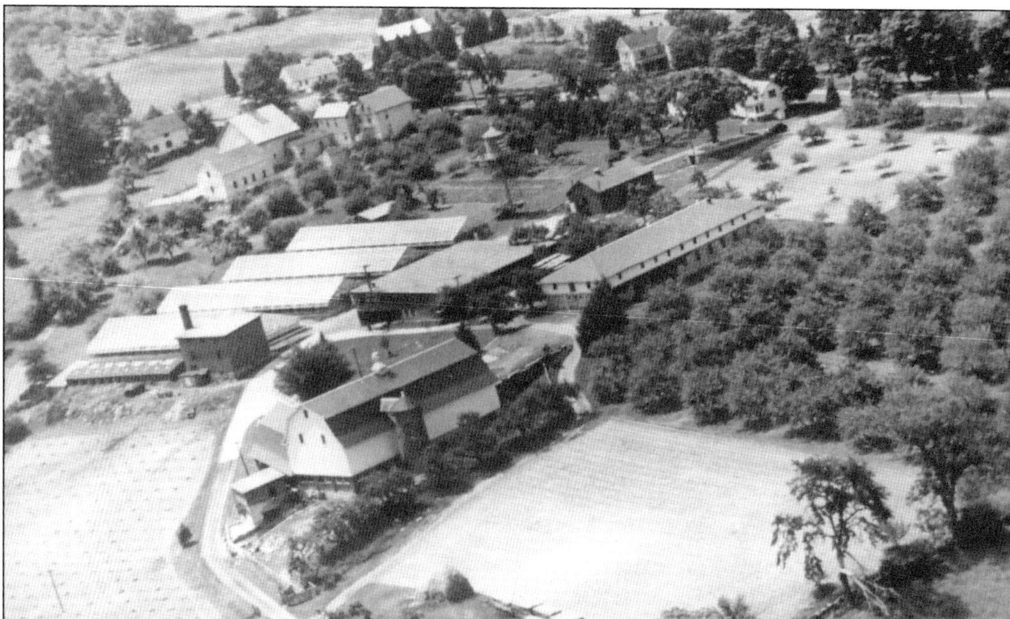

This aerial photograph shows Beaver Brook Farm, owned by the Richardson family, in 1939. In 1903, the farm's first greenhouse was built by Justice C. Richardson. Referred to as "Greenhouse No. 1," it had a furnace, allowing for the growing of seedlings during the winter. Squash was the main vegetable grown in this greenhouse; years later it was used primarily for flower seedlings.

DEDICATION OF

DRACUT HIGH SCHOOL

BUILDING

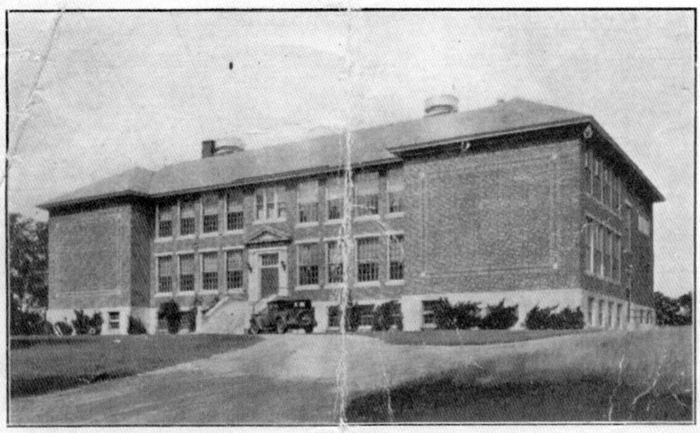

TUESDAY EVENING, JUNE 18th

NINETEEN HUNDRED THIRTY-FIVE

AT EIGHT O'CLOCK

Kindly present this program (invitation) at the door

In 1928, the Greenmont Elementary School was built. It was used as an elementary school until 1933–1934 when it was converted to Dracut's first high school. It originally opened as a two-year high school with the students finishing their junior and senior years at Lowell High School. It became a four-year high school, and the first class graduated in 1936. The principal in 1936 was James C. Riley. Greenmont was used as the town's high school until 1958 when a new high school was built on Lakeview Avenue on land donated by the Richardson family. From 1958 until 1968, the high school housed grades 7–12 when the junior high school was built (today's Englesby Intermediate School). From then until 1981, the high school housed only grades 10–12, and the superintendent's staff worked there as well. Beginning in 1981, the high school housed grades 9–12 as it still does today and the superintendent's staff was moved to the Collinsville School which was closed due to Proposition 2½. In 2011, the town meeting voted to approve a renovation of the high school. The auditorium at the Greenmont is named the James C. Riley Auditorium in honor of Dracut High's first principal.

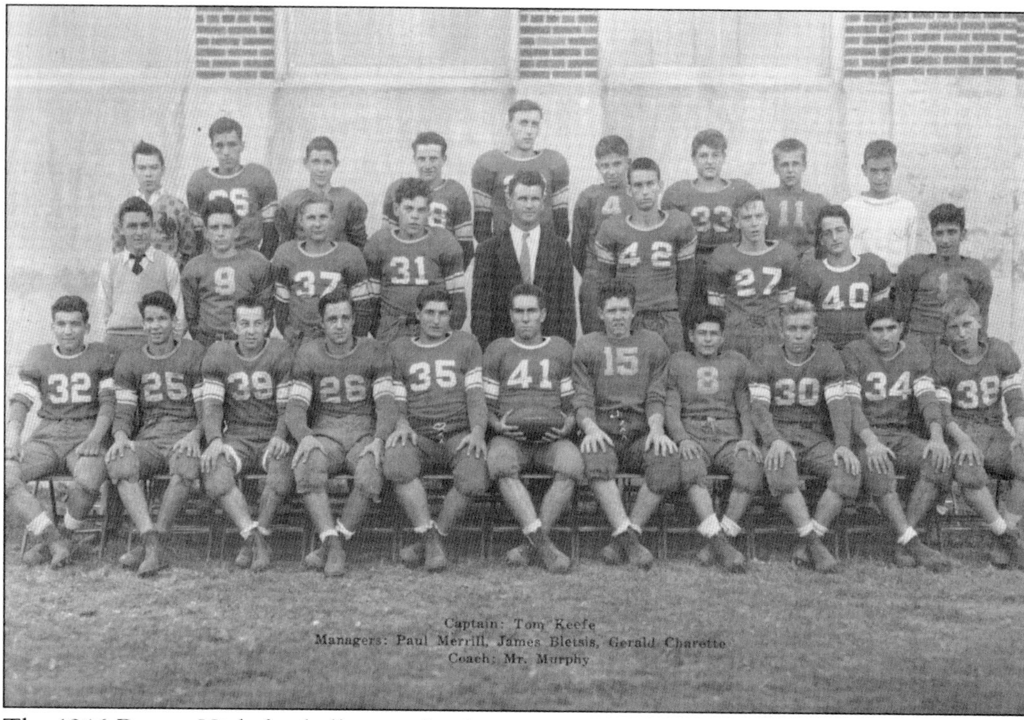

The 1946 Dracut High football poses for their team picture in Ed Murphy's first year as head coach. When the high school moved to its present location on Lakeview Avenue in 1958, the team began practicing and playing on the field there, but prior to that, they used Pleasant Street Park—now Monahan Park. In 1960, the school committee gave Pleasant Street Field back to the town for use for town activities.

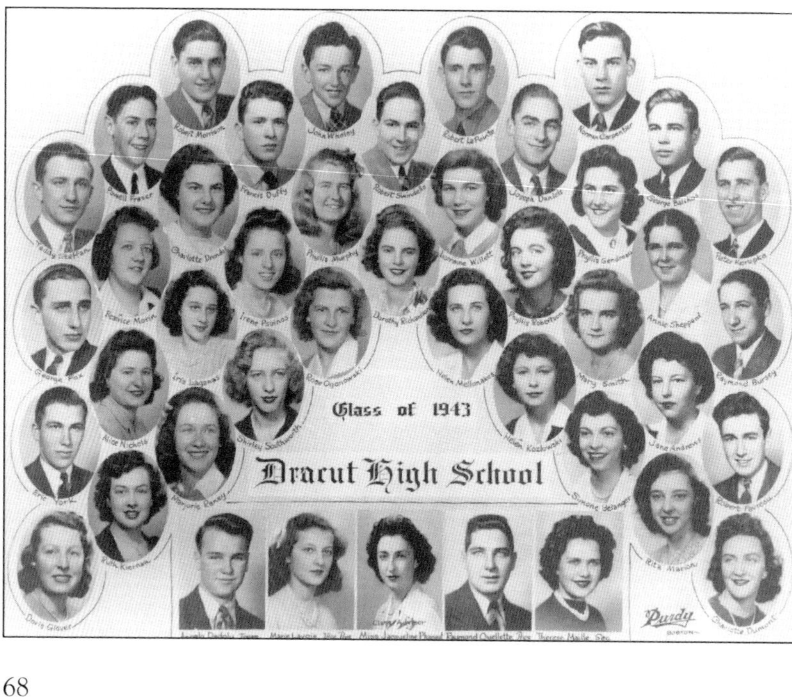

In 1943, with the country in the middle of World War II, the graduating class decided not to publish a yearbook, but they did pose for this class picture.

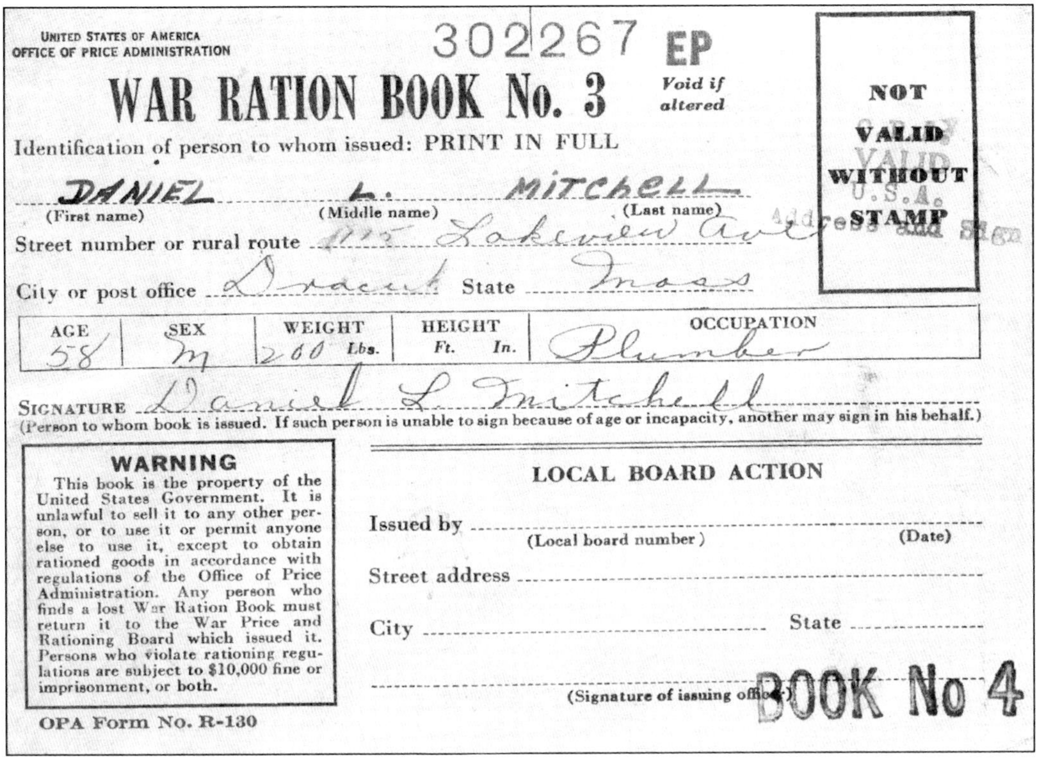
UNITED STATES OF AMERICA
OFFICE OF PRICE ADMINISTRATION

302267 EP

Void if altered

WAR RATION BOOK No. 3

NOT VALID WITHOUT STAMP

Identification of person to whom issued: PRINT IN FULL

DANIEL L. MITCHELL
(First name) (Middle name) (Last name)

Street number or rural route 115 Lakeview Ave

City or post office Dracut State Mass

AGE	SEX	WEIGHT	HEIGHT	OCCUPATION
58	M	200 Lbs.	Ft. In.	Plumber

SIGNATURE Daniel L. Mitchell
(Person to whom book is issued. If such person is unable to sign because of age or incapacity, another may sign in his behalf.)

WARNING
This book is the property of the United States Government. It is unlawful to sell it to any other person, or to use it or permit anyone else to use it, except to obtain rationed goods in accordance with regulations of the Office of Price Administration. Any person who finds a lost War Ration Book must return it to the War Price and Rationing Board which issued it. Persons who violate rationing regulations are subject to $10,000 fine or imprisonment, or both.

OPA Form No. R-130

LOCAL BOARD ACTION

Issued by .... (Local board number) (Date)

Street address ....

City .... State ....

.... (Signature of issuing officer)

BOOK No 4

This war ration booklet was found in the archives of the Dracut Historical Society. Americans had to use these during the war due to the lack of basic goods. At the bottom right, this war ration booklet is listed as OPA Form No. R–130.

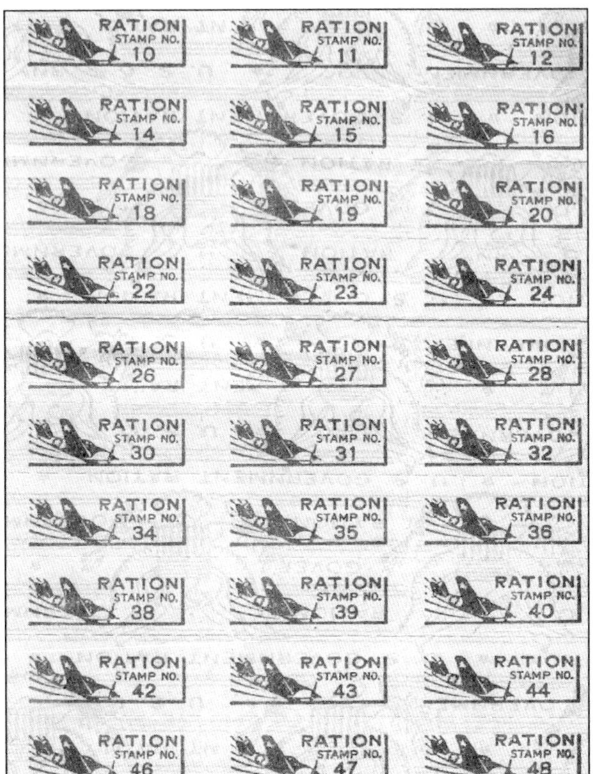

The Office of Price Administration (OPA) was created on August 28, 1941, by Pres. Franklin Roosevelt in order to control retail prices—except agricultural commodities—and to ration out the supply of other goods necessary for the war effort. Items that were rationed by OPA included tires, cars, shoes, sugar, gasoline, coffee, processed foods, and meat.

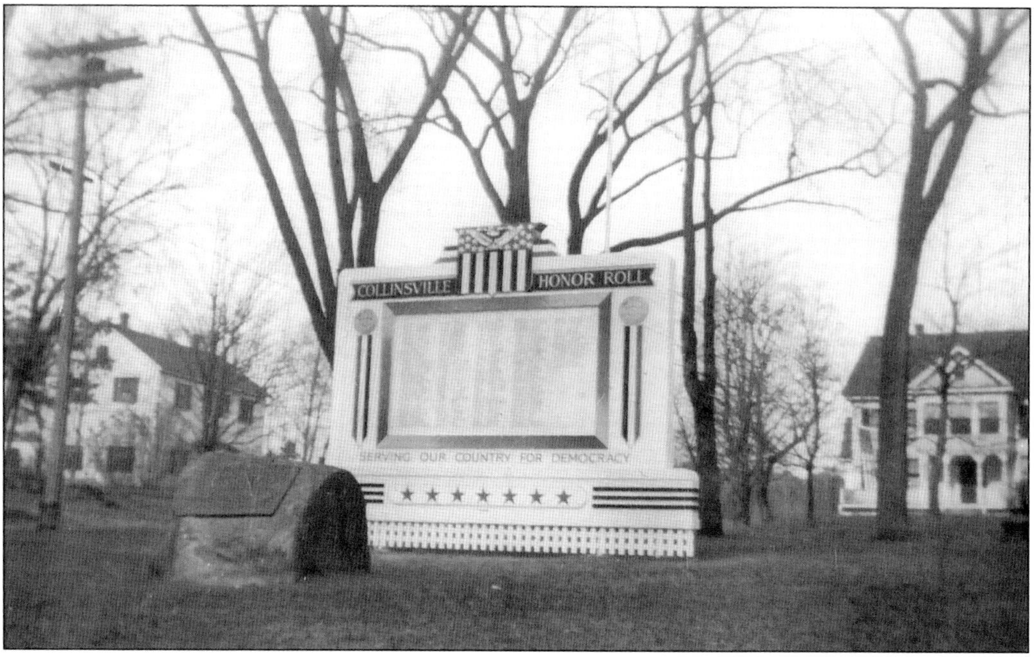

During World War II, Collinsville residents erected an honor roll in Costello Square—the intersection of Lakeview Avenue and Mammoth Road—to recognize Collinsville men who were fighting. The stone memorial in the forefront of the photograph was dedicated in 1929 to honor the four Dracut men who fought in the Spanish American War: Arthur Garland, Eden C. Walker, George H. Connell, Joseph G. Eaton.

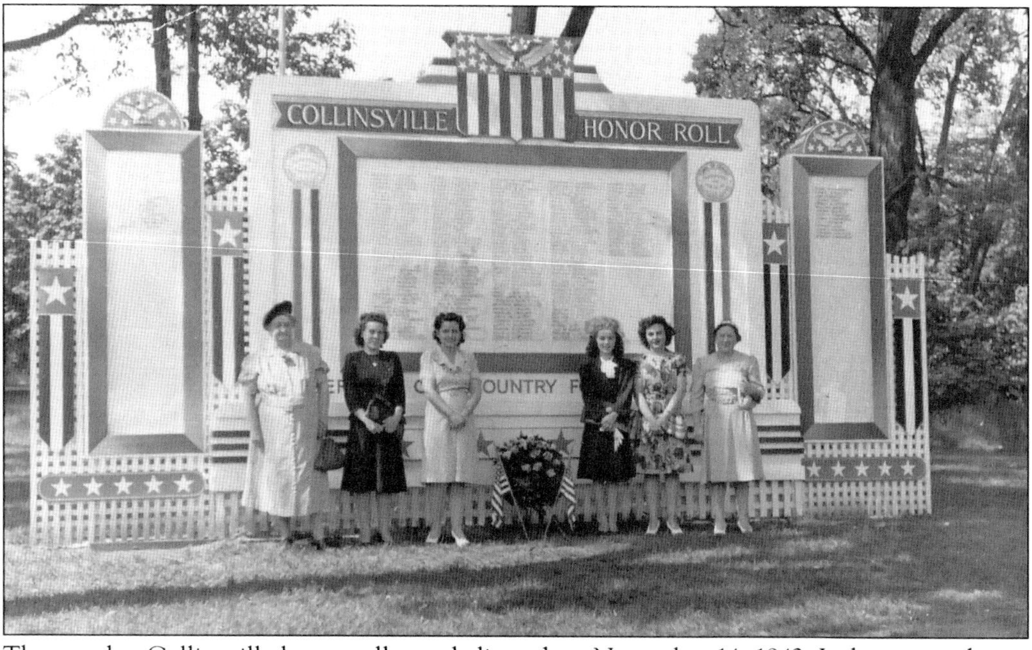

The wooden Collinsville honor roll was dedicated on November 14, 1943. It deteriorated over the years and was eventually torn down. A memorial honoring all Dracut men and women who fought in the nation's wars was later erected on the grounds of Dracut High School.

There were numerous dairy farms in Dracut. In the early 1900s, John F. Elie established the Golden Dairy on Loon Hill. Pictured here is his son Arthur Elie in the late 1930s, delivering milk. When World War II began, Arthur Elie joined the Navy and served in the South Pacific. (Courtesy Paul and Bonnie Elie.)

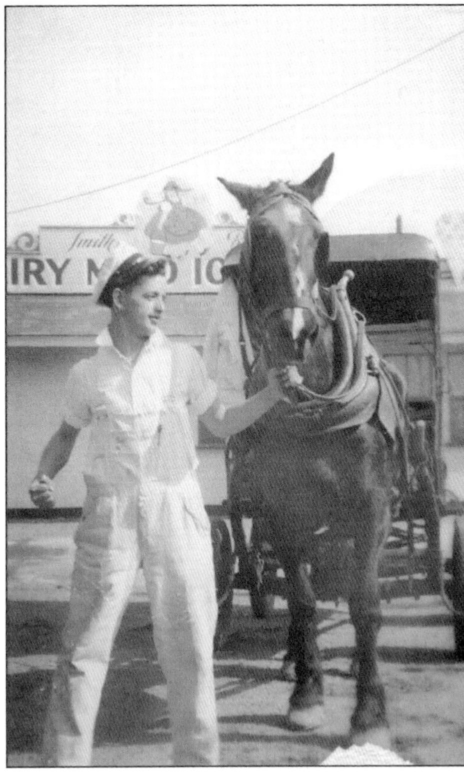

Lakeview Avenue, the dirt road on the right, looks much different today than it did in the 1940s. The house in the distance is the Oliver Coburn house, now home to the Dracut Historical Society. The field was part of the Richardson Farm, and after World War II, they leased it out as an airfield, ultimately donating the land to the school department in the 1950s. Today, Dracut High School, Englesby Intermediate School, Lakeview Junior High School, and Brookside Elementary are all found here. (Courtesy Paul Dumont family.)

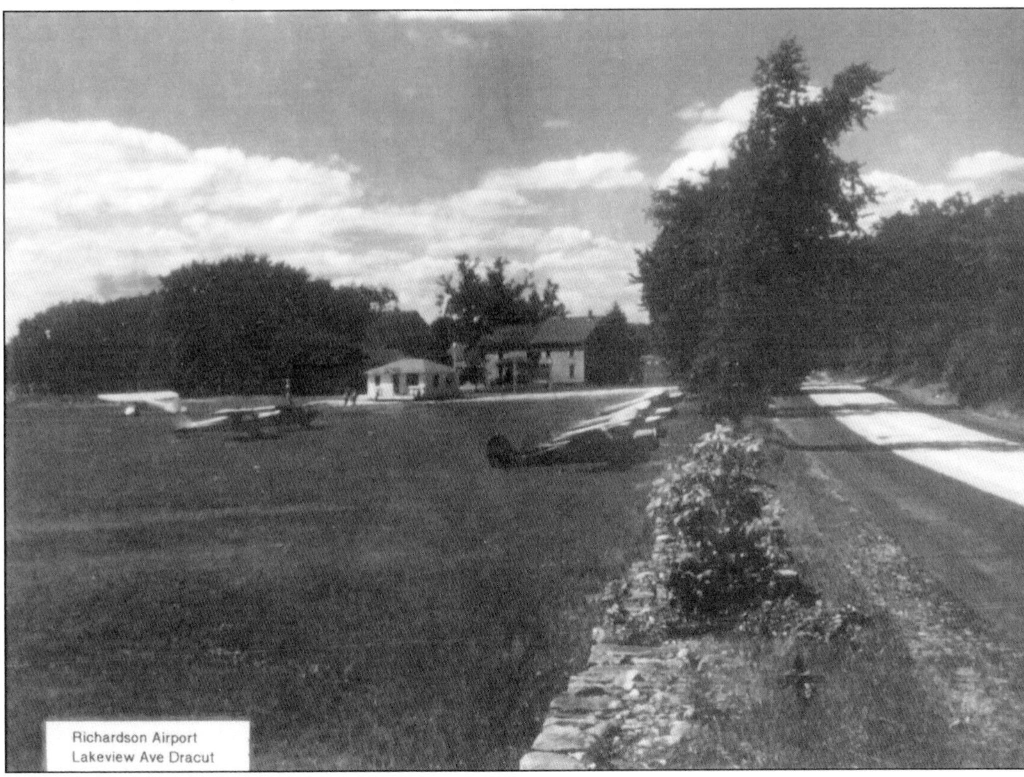

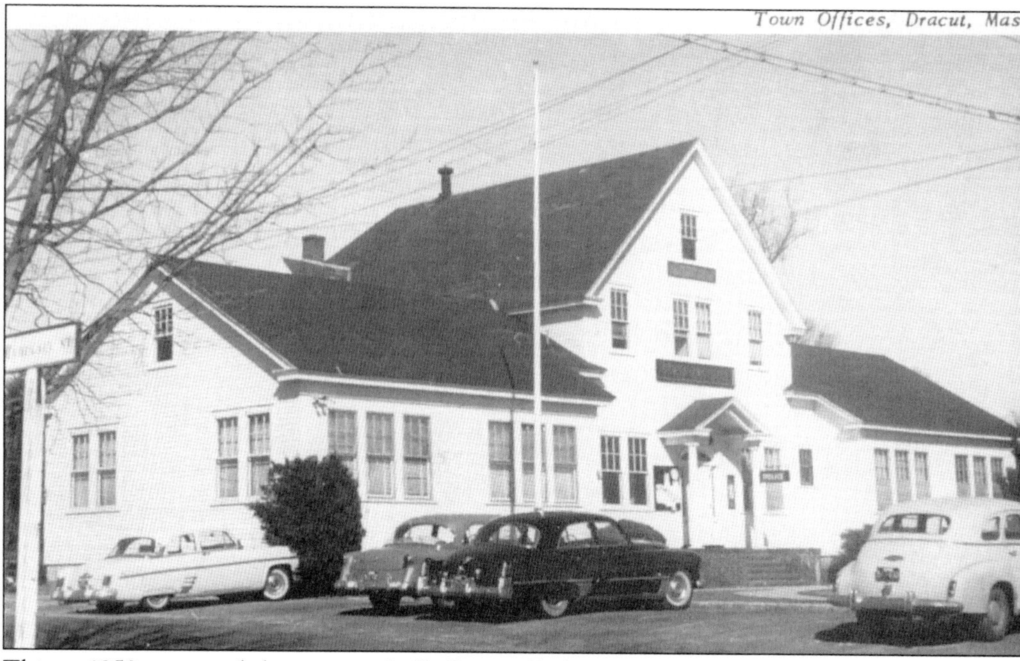

This c. 1950s postcard shows town hall. Originally built as Dracut Center School, it has been used as town offices since 1889. The current town manager is Dennis Piendak. (Courtesy Paul Dumont family.)

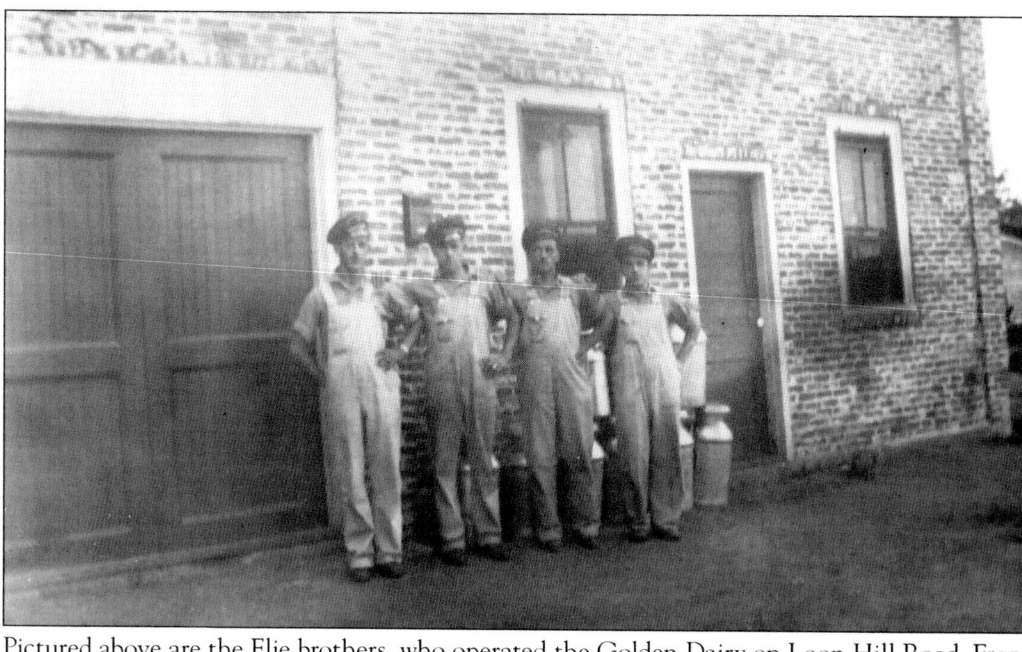

Pictured above are the Elie brothers, who operated the Golden Dairy on Loon Hill Road. From left to right are Arthur, Jerry, Fred, and Henry. They were the sons of John F. & Marie (Hebert) Elie, who established the dairy in the early 1900s. Arthur Elie was killed in an automobile accident in January 1963 on the Aiken Street Bridge. (Courtesy Paul and Bonnie Elie.)

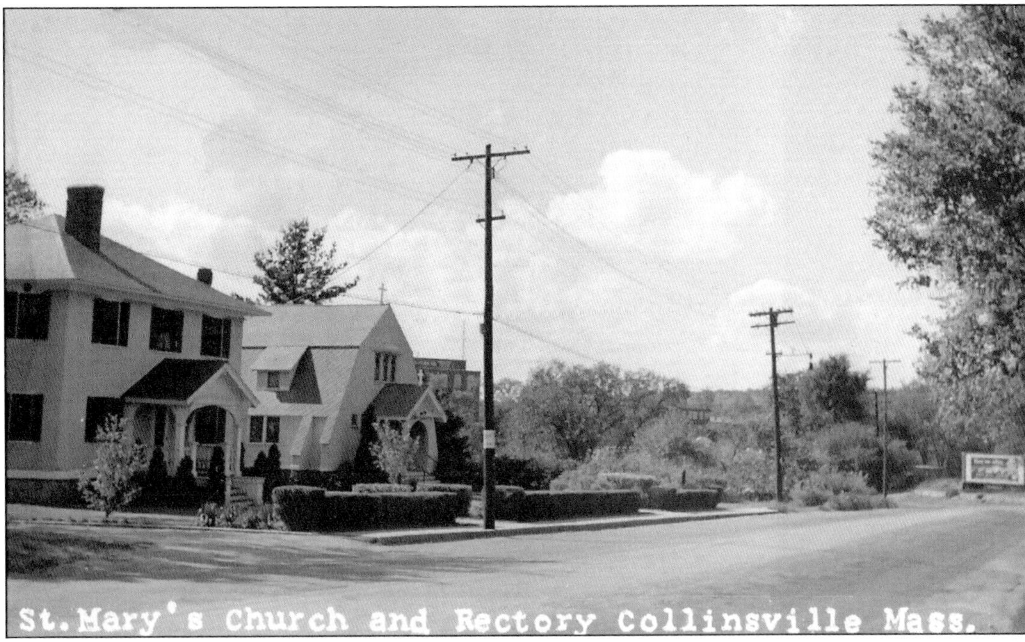

This is a postcard of St. Mary's of the Assumption Church on Lakeview Avenue, originally built by Michael Collins for his Irish Catholic mill workers. Later, after World War I, on the opposite side of Lakeview Avenue from St. Mary's, homes were built on Primrose Hill for Turkish immigrants working in the Beaver Brook Mills. (Courtesy Paul Dumont family.)

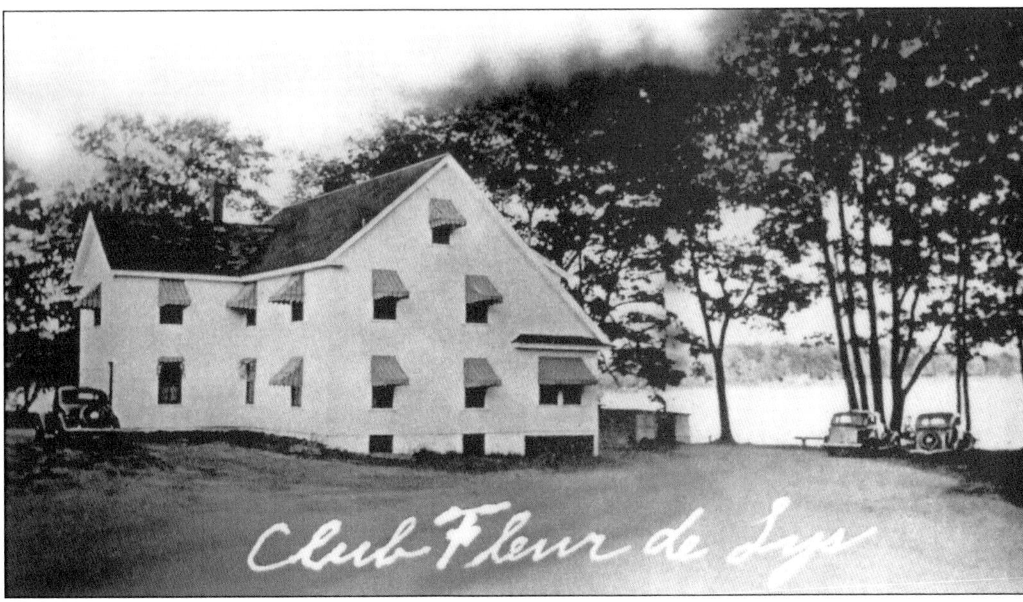

The Fleur-de-Lys Club was located on Elm Street along Long Pond. The Dracut-Tyngsborough town line goes directly through the building. It was opened as a French club by Emile Daigle and in later years was owned by Tom Clayton, who worked for WCAP Radio. During the 1950s, Clayton would fly over Dracut and broadcast from the air on the Fourth of July. (Courtesy Paul Dumont family.)

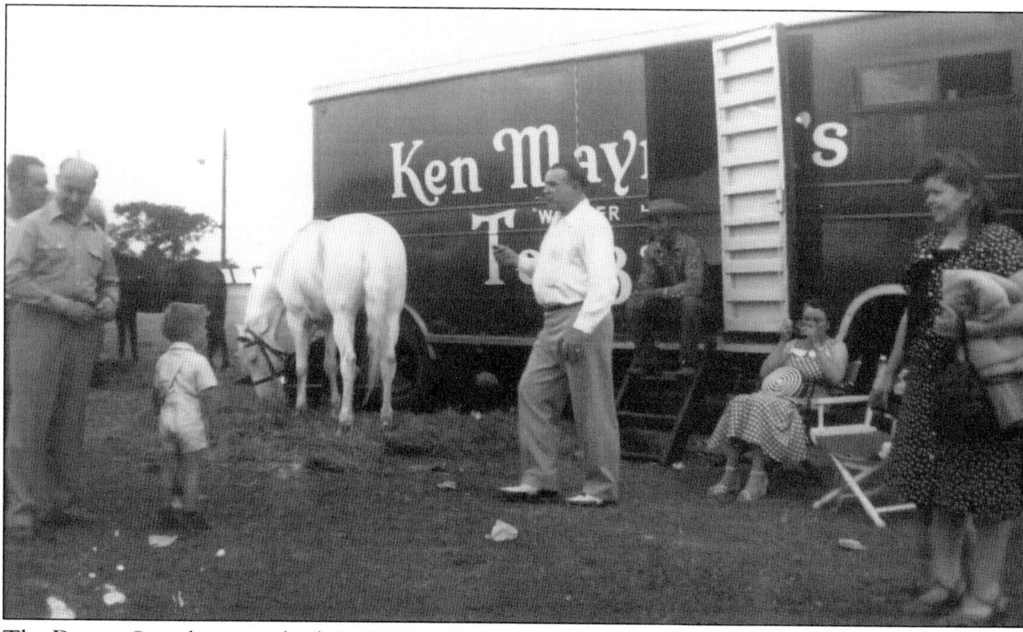

The Dracut Speedway was built in 1946 and remained open until 1955. It was located at the corner of Broadway and Loon Hill Road, which is now an empty lot. Besides racing, the racetrack was also used for other events such as this visit from rodeo performer and actor Ken Maynard, who appeared in more than 90 films.

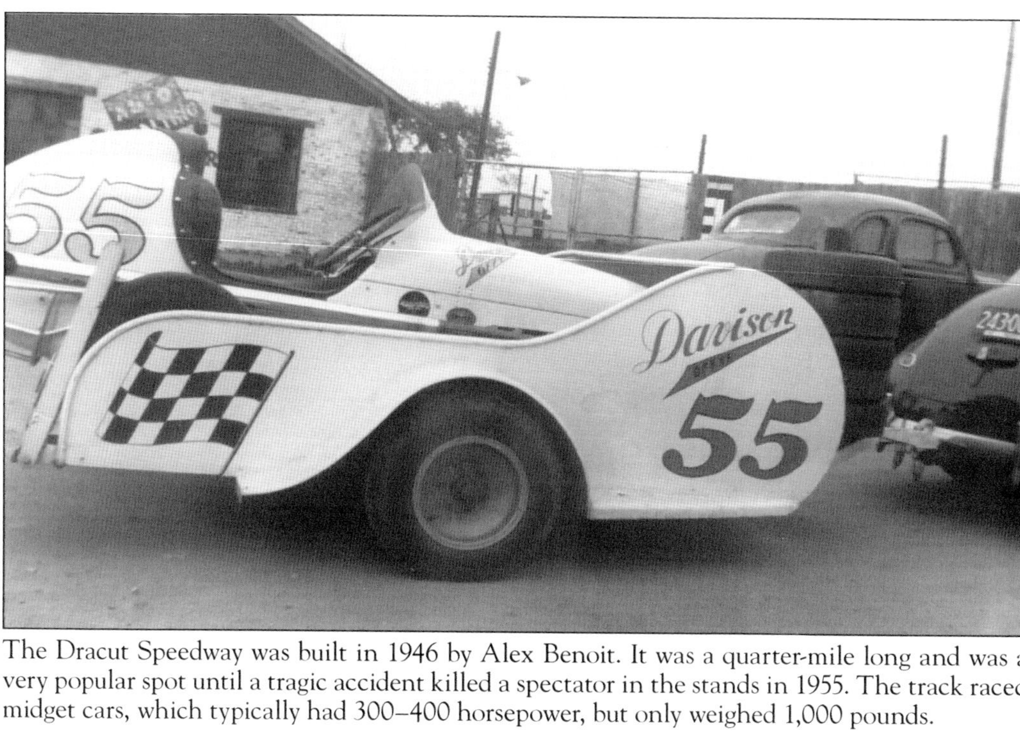

The Dracut Speedway was built in 1946 by Alex Benoit. It was a quarter-mile long and was a very popular spot until a tragic accident killed a spectator in the stands in 1955. The track raced midget cars, which typically had 300–400 horsepower, but only weighed 1,000 pounds.

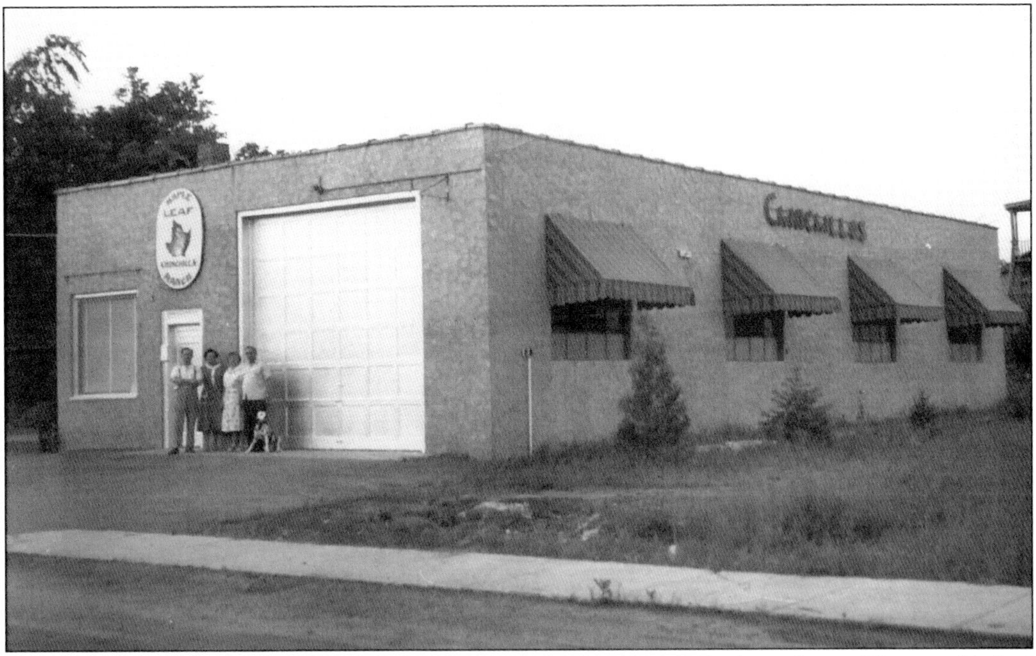

By the 1950s, the Houle family had begun investing in the Chinchilla fur industry. They established the Maple Leaf Chinchilla Ranch, pictured here, at 101 Arlington Avenue. Chinchillas are indigenous to South America and were prized for their soft and beautiful fur. The thickness and color of the fur made it unique. Each strand of fur has three colors—deep blue and white with a dark brown tip. Chinchilla fur was used for trim on ladies' evening gowns as well as stoles, jackets, and capes. About 200 pelts were necessary to make a full-length coat out of chinchilla fur.

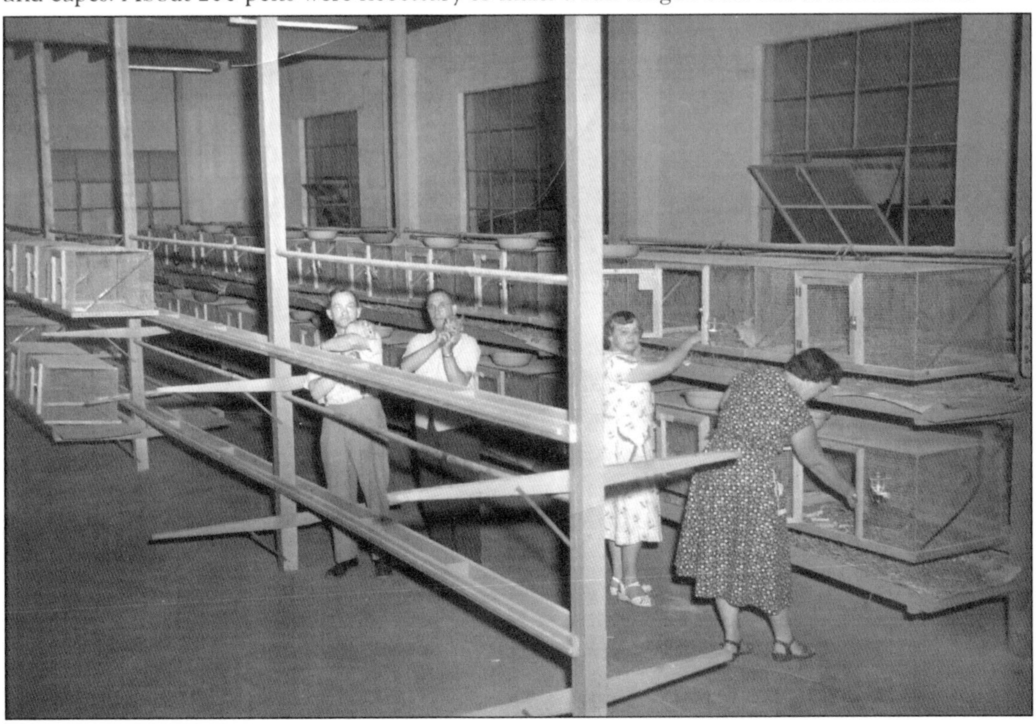

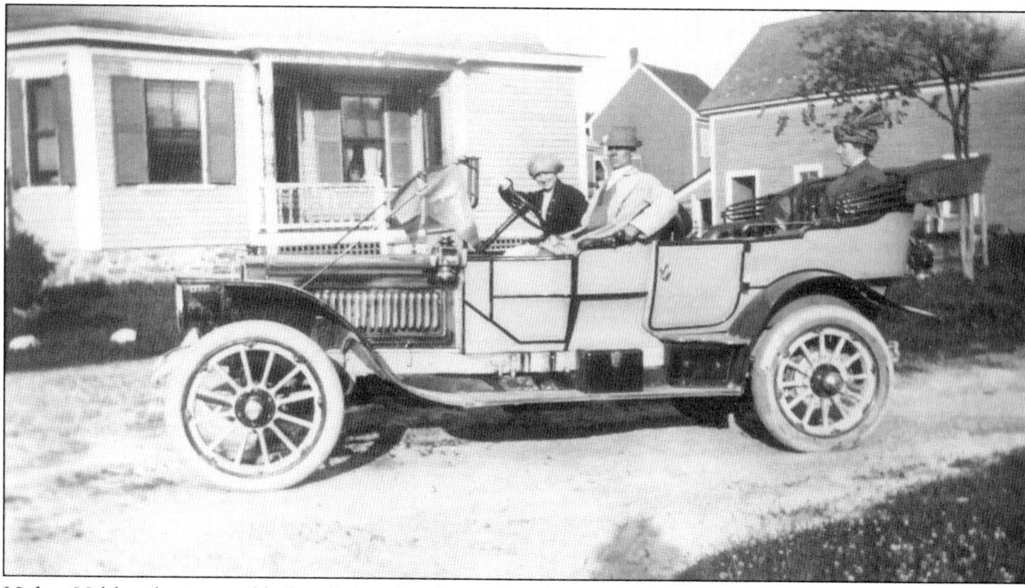

Helen Hibbard, pictured behind the wheel, returns from the beach with her neighbor and mother. (Courtesy of Willard Hibbard Jr.)

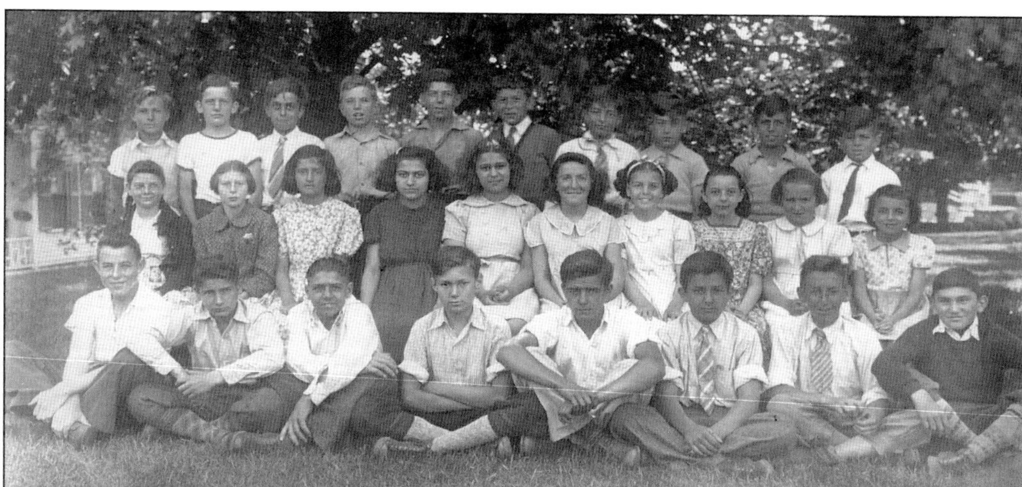

The seventh grade at Parker Avenue School in 1940–1941 included, from let to right, (first row) Phillip Rocheleau, George Alexakas, Edward Greysik, Merrill Thomas, George Babelitos, Nick Vlahokis, Charles Dunn, and Peter Stephanopalous; (second row) Theresa Harris, Marilyn Gunther, Mary Kapetenakis, Thespa Panagis, Olga Laganas, Rita Dunne, Peggy Phipps, Gloria Clark, Shirley Jouhnson, and Mary Blatus; (third row) Leonard Marshall, Dick Eklund, Chris Tournas, Charles Swallow, Charles Mellanakos, Milton Genikos, James Alenakas, Roger Comtois, Clifford Hall, and Andrew Jean. After the Parker Avenue School burned in 1922, the school was rebuilt, opening again 1924. The architect was Henry Rourke and the general contracting was done by Daniel H. Walker, who lived at 12 Thorndike Street. According to an article in the *Lowell Sun* in April 1924, the school was equipped with playrooms in the basement for the children, an innovative feature for a school building at the time. It went on to say, "The new school building was a work of art and economy."

Bob Gagnon and Warren Shaw load corn into the corn silo on the Shaw farm around 1957. Warren Shaw, standing in the front, is the current proprietor of the farm, on New Boston Road, which has been in the Shaw family since 1908. (Courtesy Warren Shaw.)

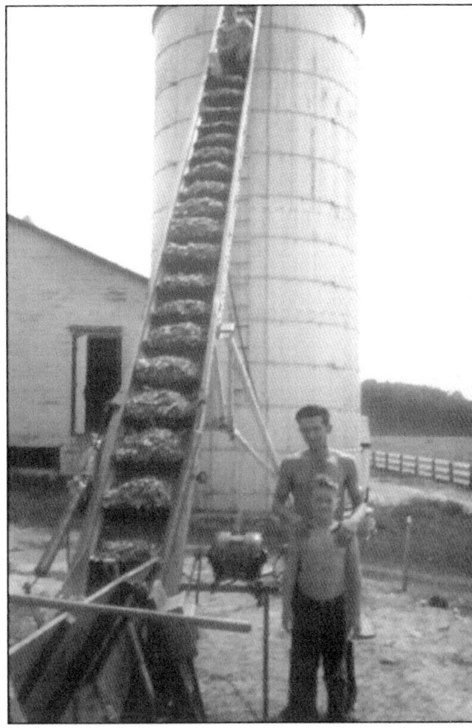

Wally Biedron Sr. is shown here working in the Shaw Farm milk bottling plant around 1952. He eventually became the milk processing manager and continued to work at Shaw Farm until his retirement in 1994. His son Walter Biedron Jr. still works on the farm as the herdsman. (Courtesy Warren Shaw.)

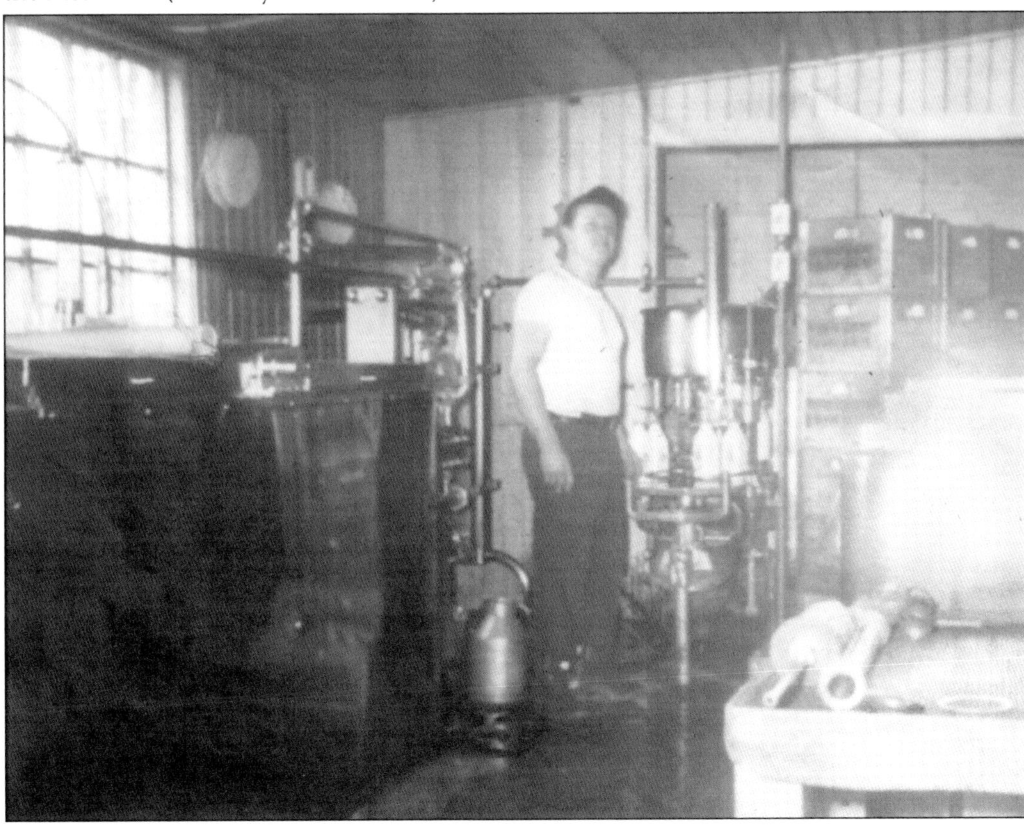

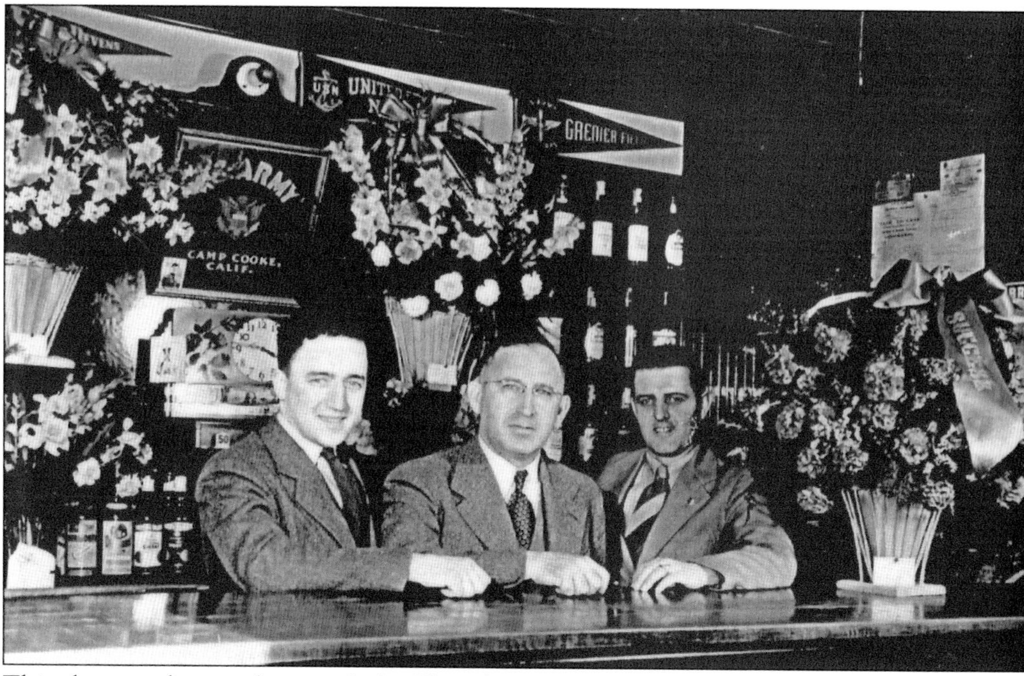

This photograph was taken inside the Fleur-de-Lys Club. From left to right are Bill McDermott, Emile Daigle, and Arthur Beauregard. After World War II, Daigle sold the club to McDermott and became the purchasing agent for the city of Lowell. The Fleur-de-Lys Club is still in operation. (Courtesy Paul Dumont family.)

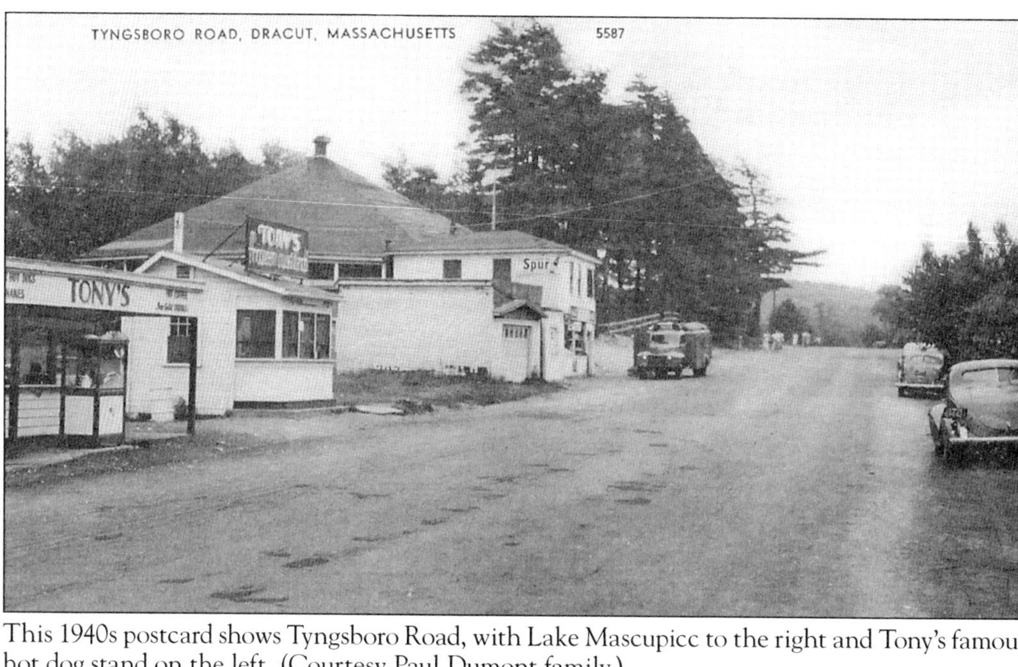

This 1940s postcard shows Tyngsboro Road, with Lake Mascupicc to the right and Tony's famous hot dog stand on the left. (Courtesy Paul Dumont family.)

Three

A New Generation 1960–1990

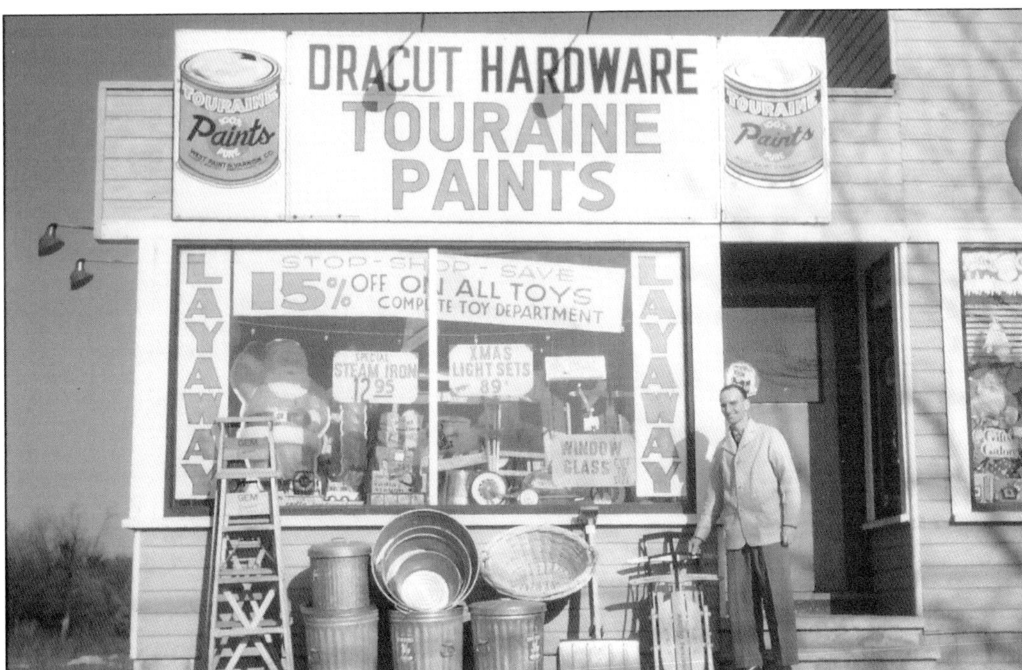

Dracut Hardware was established by Paul Dumont in 1953 in the Navy Yard District at what is now Gorman's Plaza. Later, it moved down Lakeview Avenue across from St. Therese's Church, and again in 1959 to 1982 Lakeview Avenue, where it is today, still owned and operated by the Dumont family. (Courtesy Paul Dumont family.)

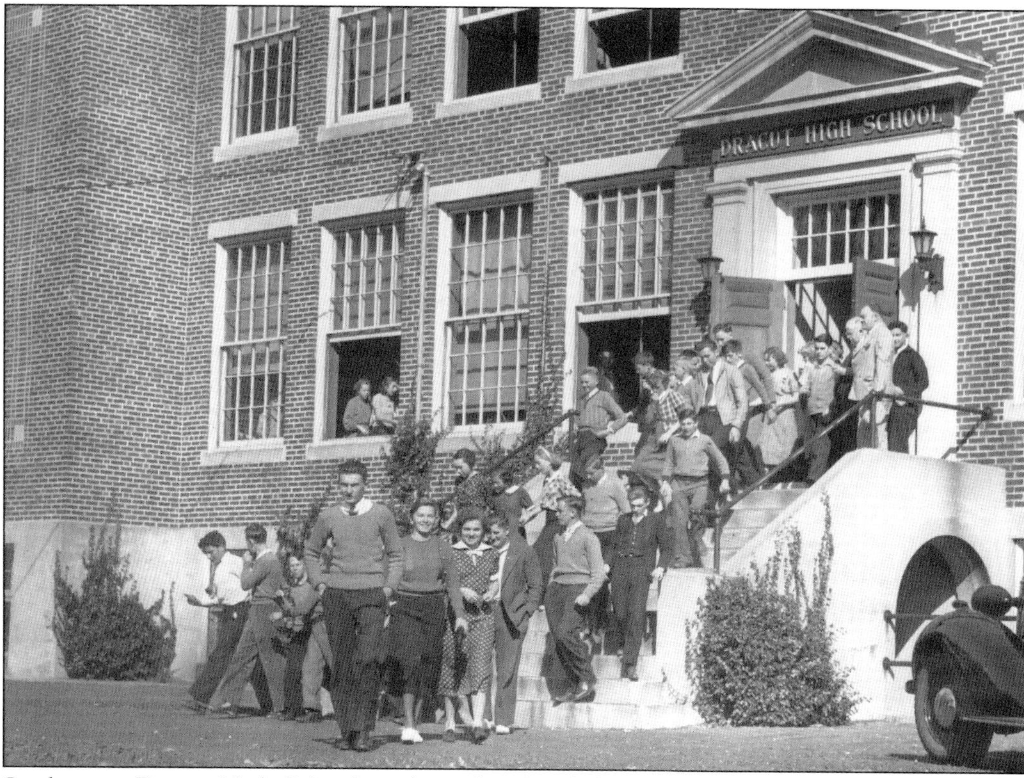

Students at Dracut High School go through a fire drill practice as superintendent of schools Charles L. Randall (top of stairs, right, with white hair) and fire chief Ernest H. Gunther (light suit next to Randall) watch. Gunther was fire chief from 1934 to 1967. A memorial for him was placed on Lakeview Avenue on June 16, 1982.

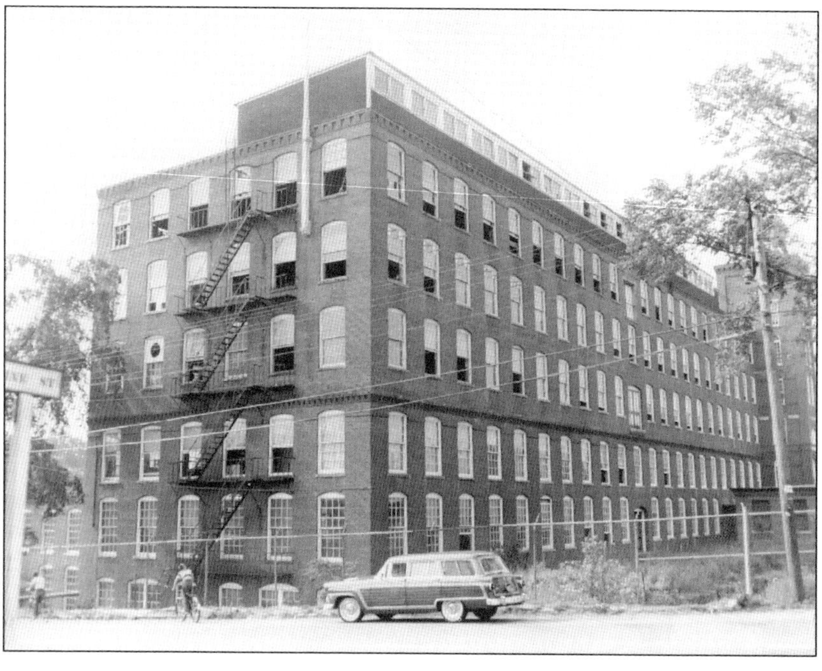

This photograph was taken on June 25, 1958, after a fire at the Beaver Brook Mills. The fire began on the top floor in the card room and caused an estimated $1 million in damage to the mills.

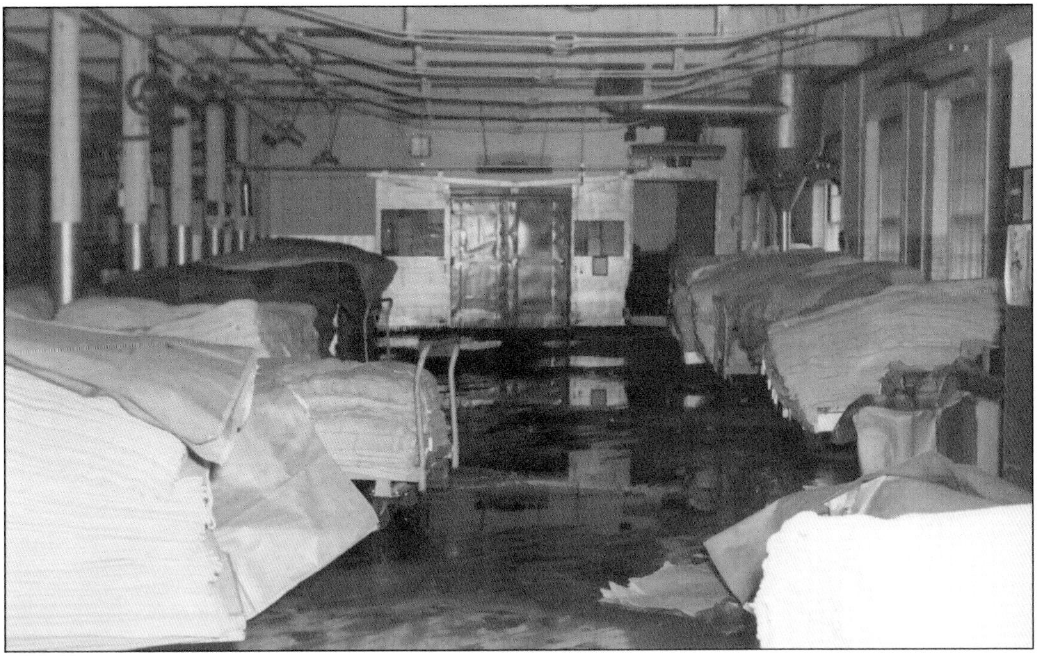

The water damage to the inside of the Beaver Brook Mills is evident in these photographs from after the 1958 fire. The tower had been tilting for years and was finally razed in 1970. The bell that had been in the tower was salvaged and was on the property of the Dracut Historical Society for a time. It is now on loan, on display outside the shops at the former Beaver Brook Mills. The millworks has been refurbished into apartment buildings, shops, and restaurants, as well as Dracut Access Television.

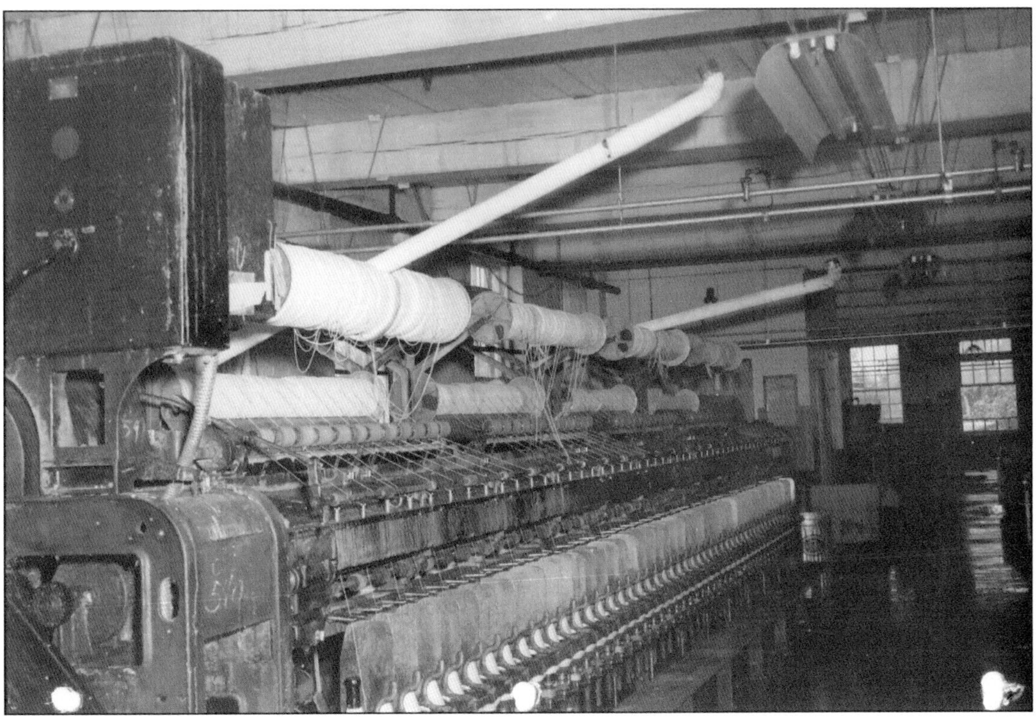

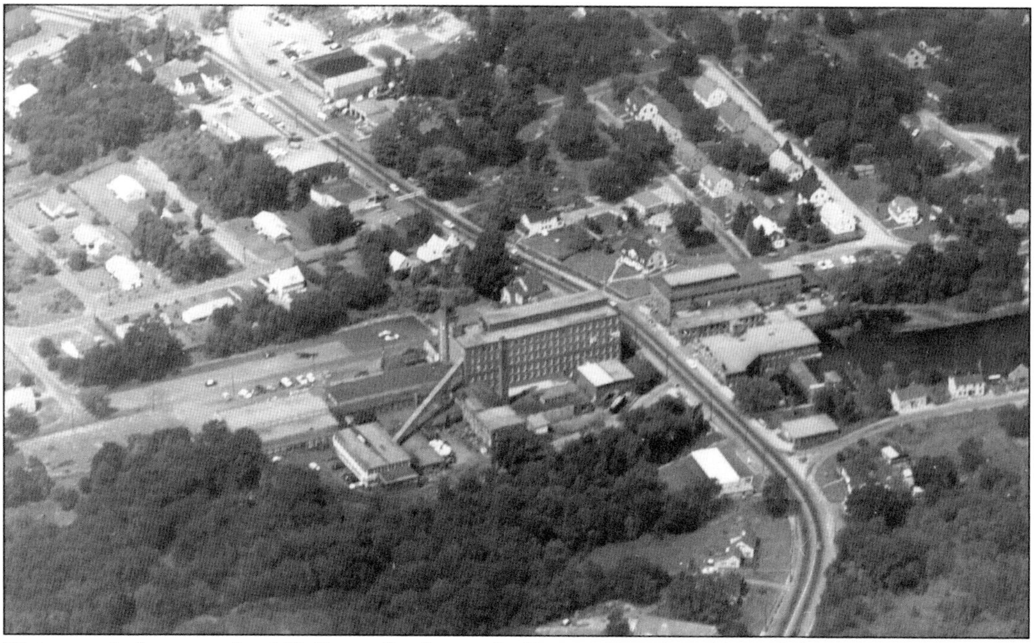

This aerial photograph of Collinsville shows the Beaver Brook Mills and the Beaver Brook falls across the street. When Michael Collins owned the mills in the late 1800s, he built a canal system utilizing the waterpower of these falls. The canal ran under the mills on the north side of Lakeview Avenue, then under Lakeview Avenue, before entering the mills on the south side. The water from the canal reenters Beaver Brook about a half-mile downstream. Collins sold the mills to the American Woolen Company, which operated the mills until after World War II. The postcard shows the Beaver Brook Mills from Mill Street. The homes on Mill Street were built by Michael Collins for the workers, and many of them still remain. This postcard comes from Paul Dumont's extensive collection of postcards from Dracut, Chelmsford, Tyngsboro, Lowell, and Hollywood and Daytona Beach, Florida.

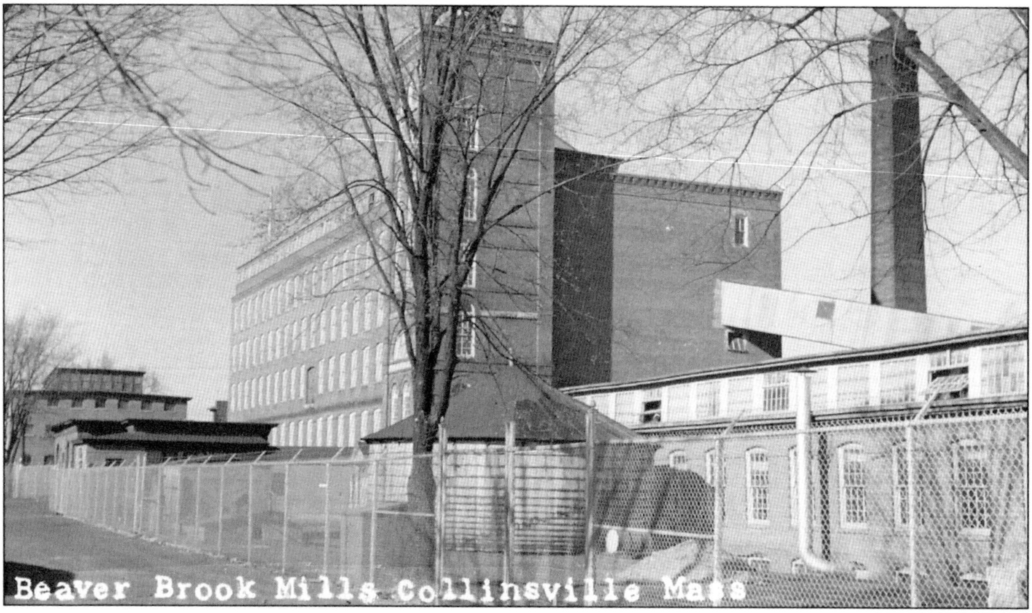

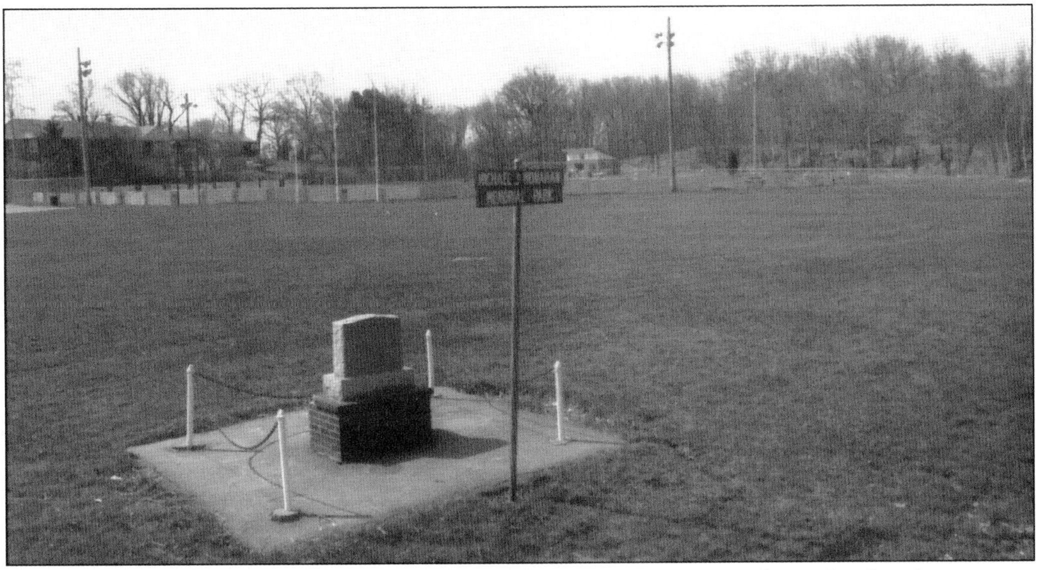

These photographs show Monahan Park on Pleasant Street across from the fire department headquarters. Michael James Monahan was born in Lowell on November 1, 1947, to James and Patricia Monahan of Malwood Avenue. He graduated from Dracut's elementary and junior high schools and Keith Academy in 1964. He studied at Boston College and had aspirations to attend medical school and become a physician. He left college in only his second year of studies in March 1966 to enlist in the Marines and serve in the Vietnam War. Deployed to Vietnam on September 1, 1966, he worked as a radio operator in the 3rd Marine Division and was killed by enemy gunfire on October 26, 1966. He was only 19 years old.

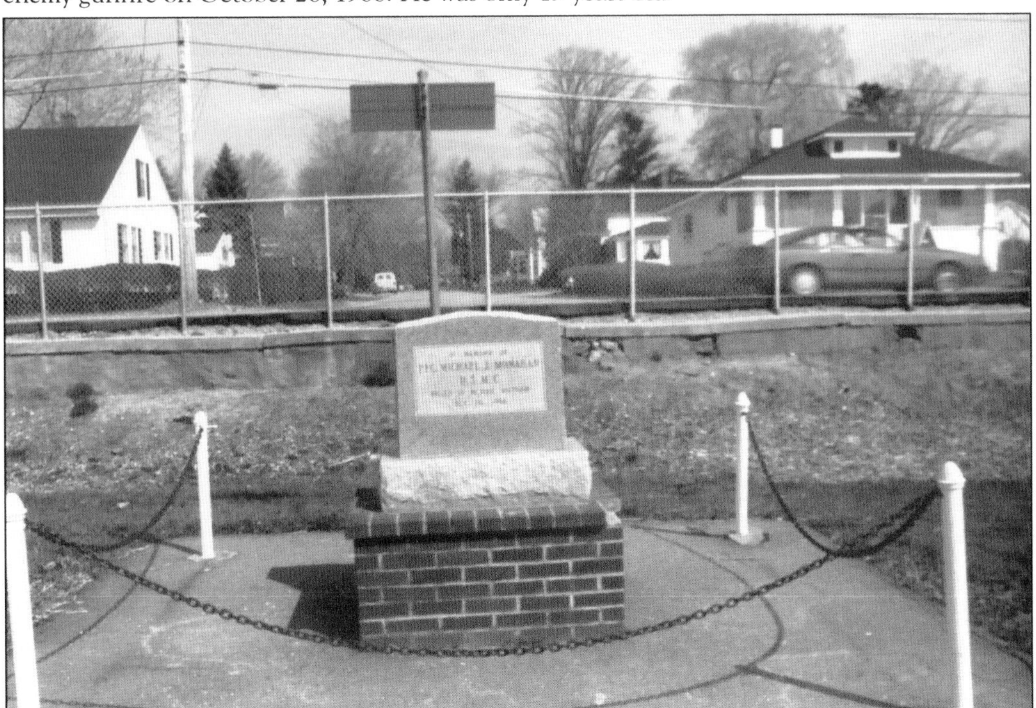

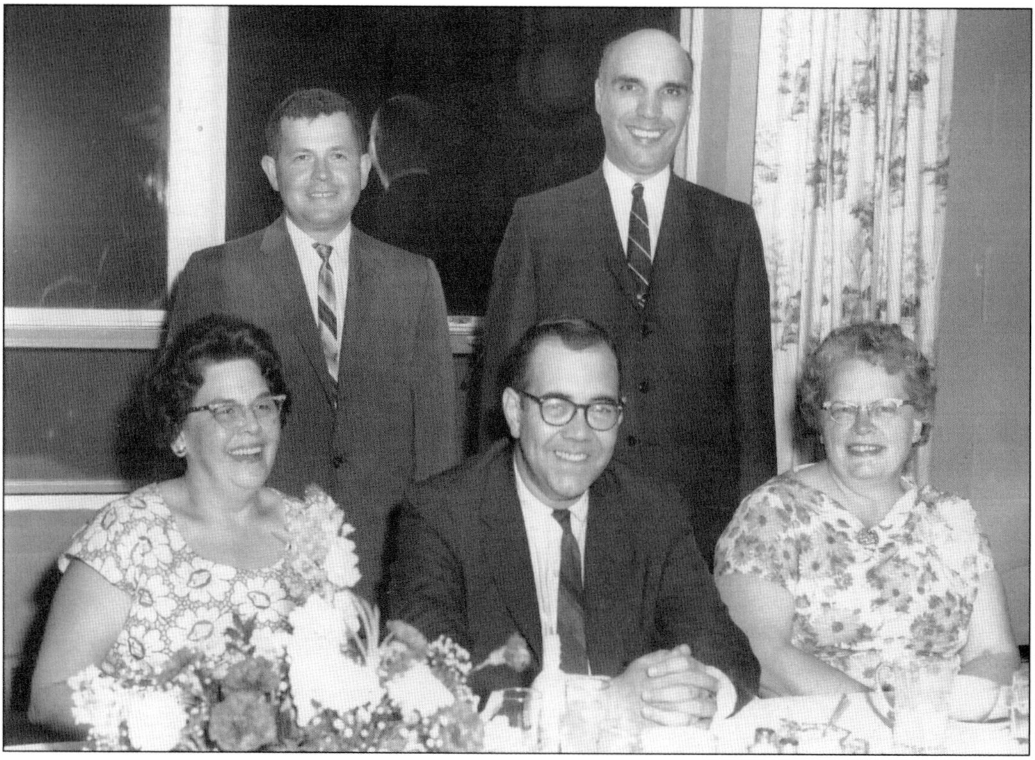

In June 1964, Dracut High School held an alumni dinner at the Harris Inn in Pelham, New Hampshire. Standing on the left is Harvey Gagnon and on the right is Dr. Christos Daoulas, the superintendent of schools from 1962 to 1998. Prior to becoming superintendent, Daoulas was principal of Dracut High School, a teacher, and a coach. In 1957, he coached the girls' basketball team to an undefeated season. Harvey Gagnon has been very active in the Dracut Historical Society and his bus company, Gagnon Transportation, served the Dracut schools until 1999. He and his wife, Loyce, established the first living trust with the Dracut Scholarship Foundation (DSF). He is also a director emeritus of the DSF along with Bruce Hutchins, former principal of Dracut High School. At the alumni dinner, seated from left to right, are Myrtle Crowe, Bradford Morse, and Pauline Varnum, a direct descendant of Samuel Varnum, who has worked in the Dracut School Department for many years. Bradford Morse (1921–1994) served as a US representative from Lowell from 1960 to 1972. In 1972, he was appointed to the position of undersecretary general for the United Nations. He is buried in Arlington Cemetery.

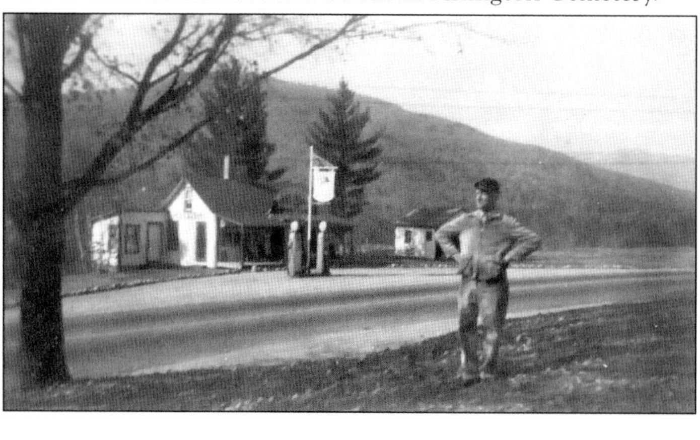

John Elie is pictured in front of his filling station on Loon Hill Road. Elie established the Golden Dairy Farm and later was an insurance salesman. (Courtesy Paul and Bonnie Elie.)

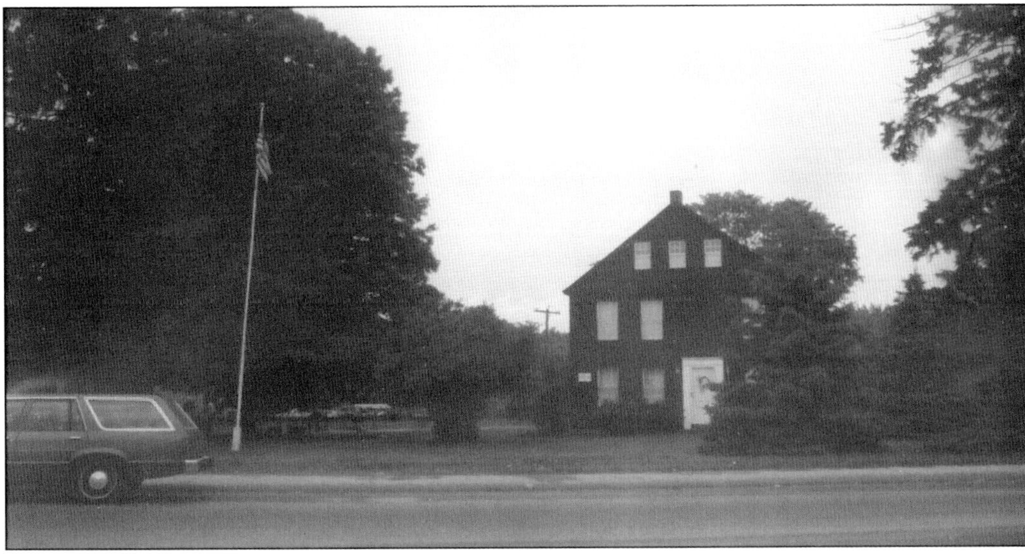

The Dracut Historical Society, which occupies the former Oliver Coburn house on Lakeview Avenue, is shown here in the 1970s. The organization owes much to John Bailey, who moved to Dracut when he was 74 years old and realized that the town's nascent museum, then housed in the town offices on Arlington Street, was in need of attention. He worked diligently to archive and to collect important town records and papers and officially organized the Dracut Historical Society in June 1928. He was elected the society's first president and today the research room at the historical society is named in his honor. Below, members of the Dracut Historical Society have their picture taken. The man on the far left is Donat Paquet, an English teacher at Dracut High School, who had his students utilize primary sources to write research papers.

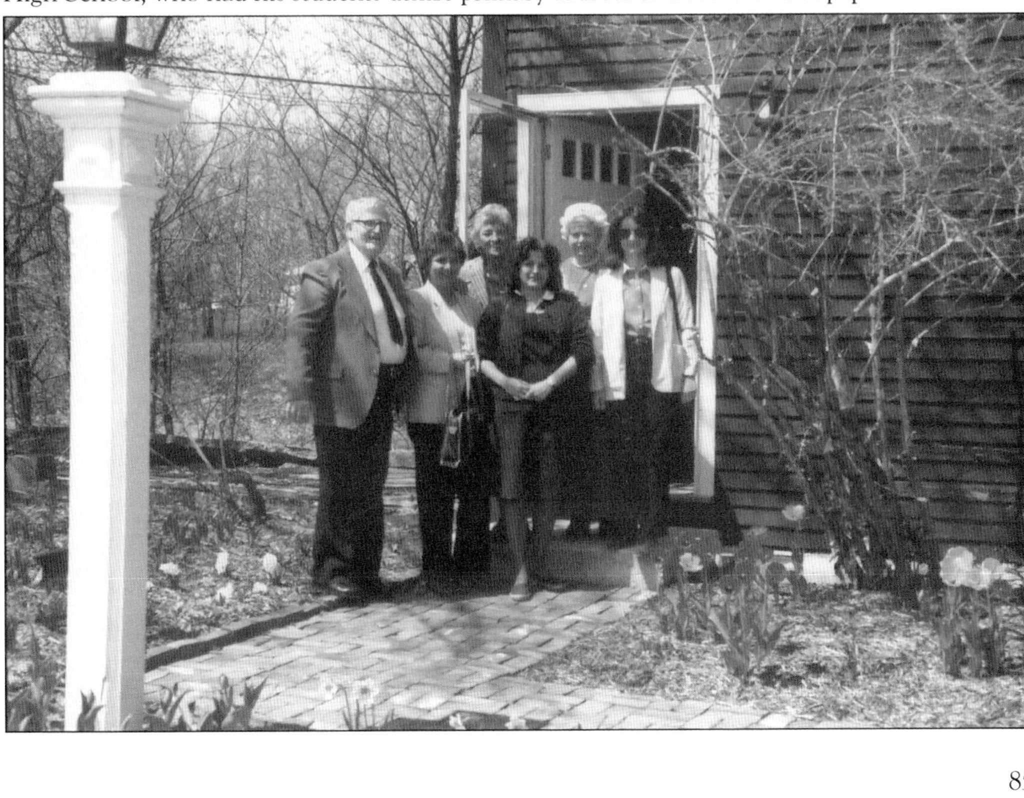

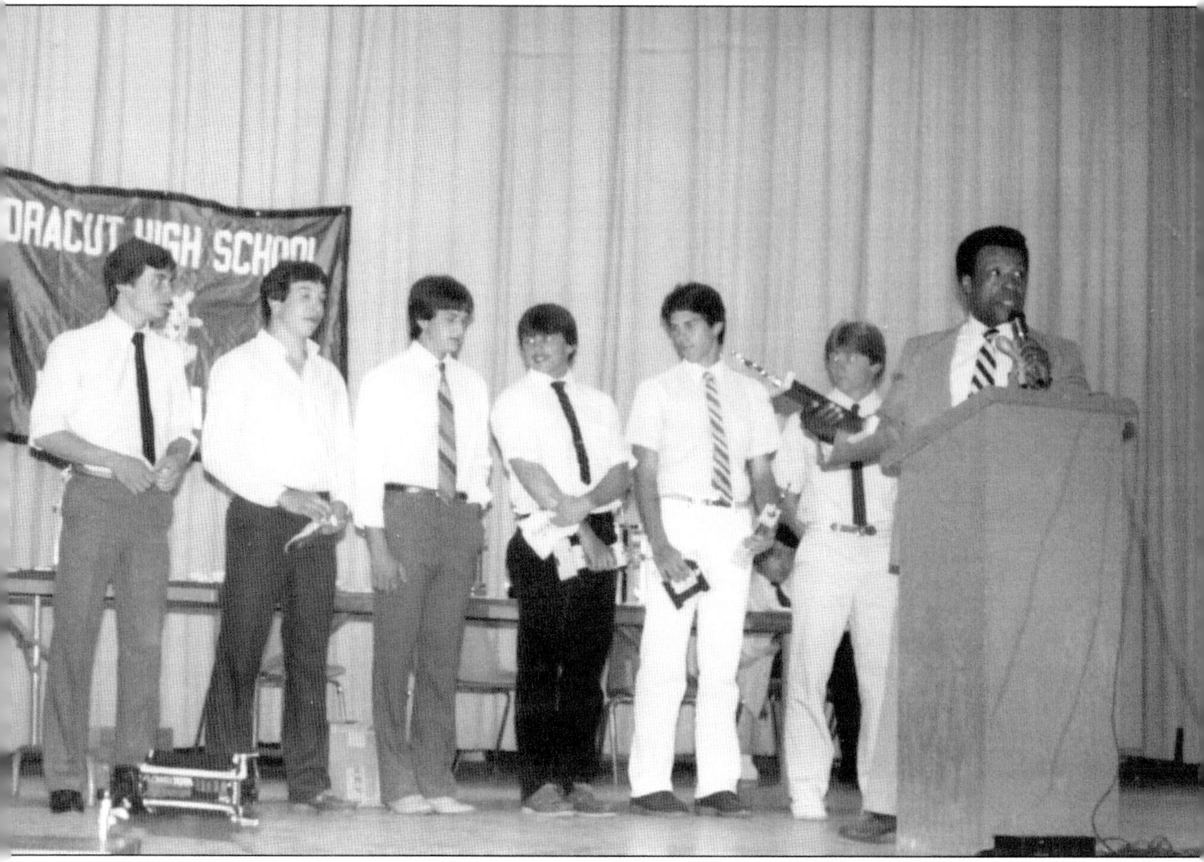

Pride Night is a Dracut High School tradition. Pictured above at the 1985 Pride Night are members of the Dracut High School basketball team being honored by vice principal and head basketball coach Dan Smith. From left to right are Joe Gangi, Peter Witts, Mike (Fuzzy) Fauvel, Rich Laboeuf, George Lafortune, and Richard McElhinney. Mike Fauvel and George Lafortune were team captains. Of special mention was the fact that the team were champions of the Greater Lowell Regional Basketball tournament that year. In addition, Mike Fauvel and George Lafortune were both in the top 10 in scoring in the Merrimack Valley Conference and were also selected as Merrimack Valley Conference all-stars. Lafortune said of his recognition at Pride Night and of receiving a scholarship from the Dracut Scholarship Foundation, "[They] were the two happiest days of [my] four years at Dracut High School." (Courtesy Norman LaFortune.)

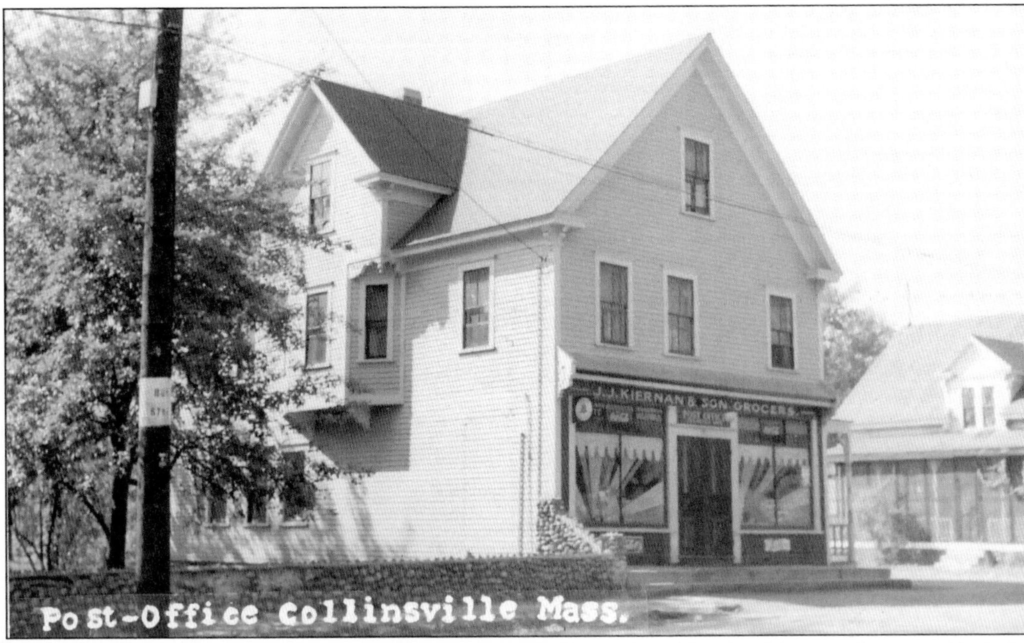

The first post office in Dracut was located in Collinsville. The building today is called the Kiernan Building, named for Dracut's longtime postmaster, H. Francis Kiernan. He was born in Chelmsford in 1880 and his family came to Dracut in 1884. He worked as a postal clerk under his father and was named postmaster in 1905. Upon his retirement, a testimonial dinner was organized in his honor and held on May 10, 1950, at the Dracut Inn. Daniel Hanson chaired the committee organizing the dinner and Irene Grondine served as the secretary and treasurer. State representative John Brox gave the toast that evening. (Courtesy Paul Dumont family.)

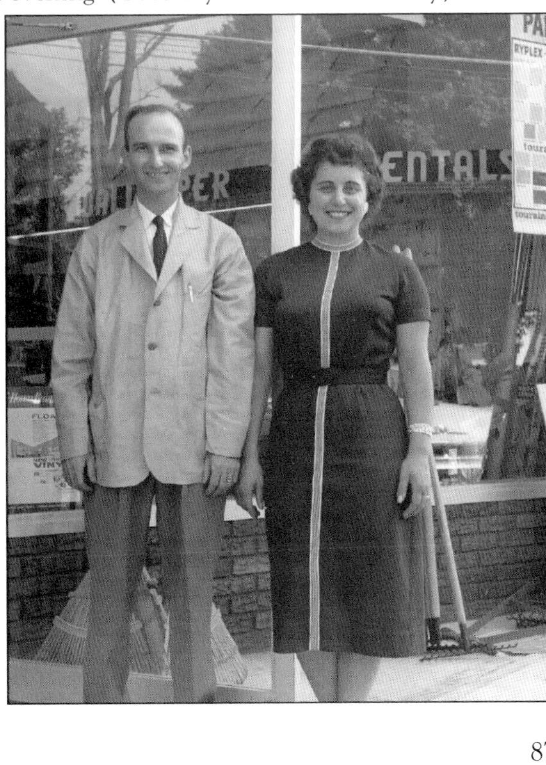

Paul and Irene Dumont stand proudly outside of their store, Dracut Hardware, on Lakeview Avenue. Dracut Hardware has been a fixture in Dracut for over 50 years. (Courtesy Paul Dumont family.)

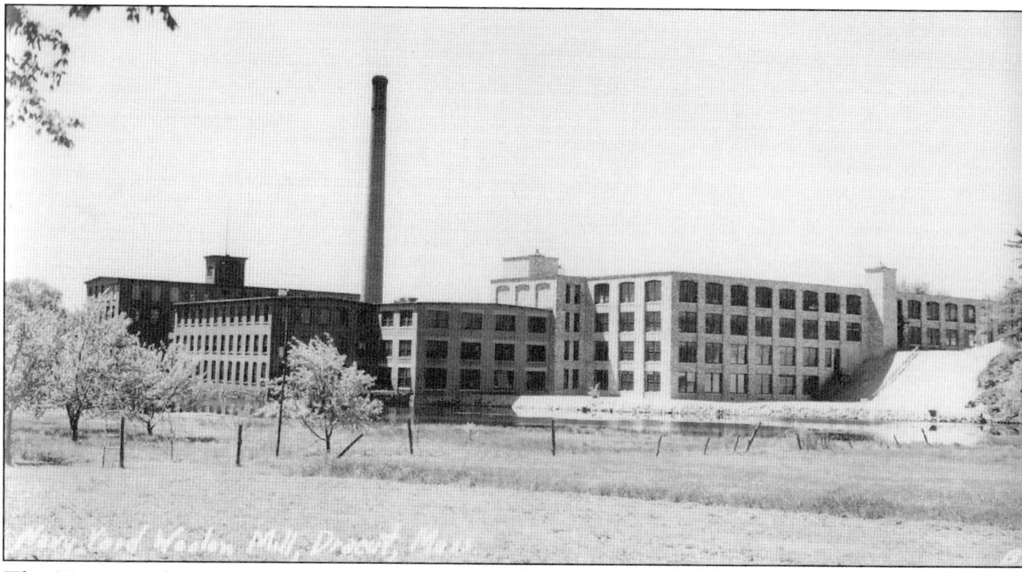

The Navy Yard District has been the site of industry in Dracut since the 18th century. There have been gristmills, paper mills, and cotton mills. Power for these mills was created by damming this section of Beaver Brook. The mill in this photograph was constructed by the Merrimack Woolen Mill Company in the 1860s. In 1862, the mill was enlarged to four stories and was known as the Navy Yard Mills. During World War II, the employees of the Navy Yard Mills produced a newsletter to send to employees who were serving overseas, entitled the *Navy Yard News*. The J.P Stevens Company eventually bought the Navy Yard Mills. (Courtesy Paul Dumont family.)

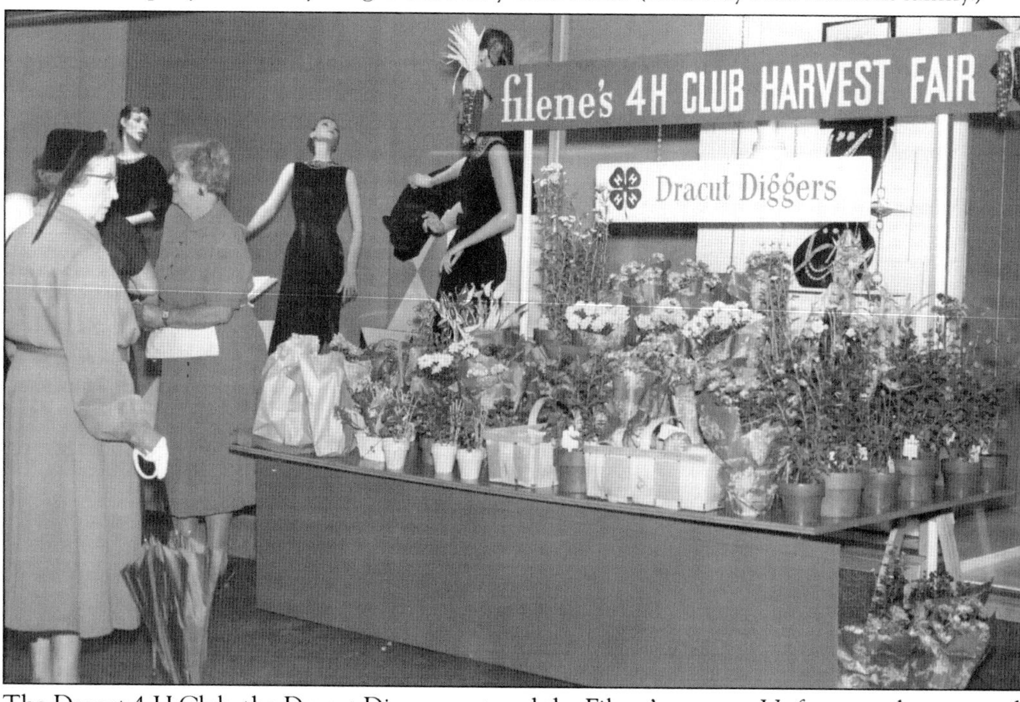

The Dracut 4-H Club, the Dracut Diggers, entered the Filene's contest. Unfortunately, not much more can be said regarding this 4-H activity. The author found this photograph in an antique store in Ogunquit, Maine. It appears as though it was taken in the early 1960s. (Author's collection.)

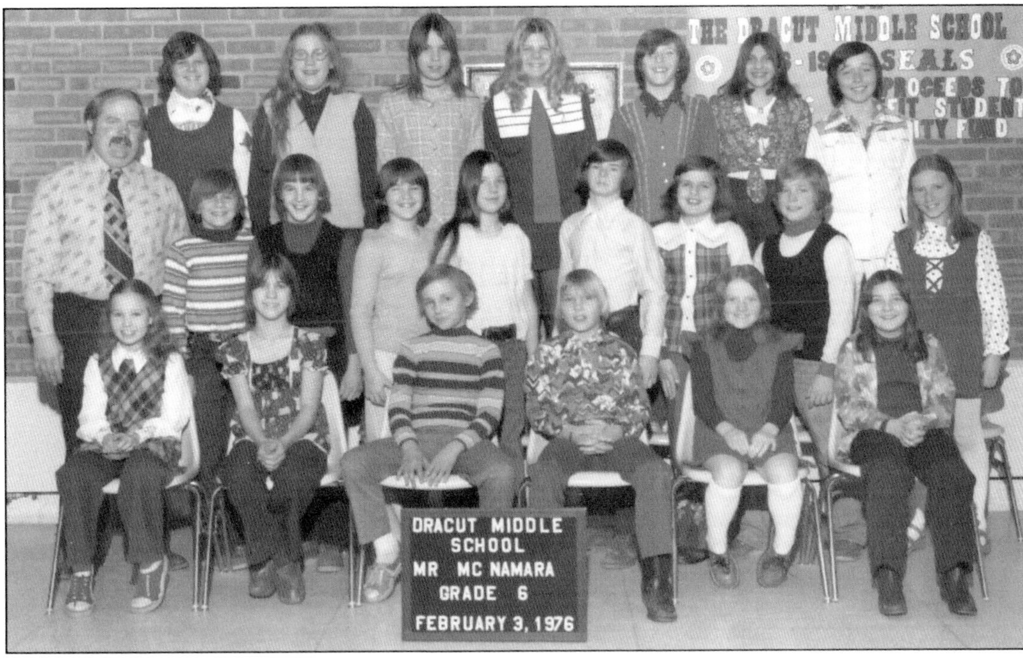

Michael McNamara's sixth-grade class at Dracut Middle School is pictured above in 1976. Amazingly, Dr. McNamara was able to recall the students' names from memory. Pictured from left to right are (first row) Charlene Corcoran, Elizabeth Ducharme, Albert Beaulieu, Gerry Chambers, Donna Breault, and Linda Paquin; (second row) Michael Dalphond, Kevin Jean, Robin Kempton, Kathy Kawa, Daniel Lepine, Iris Sousa, Bruce Hicks, and Deborah Boisvert; (top row) Paul Provencher, Sue Ellen Foss, Michelle DiComandrea, Nancy Campbell, and William Tellier. Dracut Middle School is today's Brookside Elementary School. Michael McNamara is currently on the School Committee and on the board of directors for DATV. Pictured below is Mary Riopelle's fifth-grade class in 1987 at Dracut Middle School.

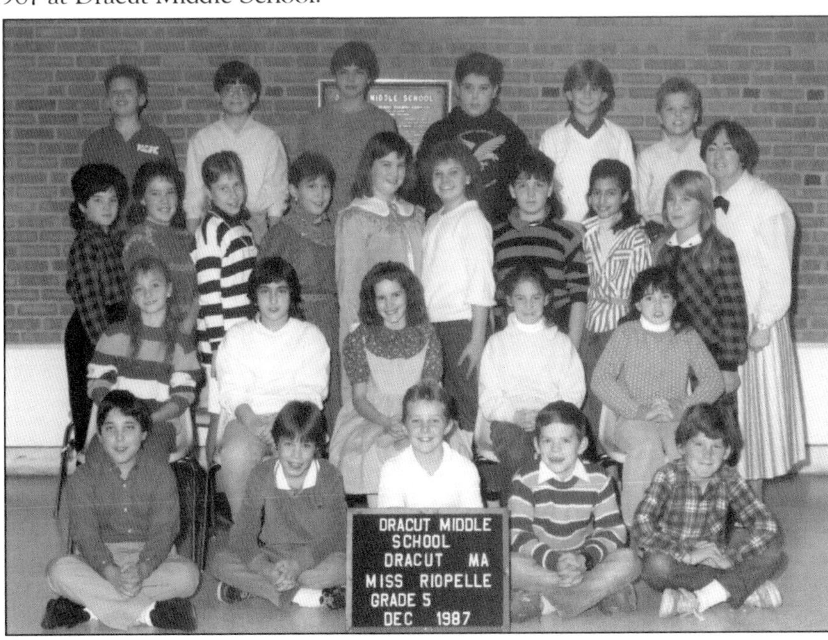

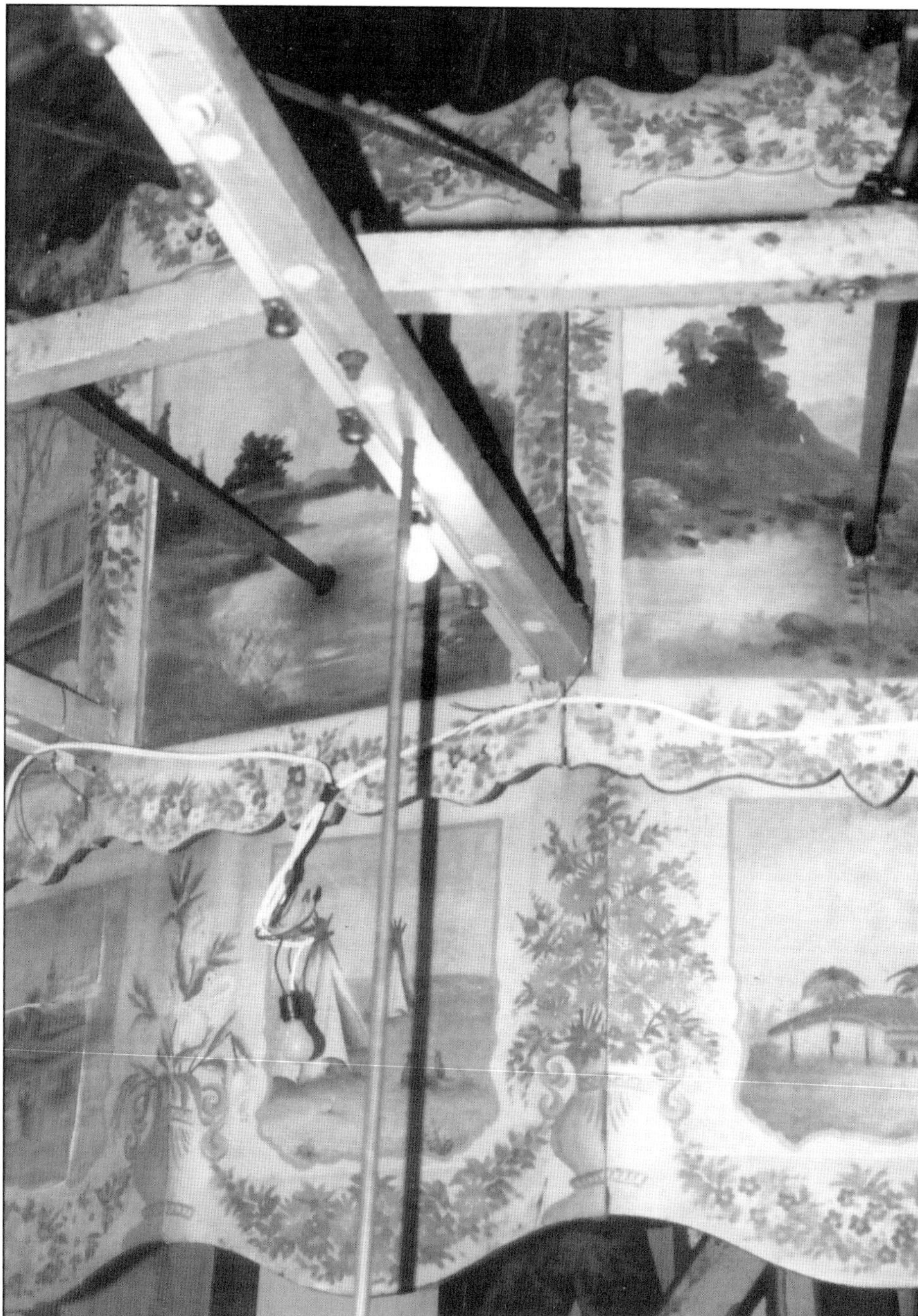

By 1970, Lakeview Park was a ghost of its former self. As the years progressed, fewer and fewer visitors came to the park and only a few rides remained. The Lakeview Ballroom was gone and apartments now stood in its place. Finally, in 1971, the owner of the unique bobbie horses at Lakeview, Aldo Barbutti, sold the carousel, which had been in his family since 1918. The decision to sell was due to declining attendance and vandalism. In 1971, vandals had broken in and caused significant damage to the carousel. The same carousel is still in operation in Forest Park, New York, having been restored by the Fabicon Company.

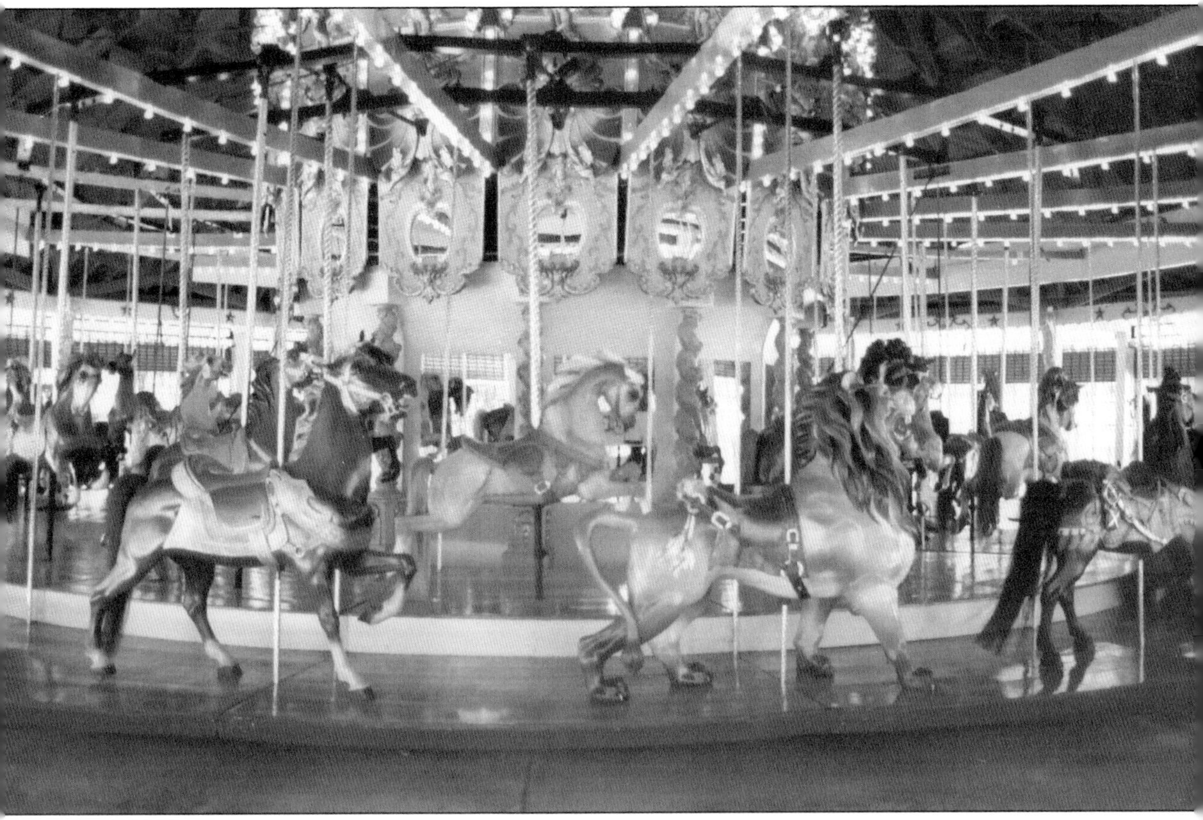

The famous carousel at Lakeview Park was hand-carved and had 13 standing horses on the outer ring. In addition, there were lions, tigers, two chariots, and a stag. There was also a goat, which was kept by the owner when the carousel was taken down in 1971. The carousel's rounding boards were not the originals; in a 1938 hurricane, the original rounding boards were destroyed. There was also a small organ. When the carousel was first sold to buyers in New York, it was dismantled and shipped. The new owners lost money on the carousel and it was almost lost forever. However, the Fabicon Company offered to restore the carousel and now it has a new home in Forest Park, New York. It was believed that the original stained-glass windows, which were part of the carousel, were destroyed when it was first dismantled in 1971, but surprisingly eight of original windows surfaced when antique dealer James Keefe began asking if any of his clients had old Lakeview carousel memorabilia. One of the panels was purchased by Dr. Michael McNamara, who had it restored and gave it to his wife as a retirement gift.

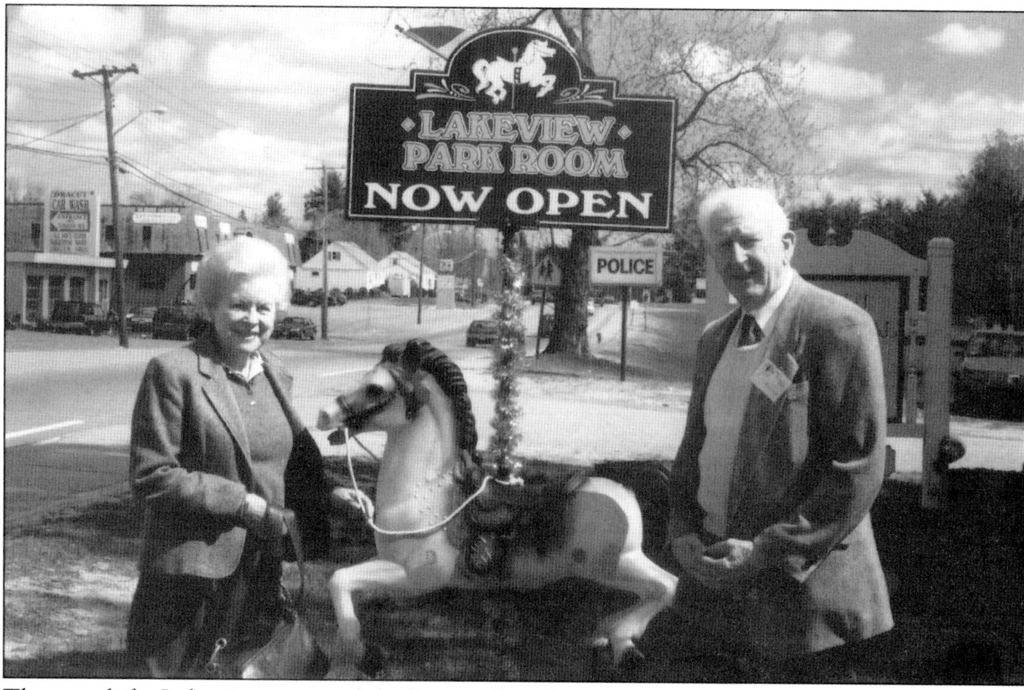

The search for Lakeview memorabilia began when Dracut artist Betty Baroni was asked to paint a picture of the Lakeview carousel. She began her research and asked antique dealer James Keefe to ask his clients if they had, or knew of, any Lakeview memorabilia. When the eight original stained-glass windows were discovered, Baroni purchased two of them from Keefe and donated one to the Fabicon Company. In return for her donation, Fabicon donated a fiber-glass casting of one of the flying horses to the Dracut Historical Society. Also, Keefe donated one of the windows to the historical society. Using theses donations, the historical society created a permanent exhibit about Lakeview. The find of the windows also helped Baroni with her painting of the carousel. She was relying on memory as to what colors to use and was pleasantly surprised when she discovered she was using historically accurate colors.

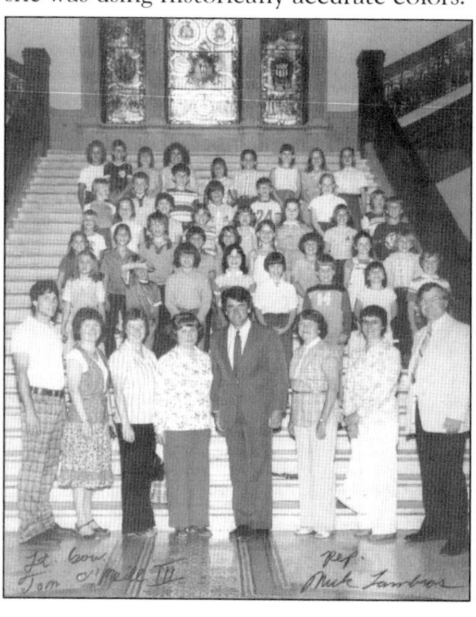

In 1975, Greenmont Elementary School students visited the state house in Boston and had their photograph taken with Lt. Gov. Thomas O'Neill III (son of Speaker of the House Tip O'Neill Jr.) and Dracut state representative Nick Lambros. Lambros was a Korean War veteran and served the town in many capacities, including as water commissioner, sewer commissioner, superintendent of Dracut Water District, selectman, and state representative. He served as state representative for 13 years. Lambros died at age 75 in September 2008.

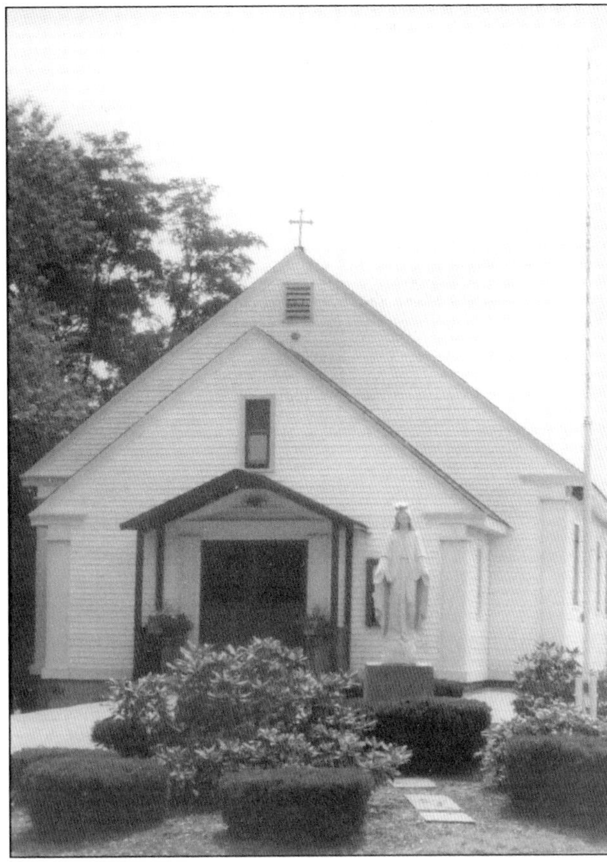

These images show St. Francis Church. The original church (at right) was established in 1939. Priests from St. Michael's in Lowell were sent to hold services at the Kenwood School for Catholic residents in that part of town. In the meantime, East Dracut residents decided to purchase the East Dracut School. The building was moved to Methuen Street in Kenwood and became St. Francis Church. Below is the current St. Francis Church, which was moved to Wheeler Road in 1996. (Courtesy St. Francis Church.)

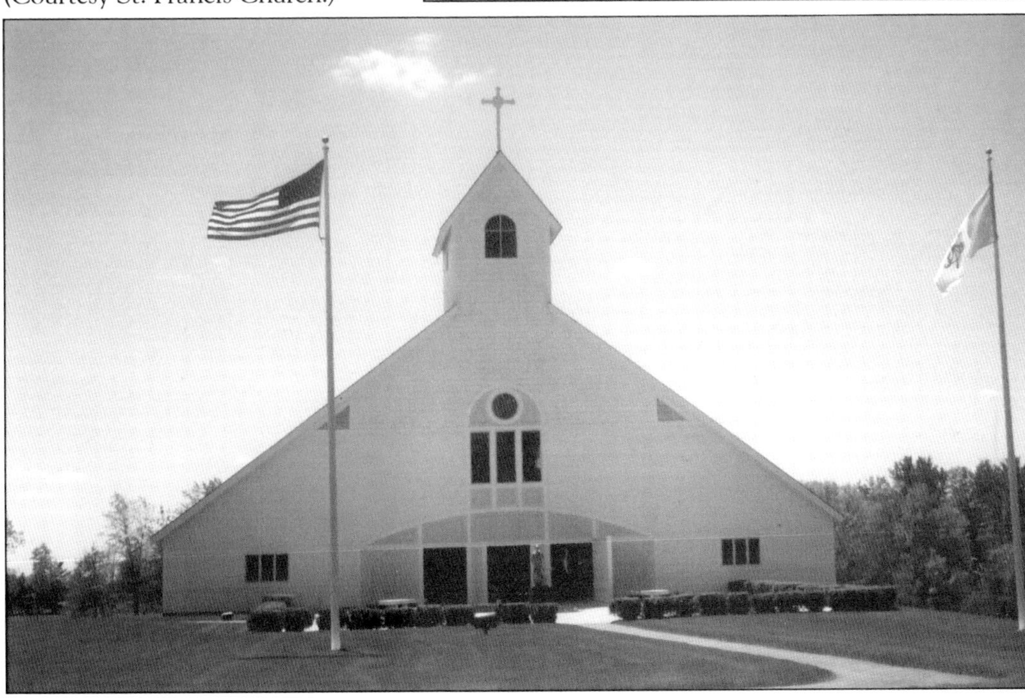

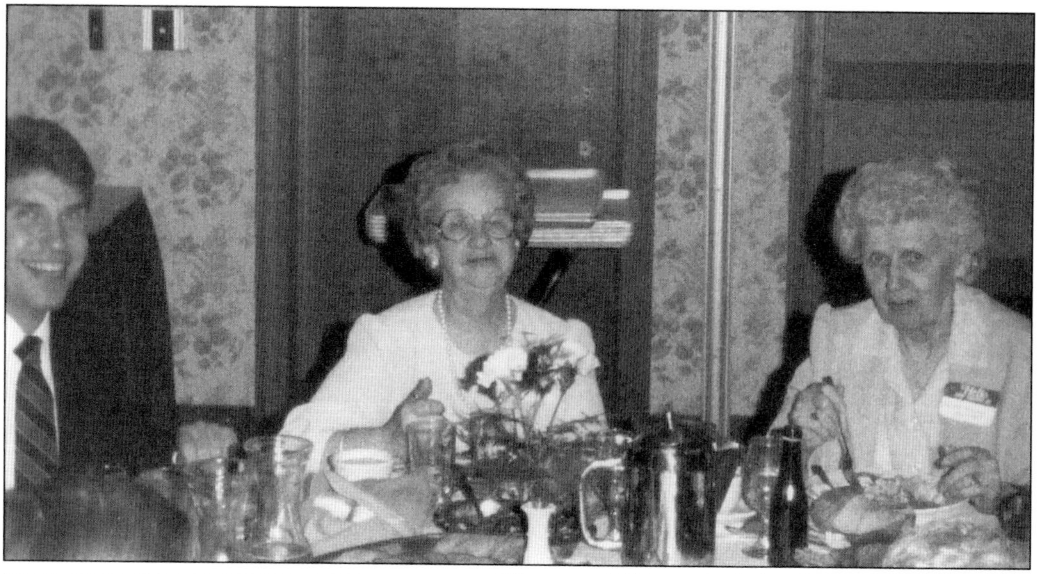

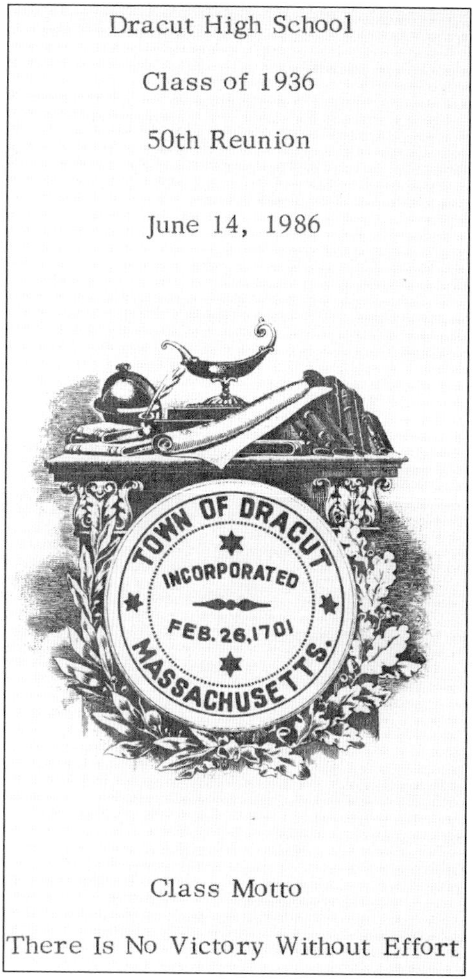
Dracut High School

Class of 1936

50th Reunion

June 14, 1986

Class Motto

There Is No Victory Without Effort

The year 1986 marked the 50th reunion of the class of 1936, the first to graduate from Dracut High School—today's Greenmont Elementary School. The class of 1936 had a commemorative brochure printed for the event, and a copy is in the archives of the Dracut Historical Society. Their class motto, "There is no victory without effort," seems appropriate for the Greatest Generation, many of whom went on to fight in World War II.

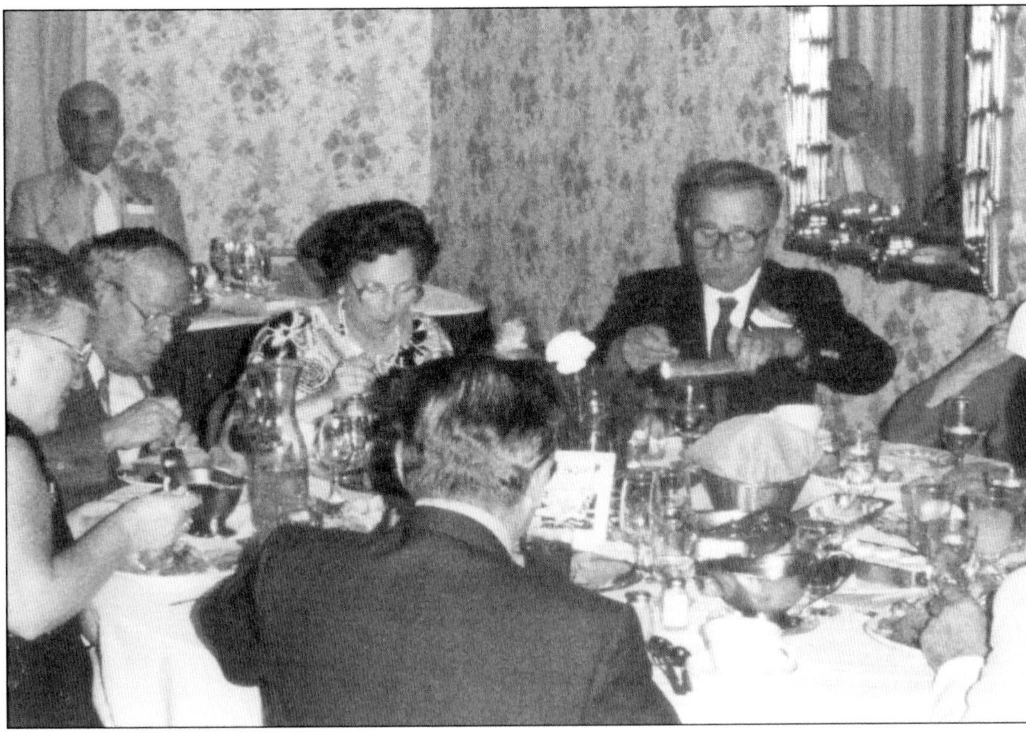

This photograph was taken at the 50th reunion for the class of 1936. As always, Dr. Daoulas is present; he is seated in the background. Dr. Daoulas was born on January 21, 1922, and was a lifelong resident of Dracut. After serving in World War II, he entered Boston University and earned a doctorate in education. He began his career in the Dracut Public Schools as a science teacher but also served as athletic director, coach, and principal of the high school. He was appointed superintendent in 1962 and served in the position until retiring. In 2005, Dracut's school complex on Lakeview Avenue was renamed the Dr. Christos Daoulas Education Complex in his honor. He passed away at the age of 85 in March 2007.

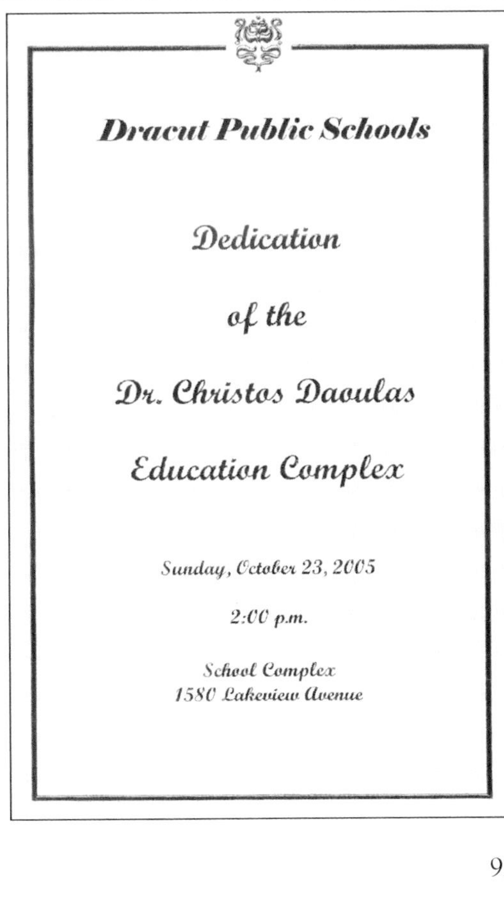

Dracut Public Schools

Dedication

of the

Dr. Christos Daoulas

Education Complex

Sunday, October 23, 2005

2:00 p.m.

School Complex
1580 Lakeview Avenue

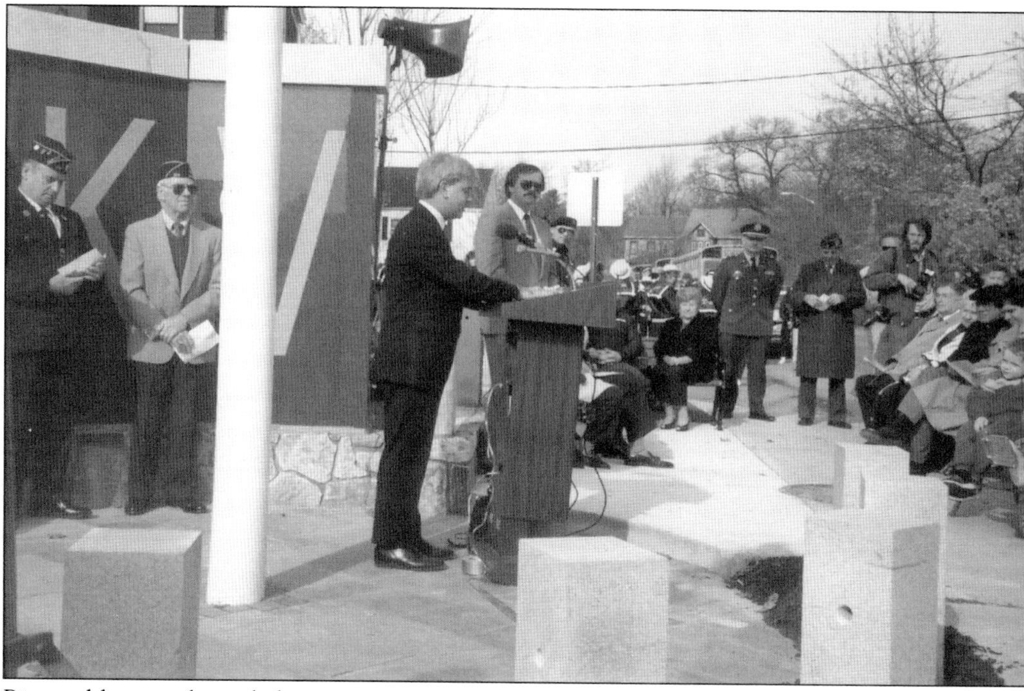

Pictured here is the rededication ceremony of the war memorial at the corner of Pleasant and Sladen Steets on November 11, 1989. In 1943, the Navy Yard World War War II Honor Roll was erected on this location and dedicated to the memory of Clarence Nichols, who died in Africa on December 18, 1942. The honor roll deteriorated over time and was eventually torn down. Frank and Darlene Gorman rededicated the site to Clarence Nichols and his brother Edmund, who was killed in Korea, and erected a new memorial to them and all Dracut servicemen who served in World War I, World War II, the Korean War, and Vietnam.

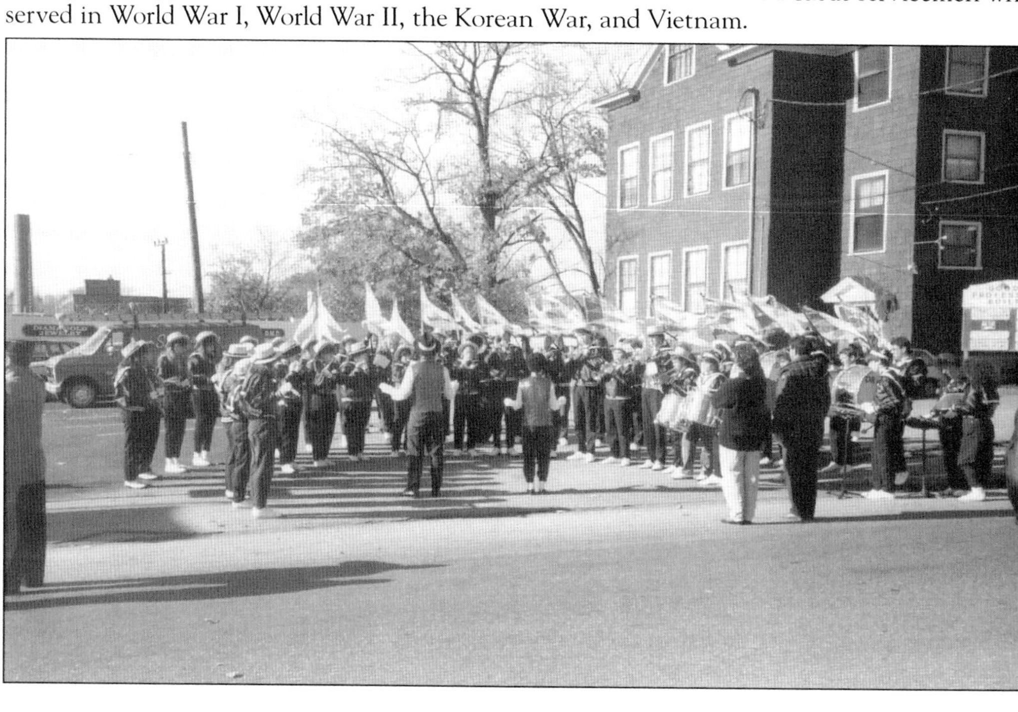

Four

A New Century Begins

1990–Present

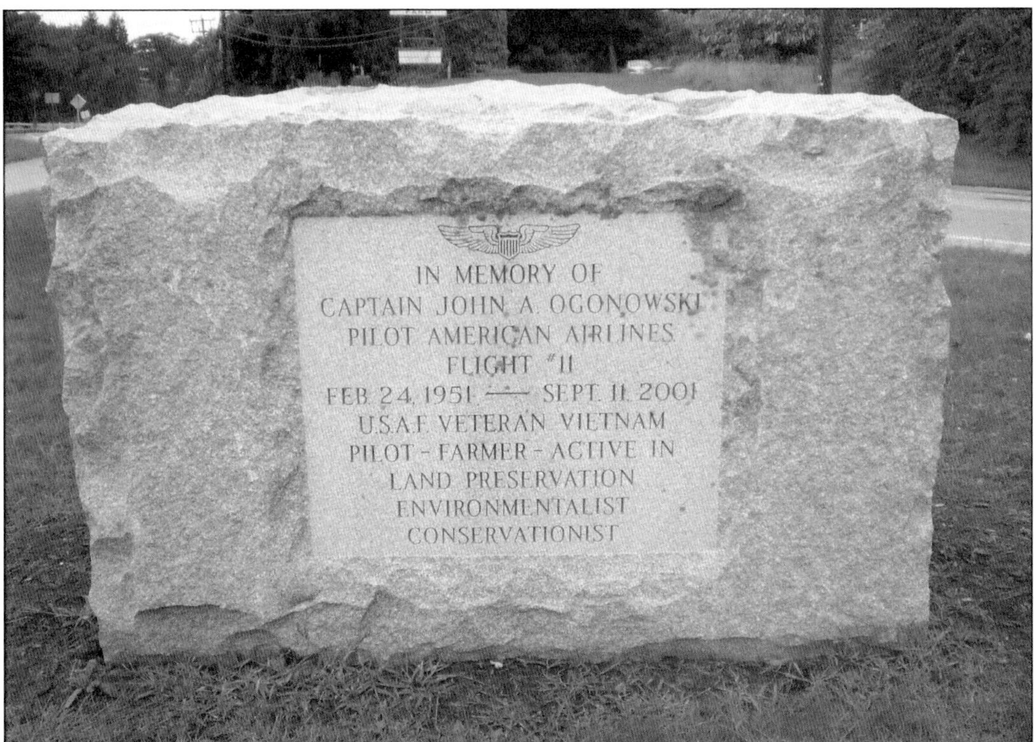

At the beginning of another century, Dracut found itself having to memorialize its own when tragedy struck on September 11, 2011. Capt. John Ogonowski was the pilot of American Airlines Flight 11, which struck the north tower of the World Trade Center. Captain Ogonowski was a well-respected member of the community; in addition to being a pilot, he was an activist for farmers. This memorial is at the intersection of Jones and Broadway Avenues. (Author's collection.)

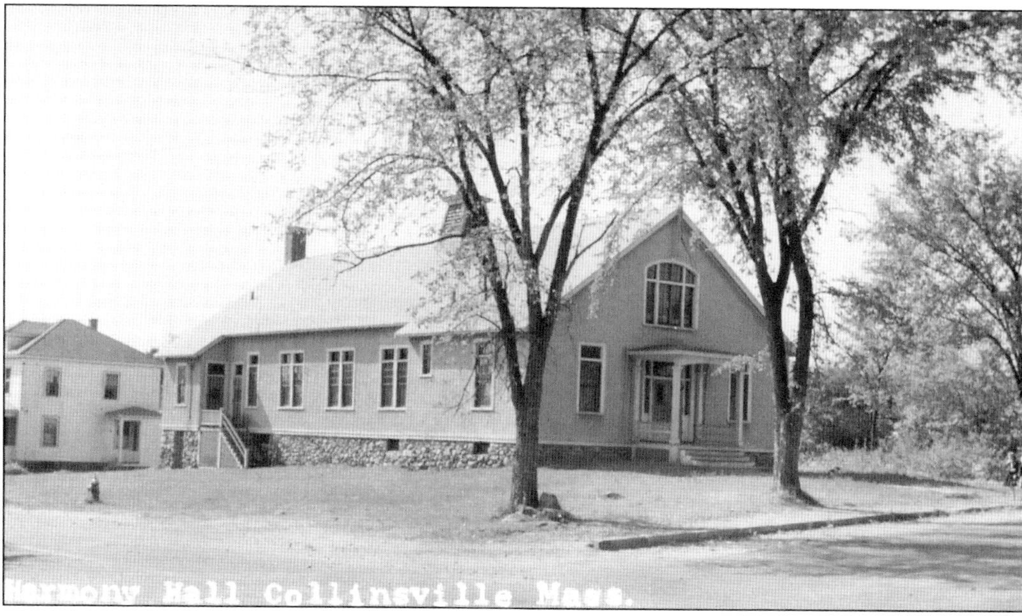

The postcard above shows Harmony Hall in its original location in Collinsville on the corner of Lakeview Avenue and Mammoth Road. In 1994, it was saved from the wrecking ball and moved to its present location at the Dracut Historical Society. It was refurbished and reopened in April 1997. Harmony Hall was connected to the meeting room at the historical society and is now used for community meetings and events.

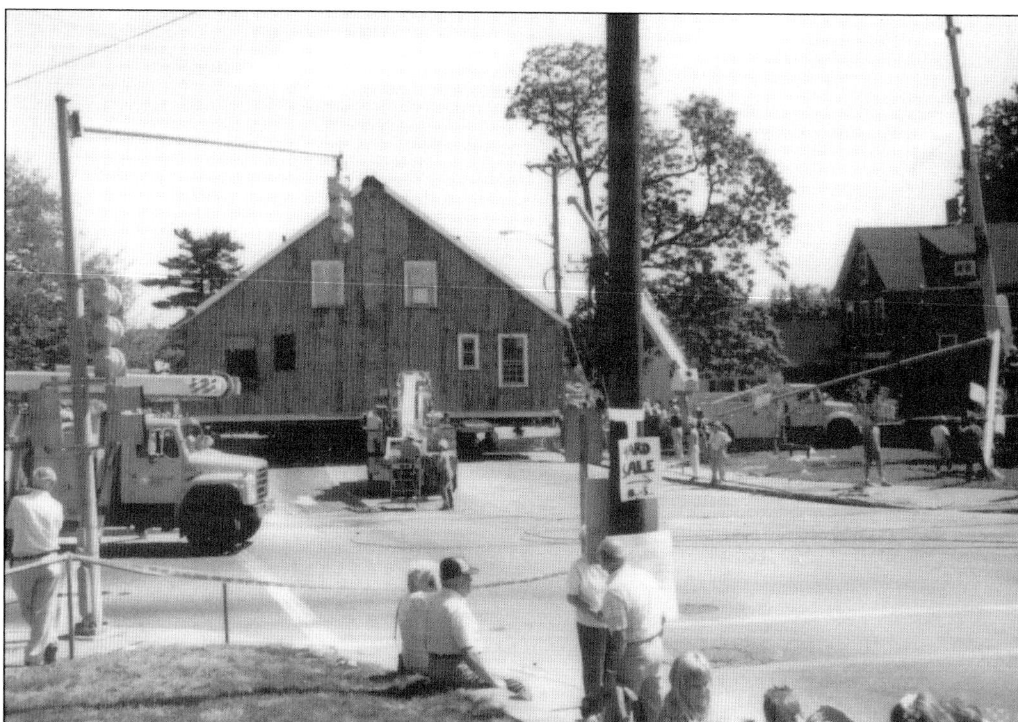

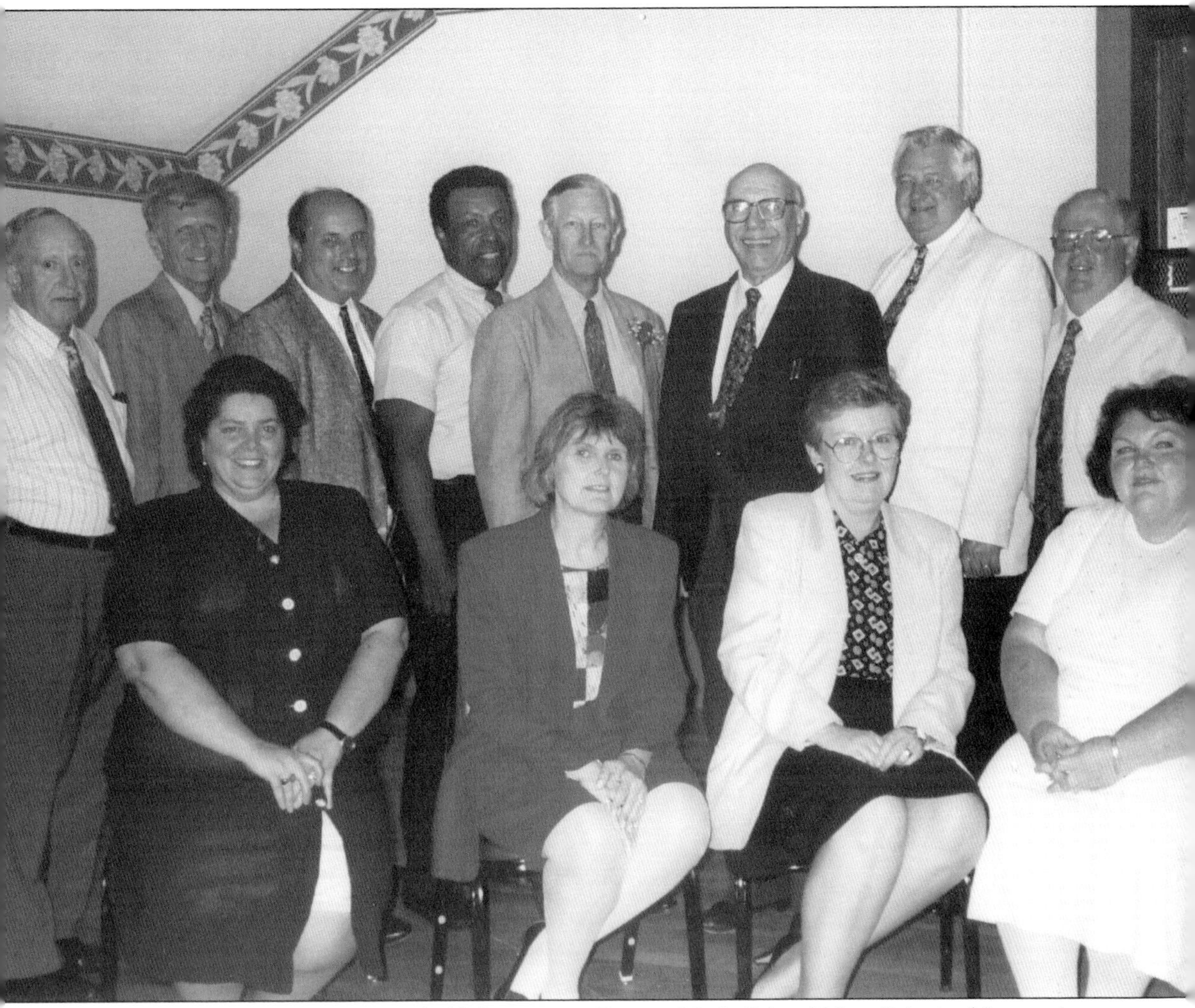

In 1994, a retirement party was held for retiring Dracut High School Vice Principal James Ace. The attendees included, from left to right, (seated) Linda Trouville, principal of Dracut Middle School; Linda Pacheco, vice principal of Campbell Elementary; Margaret Deslauriens, principal of Parker Elementary; and Marcia Brasil, vice principal of Greenmont Elementary; (standing) Donald Owens, vice principal of Dracut Middle School; Roger Dumont, principal of Dracut Junior High; Bruce Hutchins, principal of Dracut High School; Daniel Smith, vice principal of Dracut High School; James Ace, vice principal of Dracut High School; Christos Daoulas, superintendent; Leonard Smith, director of special education; and Michael McNamara, principal of Greenmont Elementary.

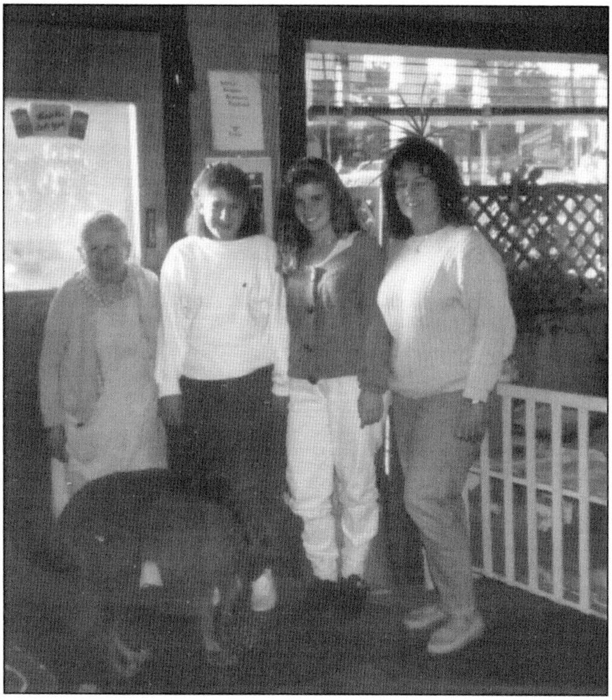

Polly Urquhardt was a fixture in Dracut from the 1940s through the 1980s, delivering newspapers and running Polly's Variety on the corner of Lakeview Avenue and Mammoth Road. Before she took over the corner store, it was known as the Lotus Filling Station. This 1991 photograph from the historical society's archives shows Polly closing her store with her family and faithful dog by her side. Mammoth Road was built at the end of the 18th century to provide a direct route to Manchester, New Hampshire.

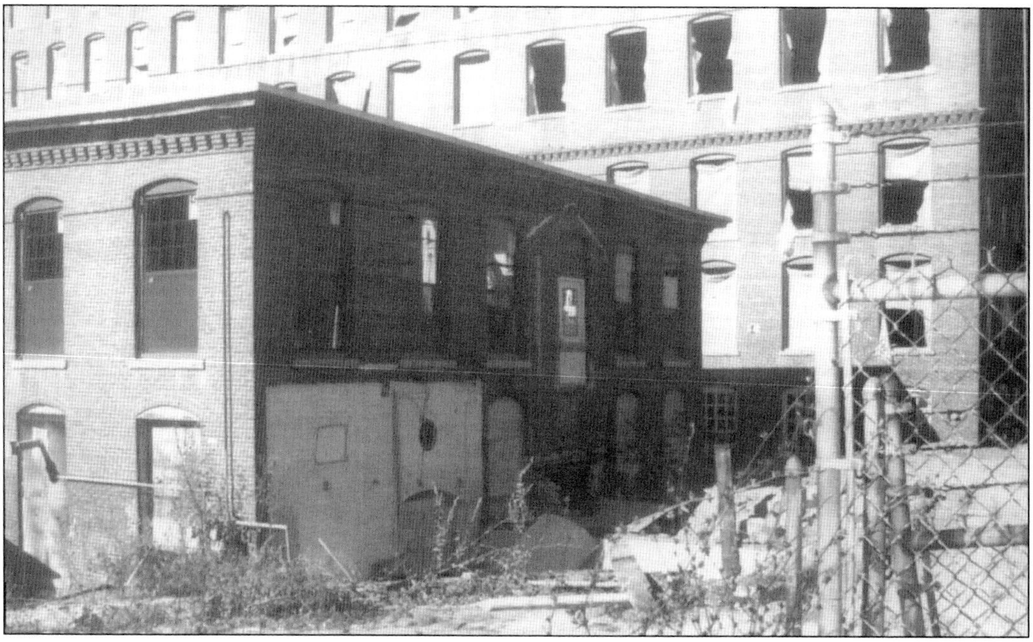

Though once a thriving industry in Dracut, the mills in Collinsville, like virtually all mills in the area, had seen a decline in their production by the end of World War II when the textile industry moved production to the South. In 1989, at the suggestion of then selectman Warren Shaw, Frank Gorman decided to purchase the former Collinsville Mills and convert them into retail and residential space. Gorman purchased the 13-acre site for $1.4 million. Prior to Gorman's plan for revitalizing the mills, the site had been used as a flea market and a few stores. The buildings had fallen into disrepair. (Courtesy Frank Gorman.)

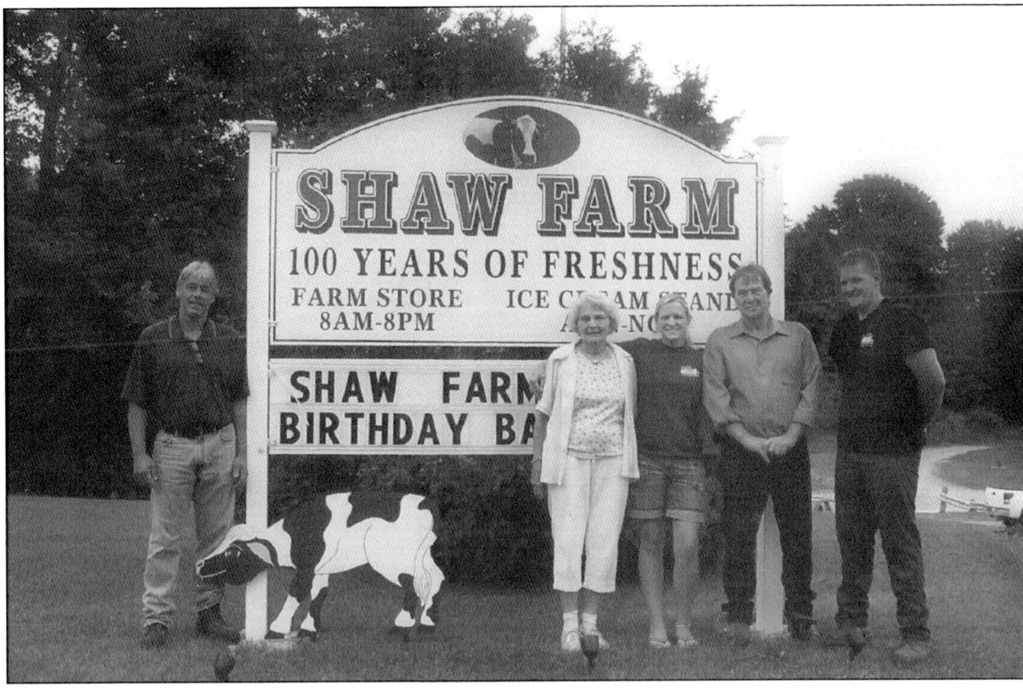

Shaw Farm celebrated its centennial in 2008. Since its inception, Shaw Farm has experienced many challenges and has continuously faced them and created a successful business. In the 1960s, supermarkets posed a threat to the business by impacting the amount of home delivery customers. Consumers were choosing to use the local supermarket and many dairy farms at this time were selling their land to developers, but Shaw Farm was able to survive. In the 1970s, Warren Shaw and Wally Biedron Jr. became full-time employees. In the 1980s, Shaw Farm expanded its retail business into ice cream, and sales grew rapidly. By 2000, the farm was self-sufficient, with 100 percent of the milk produced coming from the Shaw Farm herd. Pictured below is the Shaw Farm ice cream stand before it was expanded in 2009 to the current store. (Both images courtesy Warren Shaw.)

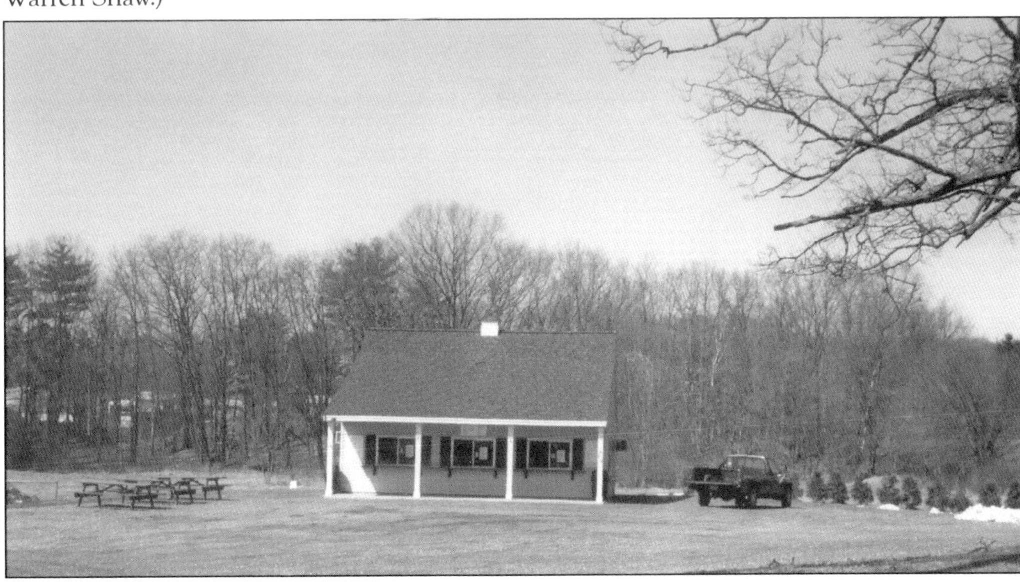

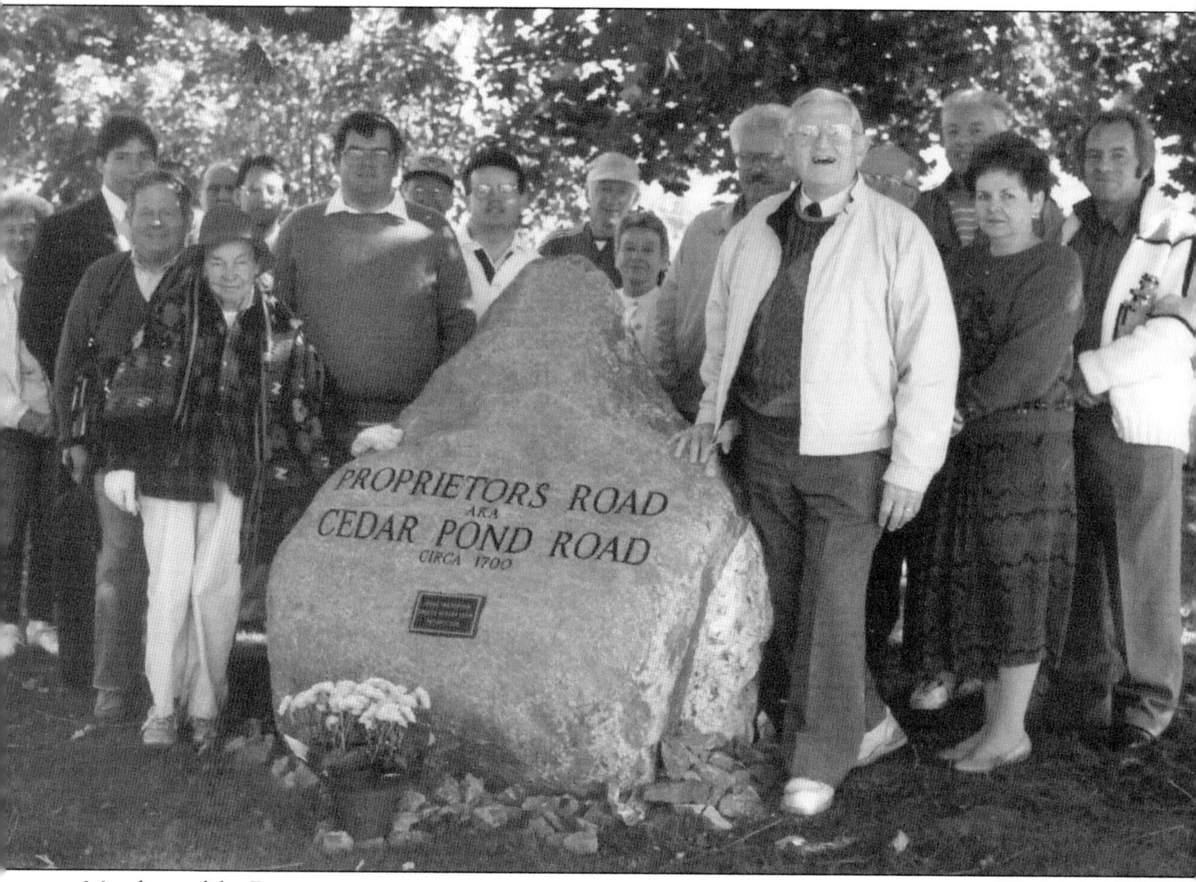

Members of the Dracut Historical Society pose in front of the Proprietor's Lane marker. Proprietor's Lane was on Marsh Hill and was used by farmers from 1700 up to the 1960s, when farms began to disappear. The farmers who owned land along Proprietor's Lane were George Callahan, whose farm was on Broadway Avenue across from Fox Avenue, Clinton Fox, who owned 20 acres bordering Proprietor's Lane, Everett Fox, whose land was near Callahan's, and the Lachut brothers. The proprietors' books are the original town records, which are in the collection of the research department of the Parker Library. The original proprietors' books were destroyed in a flood while stored in the library's basement. Fortunately, they had been scanned onto microfilm and can still be accessed.

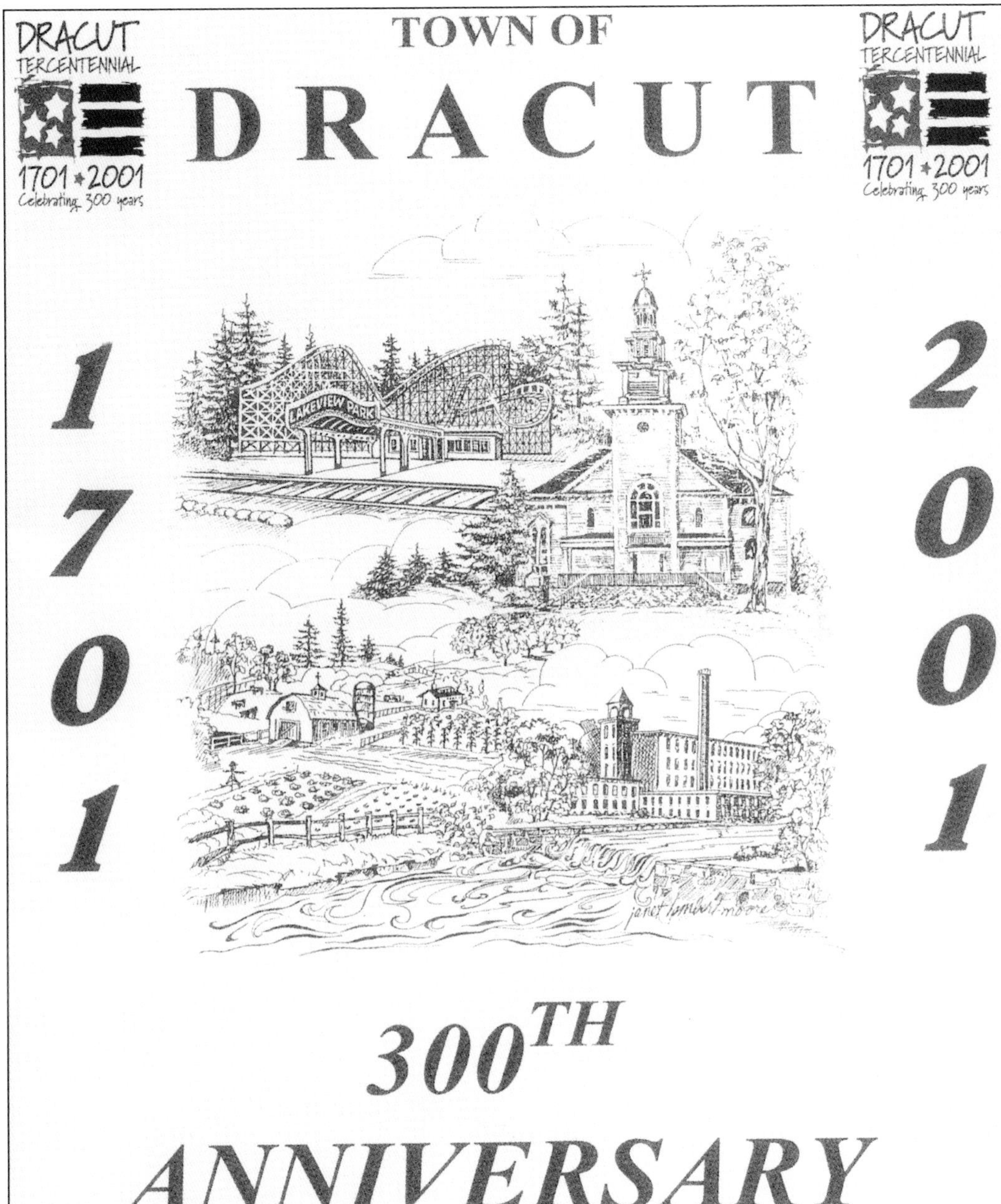

After 300 years of incorporation, Dracut celebrated its tercentenary in 2001. In 1701, 23 families lived in Dracut, but they had to pay taxes and vote in Chelmsford. They wanted to establish their own township and appealed to the Massachusetts General Court. Dracut was established on February 26, 1701. The exact origin of the name is unknown, although there is some speculation that the name is in reference to Draycotte Foliat, located near Salisbury Plain, England. John Evered Webb, Dracut's first settler, was from that area of England. Regardless, there is no other town, anywhere, with the name Dracut.

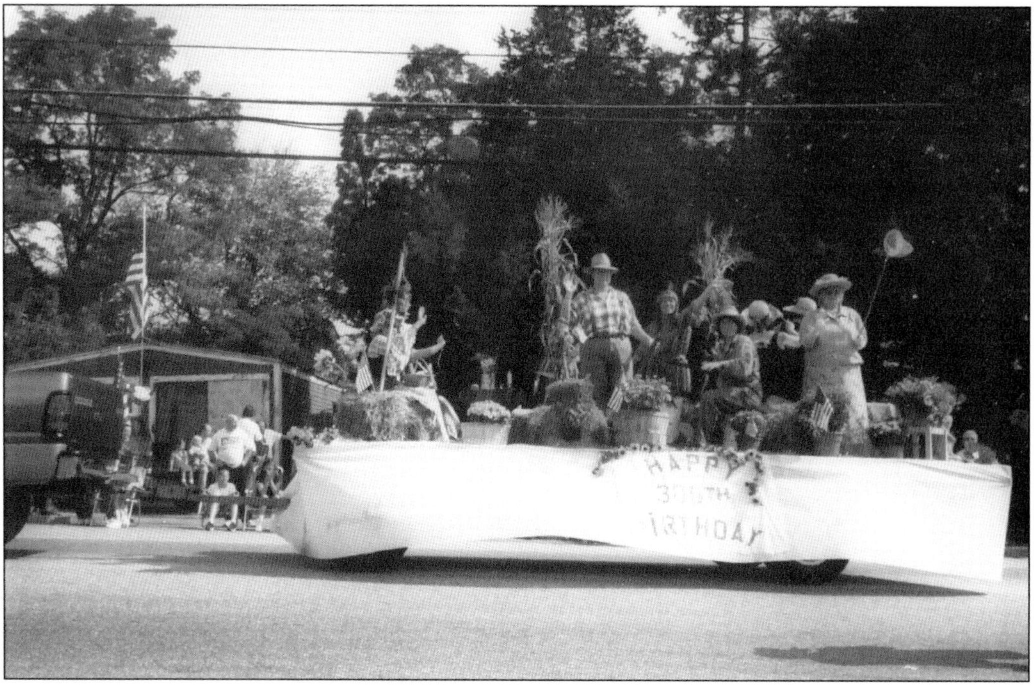

One of the events planned for the celebration of the town's tercentenary was a parade. The town originated along the Merrimack River in today what is the Pawtucketville section of Lowell. The town's first cemetery, Claypit Cemetery, is located in Pawtucketville. Several members of the Coburn family are buried there, including Moses B. Coburn, who served in the Revolutionary War. The Varnum Garrison house was built in this section of town to protect the settlers from attacks by the Native Americans. Dracut was the first permanent white settlement on the north side of the Merrimack River.

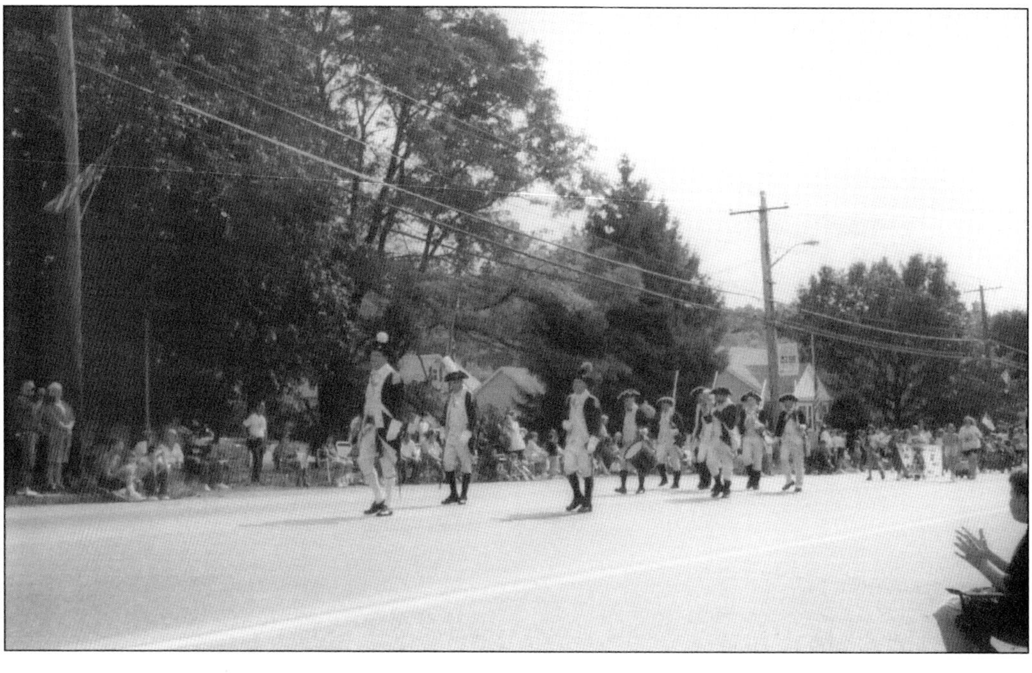

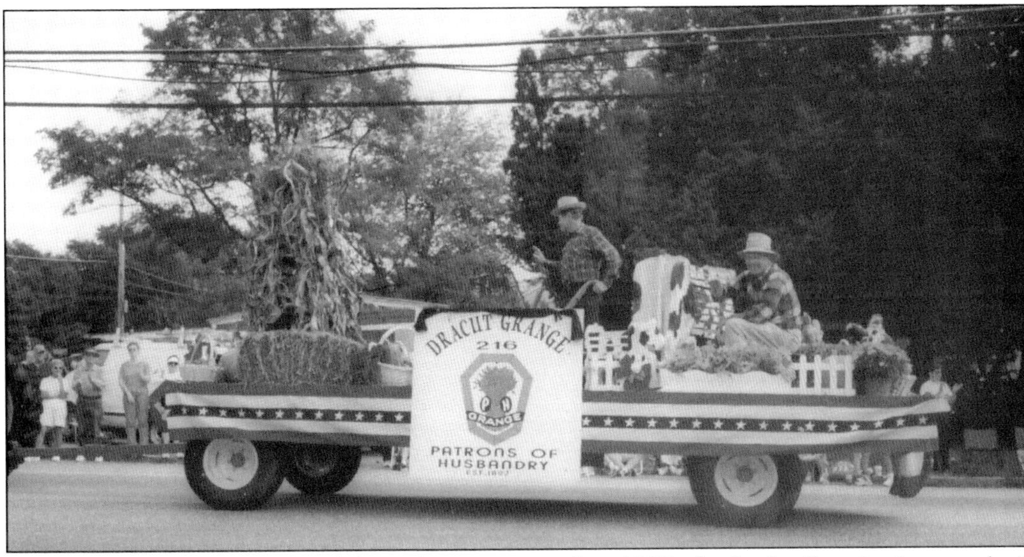

The Dracut Grange, which celebrated its centennial in 1997, also had a float in the parade. It was organized on March 8, 1897, in the Pawtucket church. George A.H. Richardson was elected master and there were 38 charter members. The Grange met in the Yellow Meeting House until 1903 when land was donated and the Grange Hall was built. Granges were formed all across the United States following the Civil War to help farms. By 1909, the Dracut Grange had over 350 members and was one of the earliest granges in the state to contribute to the State Grange Educational Aid Fund, which provides scholarships. The photograph below shows the Grange Building in 1907. (Below image courtesy Lenny Proposki.)

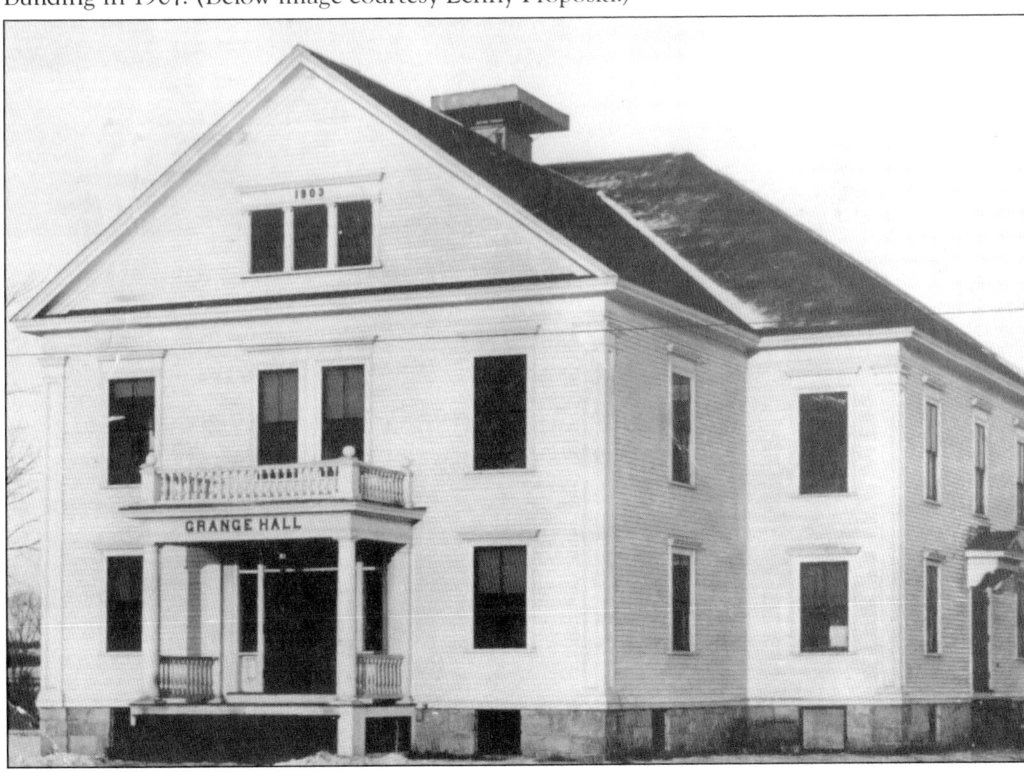

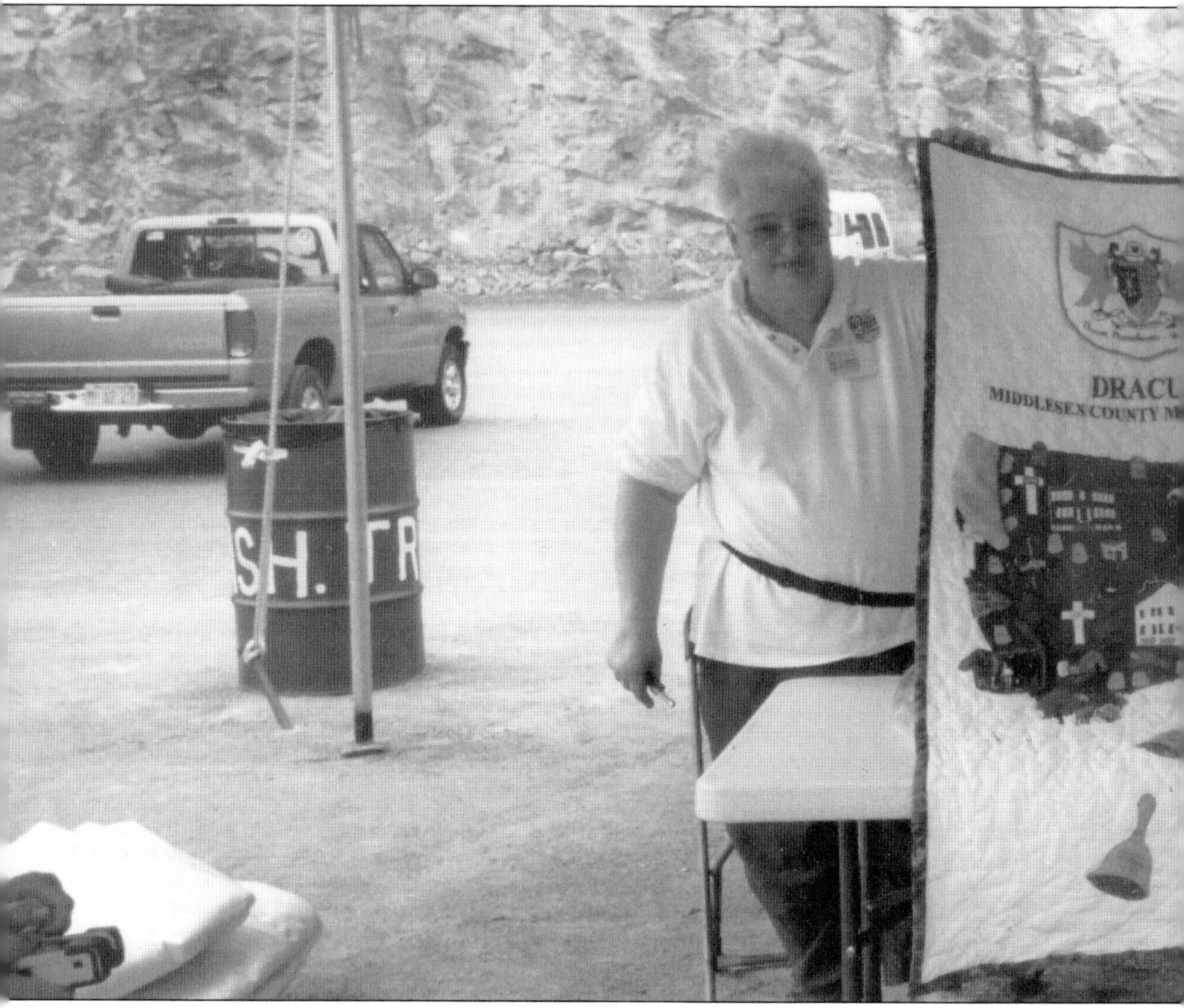

Alma Reeves (left) and Barbara Updyke hold a handmade quilt commemorating the tercentennial at the "Concert in the Quarry" in June 2001. This was one of the many activities planned through the course of the year. Both ladies are long-standing members of the Dracut Historical Society. The society had its formal opening in 1965, with 500 people in attendance. In 1980, an addition was built onto the back of the Coburn House providing additional meeting space for the society.

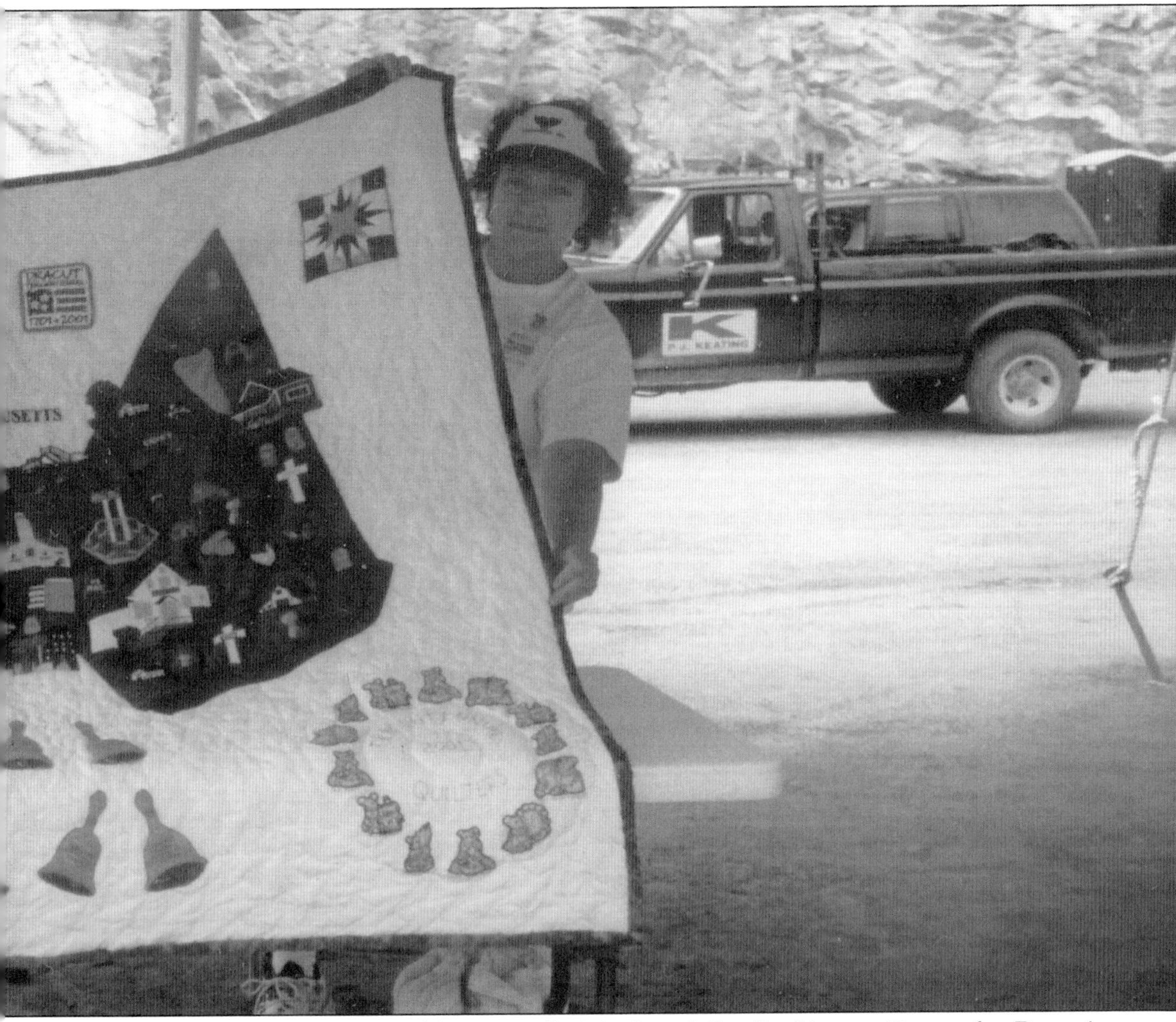

The meeting room in the new addition is called the Joseph Bradley Varnum Room after Dracut's famous military and political leader. Today, as people enter the society through this entrance, they will pass the Orpha Fox Memorial Garden, whose namesake worked tirelessly to record and write about Dracut's history. The Fox family was one of the earliest families to settle Dracut.

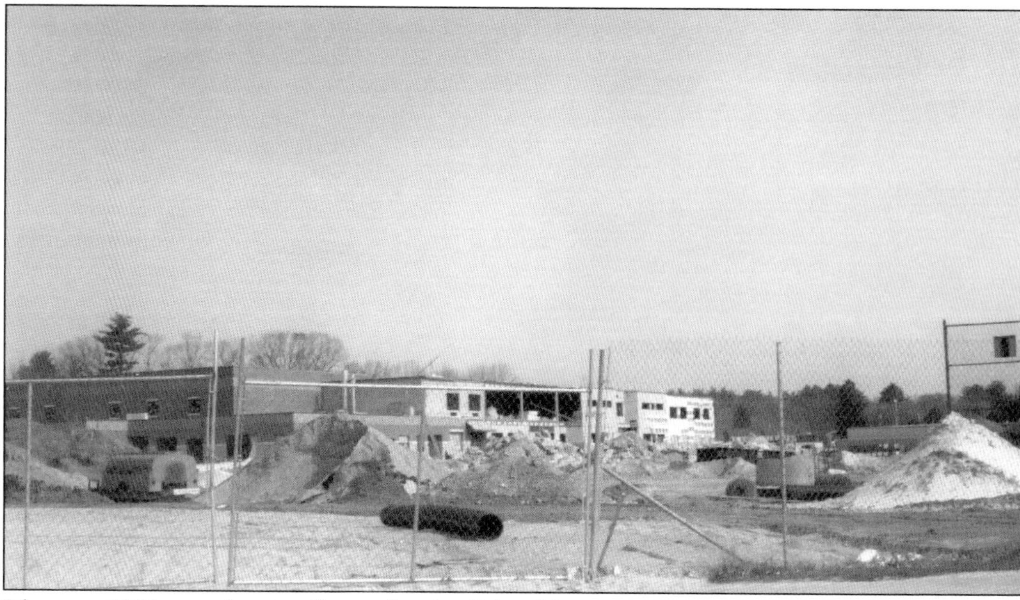

The year 2001 was also significant for the School Department. Dr. Daoulas retired in 1998 as superintendent. His successor was Elaine A. Espindle. In 2001, the town's new junior high school was built. It was the first major construction in the School Department since the Joseph Campbell Elementary School was built in 1973. With the new junior high school, a grade reorganization was planned. Elementary schools would house grades K–4, the intermediate school grades 5–6, the junior high school 7–8, and the high school 9-12. In September 2001, two schools opened: the Lakeview Junior High School and the George H. Englesby Intermediate School. At 138,000 square feet, the new junior high school was considerably larger than the previous one. With the new junior high school, the Brookside, Campbell, and Greenmont Elementary Schools had their numbers decreased, which helped alleviate overcrowding at all three schools.

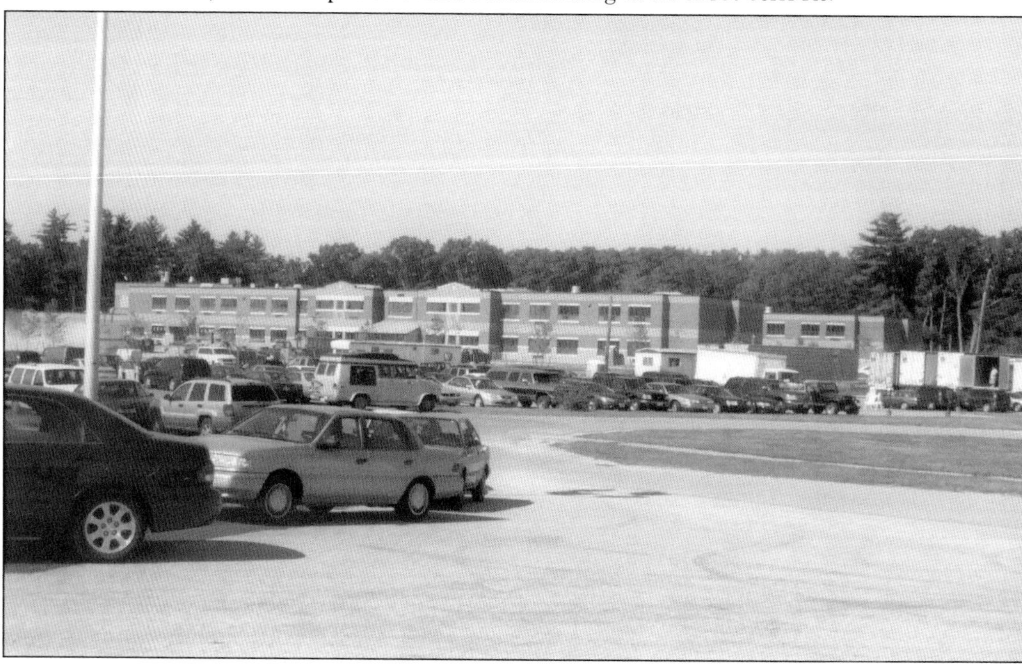

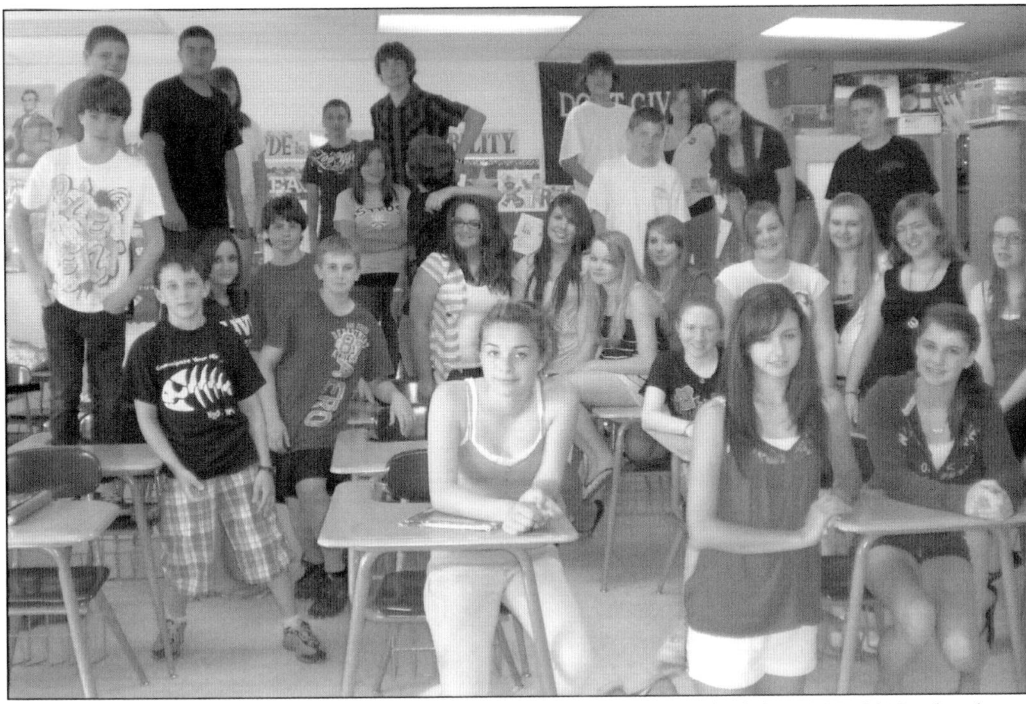

These photographs were taken in the author's classroom at the end of the 2009–2010 school year, and the author has little doubt that many of these students will be future recipients of scholarships through the Dracut Scholarship Foundation. When the Junior High School was constructed, the Englesby School was converted into an intermediate school for the town's fifth and sixth grades. The building of the junior high school was a major accomplishment by former superintendent Espindle, who remembers with pride the building of the junior high school and creation of the intermediate schools as "a dynamic era for all" that drew "excitement from all aspects of the school system." (Author's collection.)

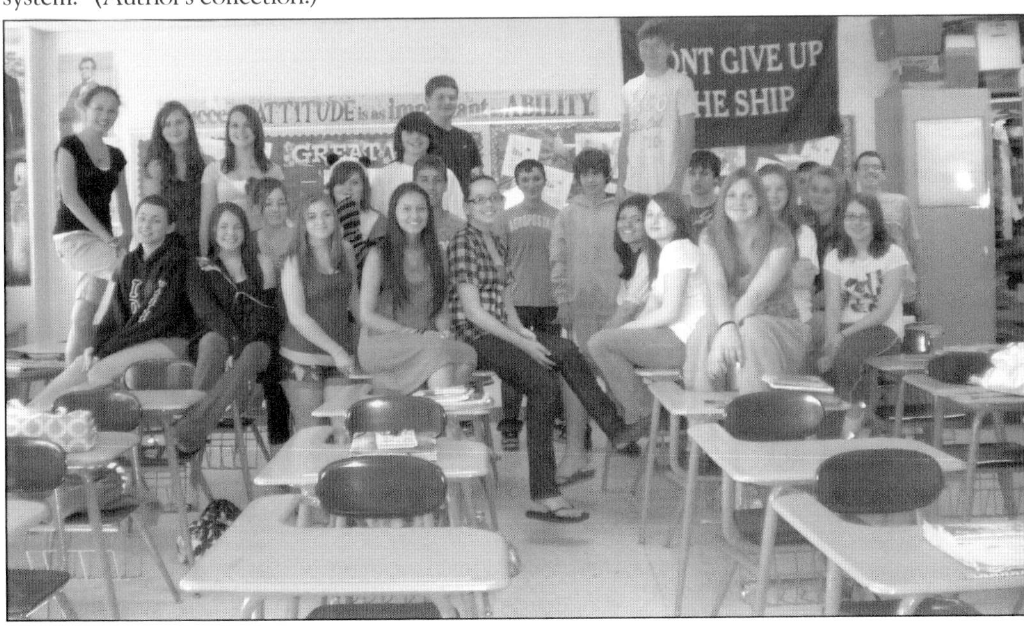

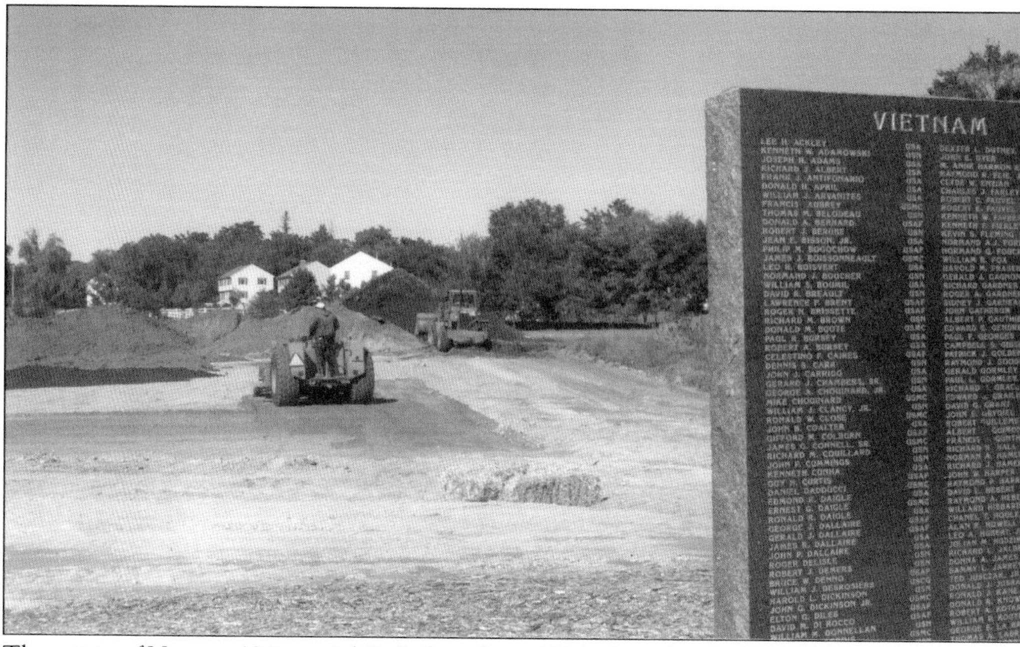

The origin of Veterans' Memorial Park dates from 1996 when the town purchased 23 acres along Broadway. The purchase was made possible because the town received a grant of $462,400 from the state's Division of Conservation Services. The grant accounted for 68 percent of the purchase price of the farmland. Once the land was purchased, the Board of Selectmen appointed a 47-member committee to help guide and advise on the development of the park. These 47 committee members created three subcommittees to accomplish their charge. By April 1999, enough fundraising had been done so that construction on the park could begin and a ground-breaking ceremony took place. In 2007, the concession stand opened and sales from it help to support the park which today is a total of 26 acres.

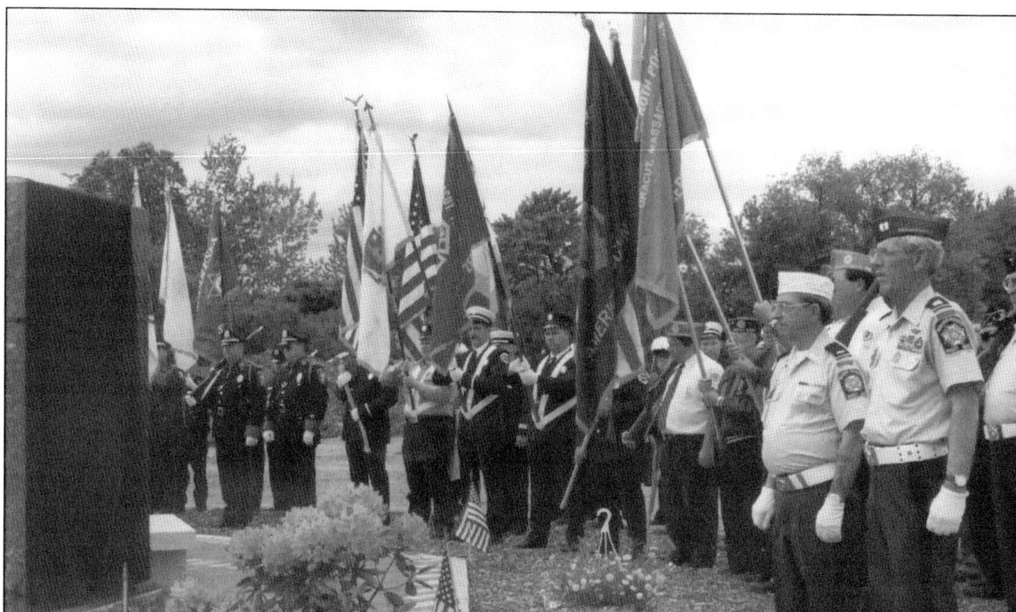

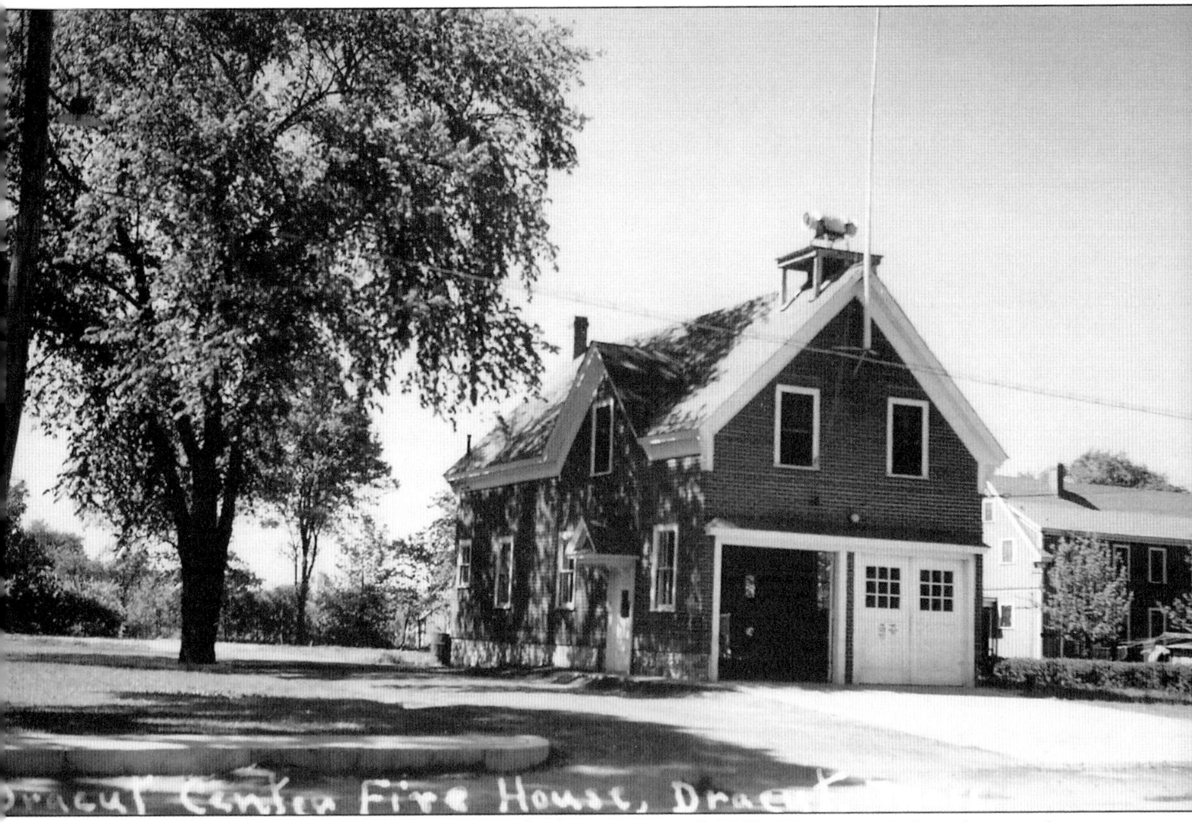

This postcard shows the Dracut Center firehouse around 1950. The town's first fire truck was purchased by Frank Gunther and his fire company. Ernest Gunther was appointed fire chief in 1934, a position he held until his retirement in 1967. This postcard, as well as all the postcard images in this book, comes from the collection of the late Paul Dumont, former owner of Dracut Hardware. When Dracut Hardware relocated in 1960 from the Navy Yard to Lakeview Avenue, there was a house on the property, which was moved to 506 Nashua Road to become the family home of Paul and his wife, Irene. After the house was moved, the Dumonts decided to build a small strip mall, which was occupied by the Tasty Pastry Shop and Union National Bank. The Tasty Pastry was operated by Paul Dumont's twin brother Emile as a second location to his already established business in Chelmsford. Over the years, the stores in the strip mall moved out and Dracut Hardware was able to expand into the space.

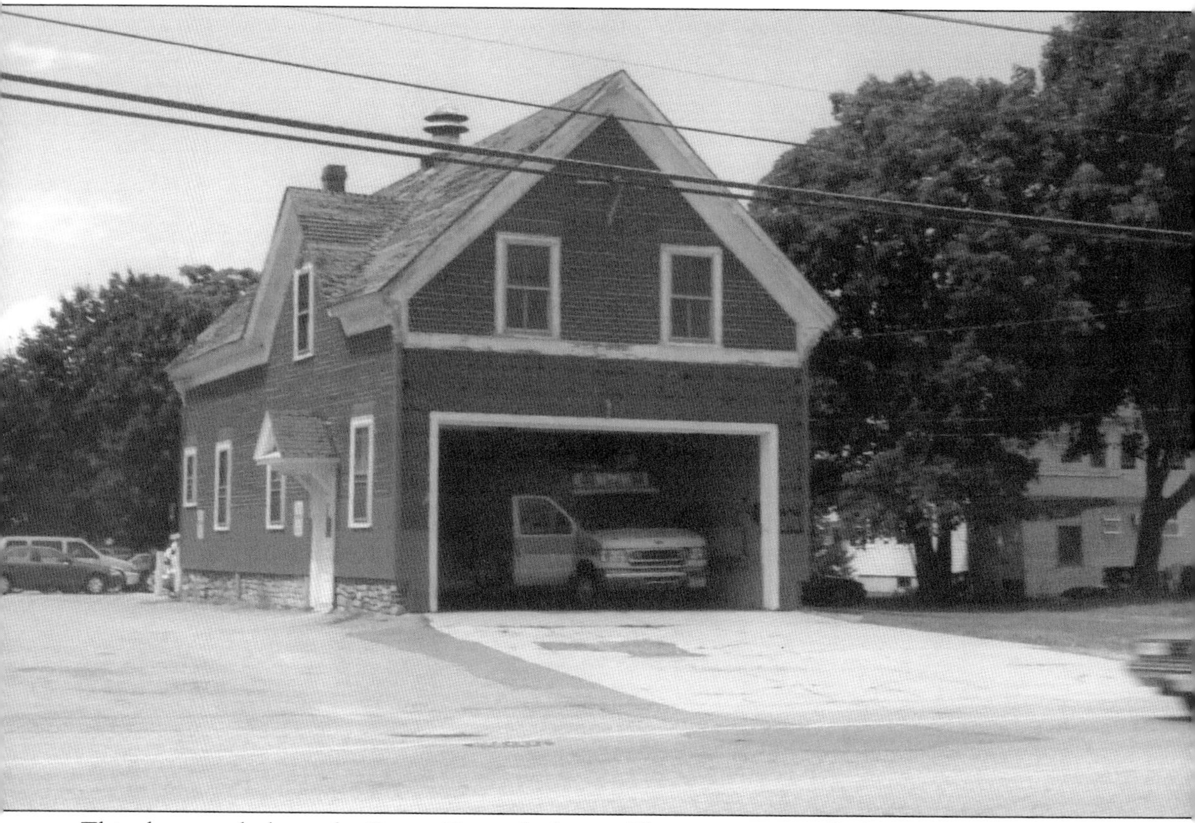

This photograph shows the Dracut Center firehouse. There were originally four stations throughout the town: one in Kenwood near the Kenwood School, one in Dracut Center near the library, the old central station on Pleasant Street, and a fourth in Collinsville next to Dracut Hardware, which is still used. For many years, Dracut had a "call department." Volunteers would respond to the station in their district according to where they lived. From there, they would man the trucks and respond to fires. Each station had a very large horn on its roof—seen in the previous image—to notify volunteers of a fire. In later years, those horns were used to notify the town of school closings due to snow. (Courtesy Paul Dumont family.)

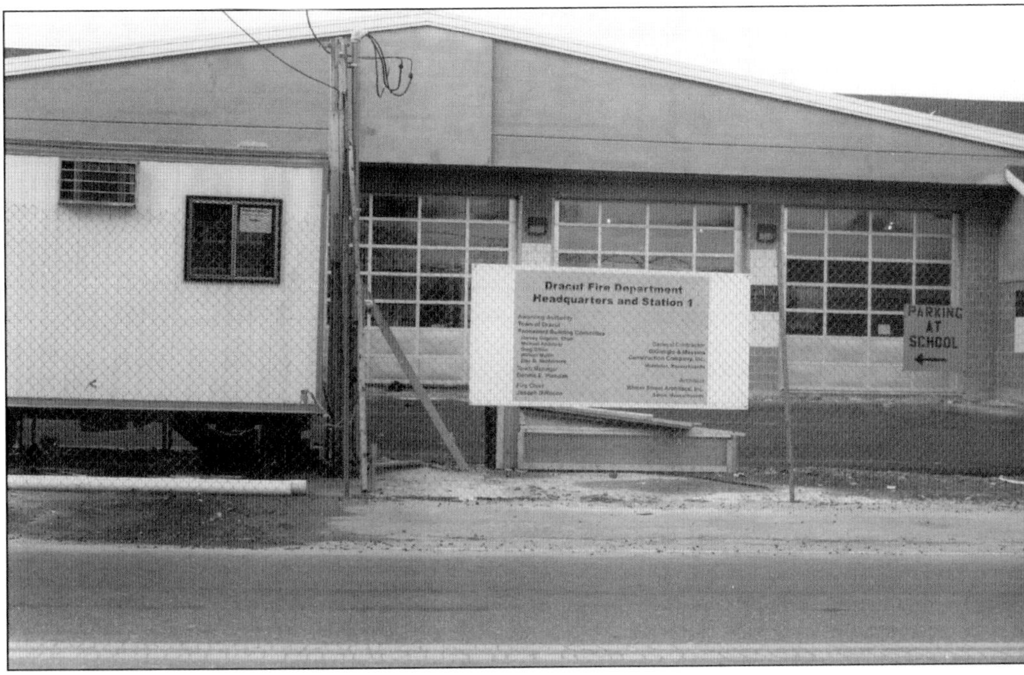

A new fire station was built on Pleasant Street to replace the old one, which had been in use for several decades. It was constructed during the tenure of fire chief Joe DiRocco across from Monahan Park. The current fire chief, Leo Gaudette, is retiring this year after serving as chief since 2002. Captain David Brouillette was named Gaudette's successor by Town Manager Dennis Piendak.

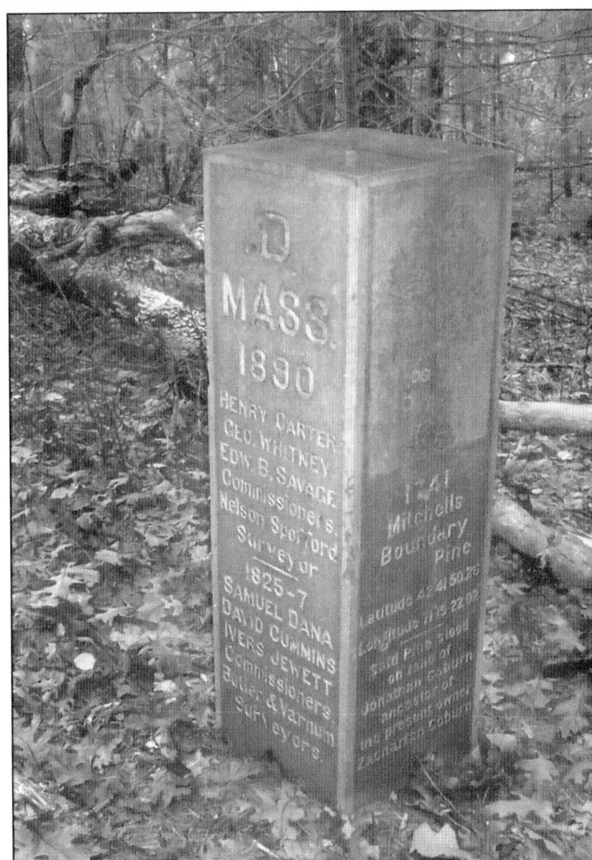

Dracut's boundaries have changed much over time, and the town is much smaller than it had originally been in 1701. In 1741, the boundary line between New Hampshire and Dracut was finalized and Dracut's size was cut in almost half. In the 19th century, Dracut lost Centralville and most of Pawtucketville when those neighborhoods were annexed to Lowell. Pictured on the right is the Pine Tree Marker, which marks one of Dracut's boundaries. It is located near Black Oak Lane and Coburn Avenue.

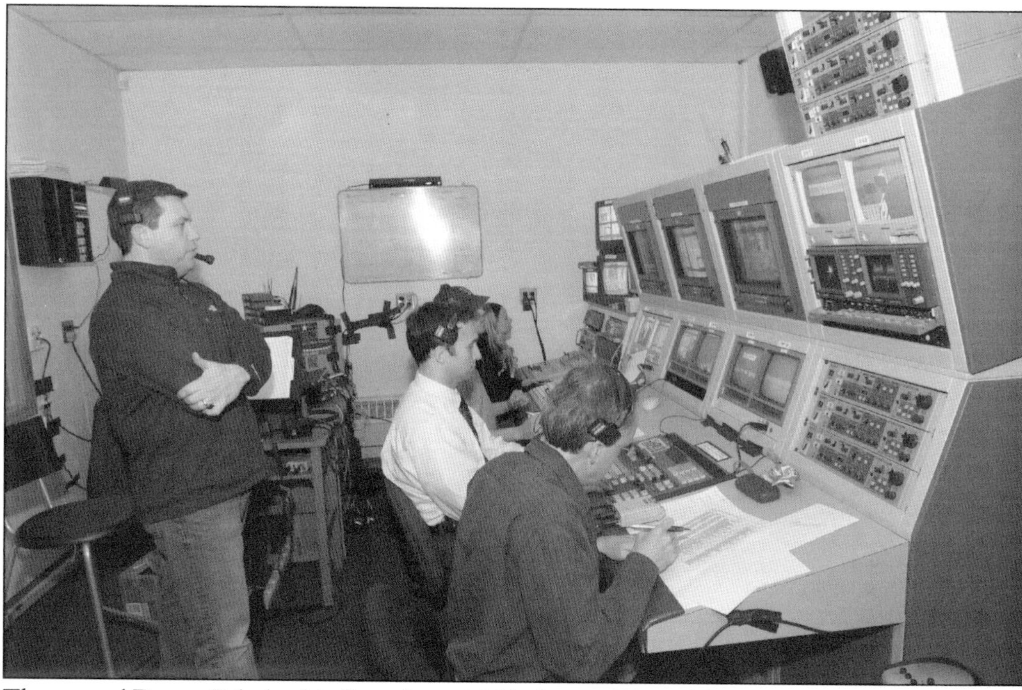

The annual Dracut Scholarship Foundation's Telethon will be celebrating its 30th anniversary in 2013. The heart and soul of the event is the television control room at Dracut High School. Gary Meuse, pictured standing at left, has produced the telethon since its inception. In 2012, the telethon raised a record $130,000. (Courtesy Lenny Proposki.)

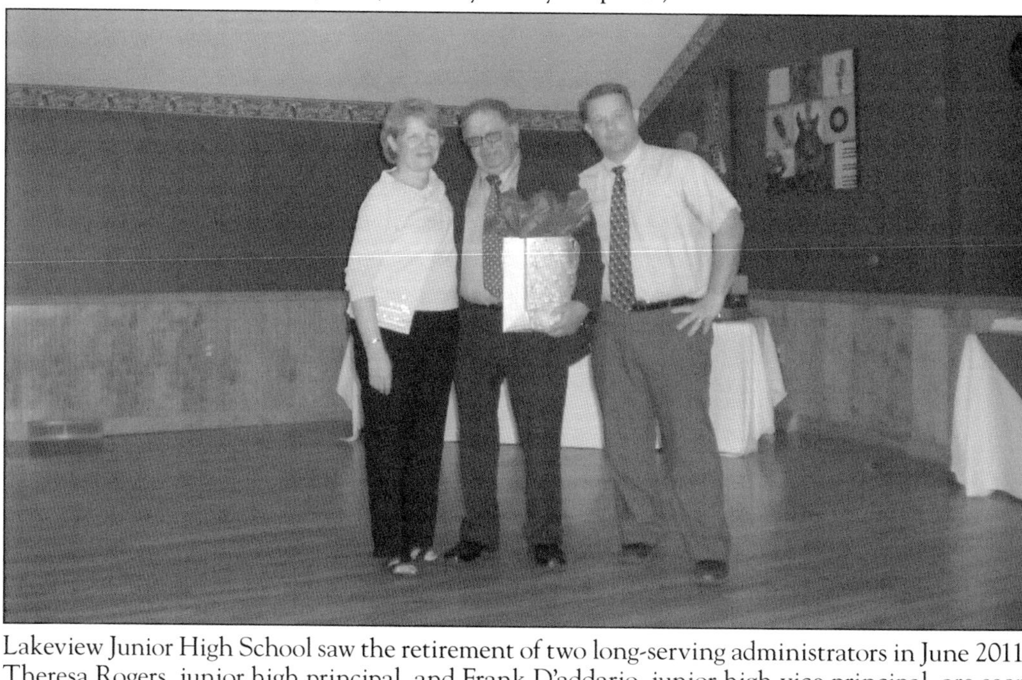

Lakeview Junior High School saw the retirement of two long-serving administrators in June 2011. Theresa Rogers, junior high principal, and Frank D'addario, junior high vice principal, are seen here at their retirement party at the Village Inn. On the right is the current junior high vice principal, Robert McGrath. (Author's collection.)

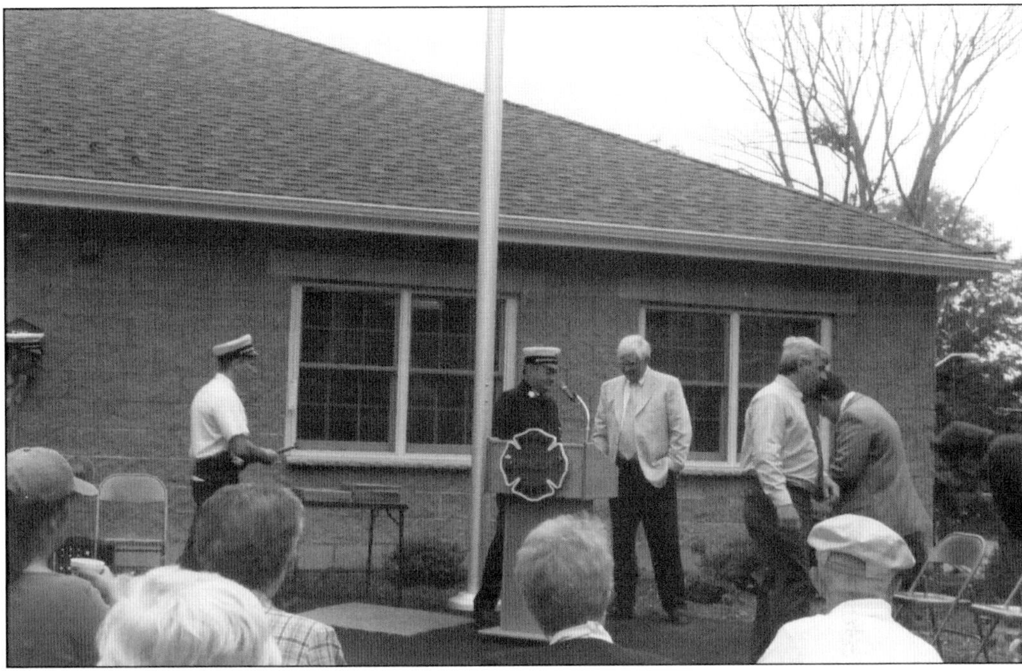

The dedication of the East Dracut fire station at the corner of Jones Avenue and Broadway Avenue took place in June 2000. The station was the culmination of the efforts of many in town, including Town Manager Dennis Piendak, selectmen, and fire chiefs Joe DiRocco, Gerard Carle, and Robert Kohanski. In 1985, a town meeting appropriated $45,000 for the lot the station sits on, and the total cost for the completed facility was just under $1 million. It is 870,000 square feet, and its presence has cut response time in that section of town from 12 minutes to 3 minutes.

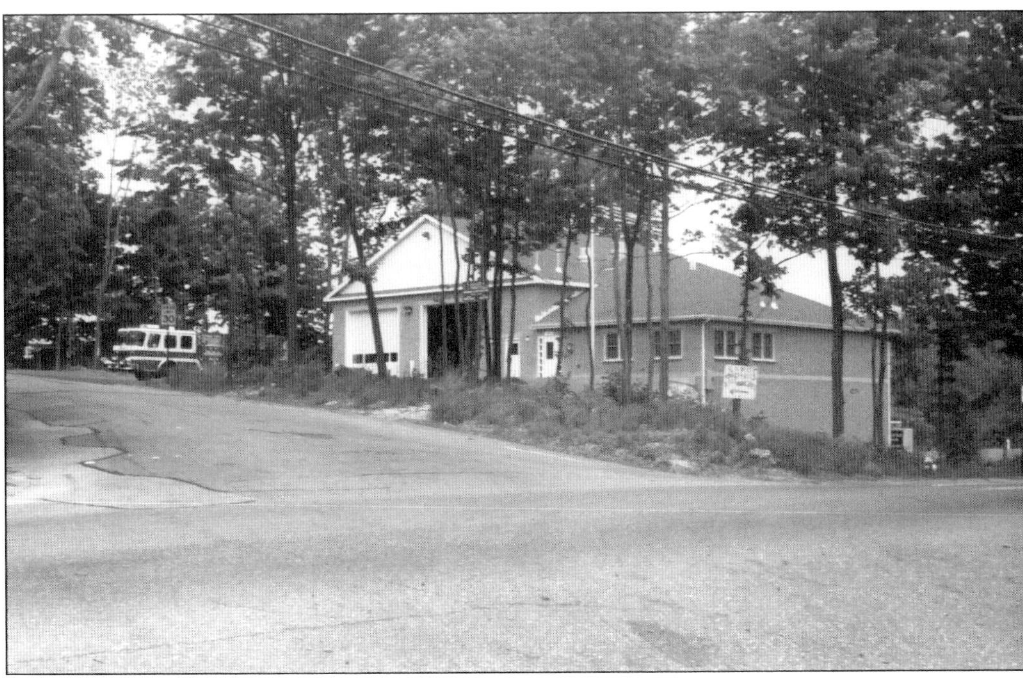

DRACUT TERCENTENNIAL 1701 ★ 2001 Celebrating 300 years

"DRACUT TERCENTENNIAL"

GALA CELEBRATION

Saturday, February 24, 2001

THE MILL HOUSE RESTAURANT
Route 110, Dracut, Massachusetts

6:00 - 7:00 Social Hour
7:00 PM Dinner - 8:00 PM Program

9:00 PM - Enjoy & Dance To
"THE CONTINENTALS"

$30.00 Per Person

Dracut celebrated its tercentenary in 2001 with events such as those shown here, but the town's history would be incomplete without mentioning Passaconaway. His name means "Chief of the Bear" and he was the sachem, or chief, of the Penacook tribe, which had a settlement at Pawtucket Falls. Pawtucket is an Algonquin word meaning "at the falls in the river." There is a statue of Passaconaway on Lowell's Edson Cemetery, and the Kancamagus Highway in New Hampshire is named after his grandson.

DRACUT TERCENTENNIAL 1701 ★ 2001 Celebrating 300 years

P.J. KEATING

DRACUT TERCENTENNIAL COMMITTEE
And
P. J. KEATING CO.
Presents
THE CONCERT IN THE QUARRY
Featuring
THE U. S. NAVY BAND
17 PIECE SHOW BAND
JUNE 24, 2001

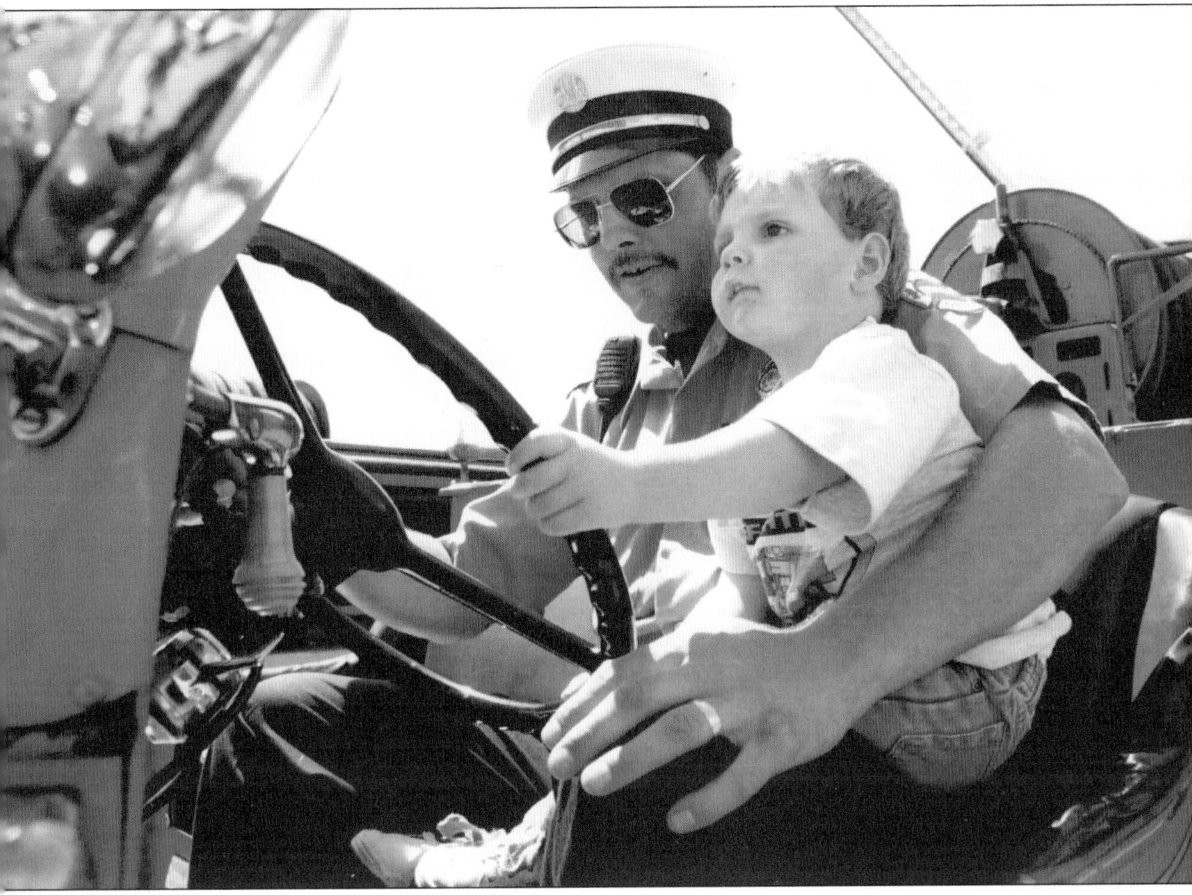

In addition to the opening of the new Lakeview Junior High School and the town's numerous tercentenary activities, the Dracut Fire Department organized the first Firefighters' Activity Day. The first Activity Day was held at the old Dracut Civic Club. There was a softball game, and the firefighters did the cooking as their way of showing appreciation to the community. In its third year, the event was moved to the school complex and has remained there ever since. From 1991 to 2000, the day was known as Firefighters' Activity Day, but in 2000, it was renamed Old Home Day and Firefighters' Activity Day. It has expanded every year since its inception. In 2011, there were over 200 booths and 13,000 people visitors. Here, firefighter Ken Wojtas and his son Nicholas celebrate Firefighters' Activity Day. (Courtesy Ken and Rhonda Wojtas.)

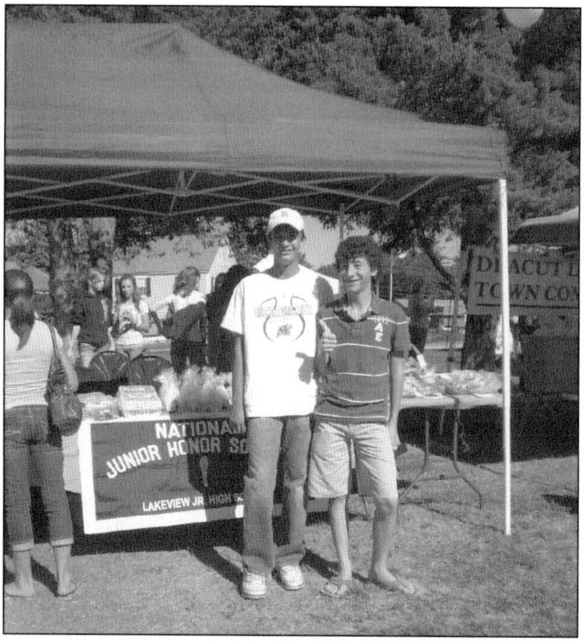

Dracut's Old Home Day takes place on the second Saturday of September. Each year, the event grows and tables and activities fill the grounds in front of the Englesby Intermediate School on Lakeview Avenue. The Englesby School was named for longtime Dracut educator George H. Englesby in 1972. In 2010, the Lakeview Junior High School's National Junior Honor Society had a table there for the first time. Ari Malliaros and Alex Corcoran, both members of the NJHS that year, are seen here. In addition to booths, there are also rides and games for children, a five-kilometer road race, and a car show. (Author's collection.)

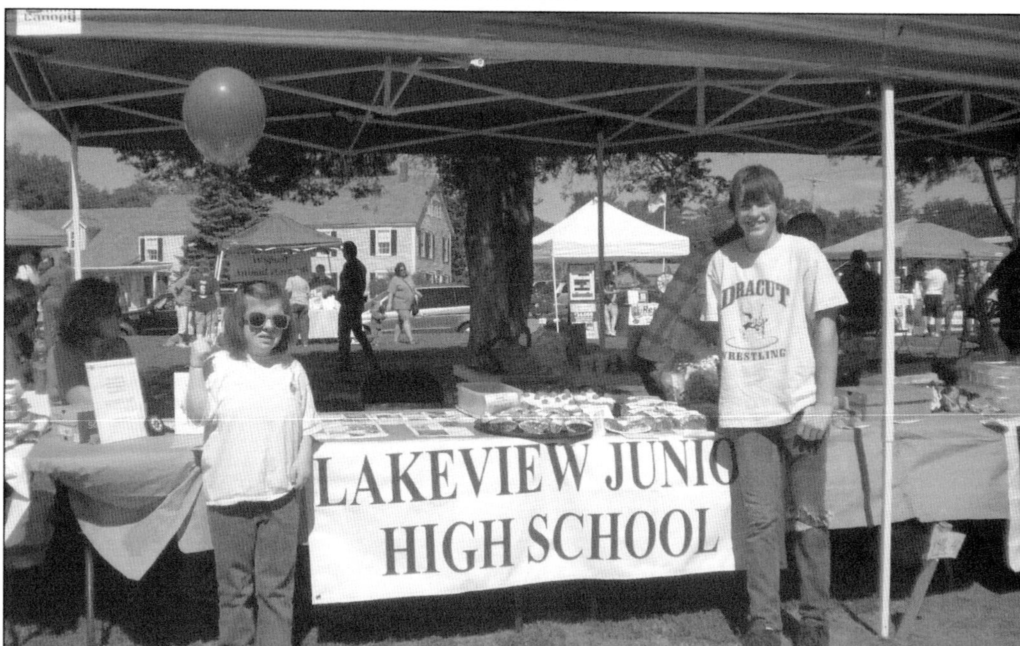

The funds raised by the Lakeview Junior High School's National Junior Honor Society at Old Home Day are used to support the group's annual "Harvest Ball," an afternoon of entertainment and refreshments at the Dracut Council on Aging. The event is held each October and students serve the Senior citizens refreshments and dance with them. It was first conceived by the JHS vice principal at the time, Frank D'addario, and NJHS advisor Bill Vogel as a community service project the students could coordinate each year. In 2010, the national office recognized the Harvest Ball as one of four outstanding service projects in the nation. (Author's collection.)

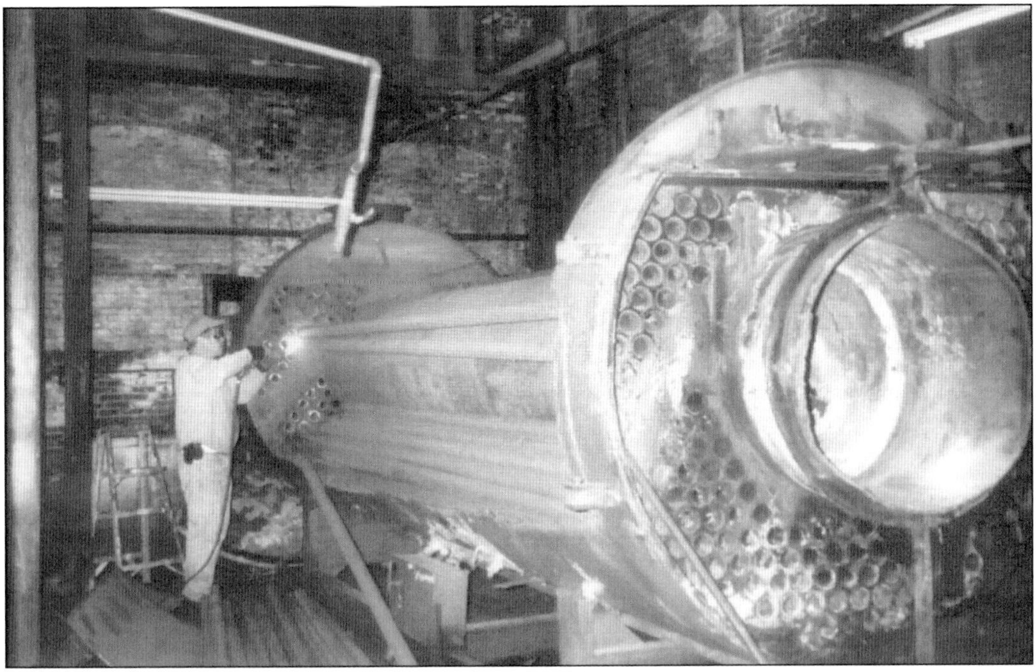

Frank Gorman's plan to renovate the Beaver Brook Mills was the first time in Dracut's history that a renovation of former textile mills had been proposed. The town was wholeheartedly behind the project, and town meeting voted to change the zoning for the site to both residential and retail use. The state also supported the project by classifying the area as an Economic Target Area. Once these issues and other financing issues were surmounted, a groundbreaking ceremony was held on December 14, 2005. These photographs show an old turbine being dismantled and taken away once construction began. The space that once housed the turbine is now used by a church. Gorman is proud of his work to revitalize the Beaver Brook Mill site: "I've been able to make a good living doing what I love. And I think I've been able to do some good things for the town I love." (Both images courtesy Frank Gorman.)

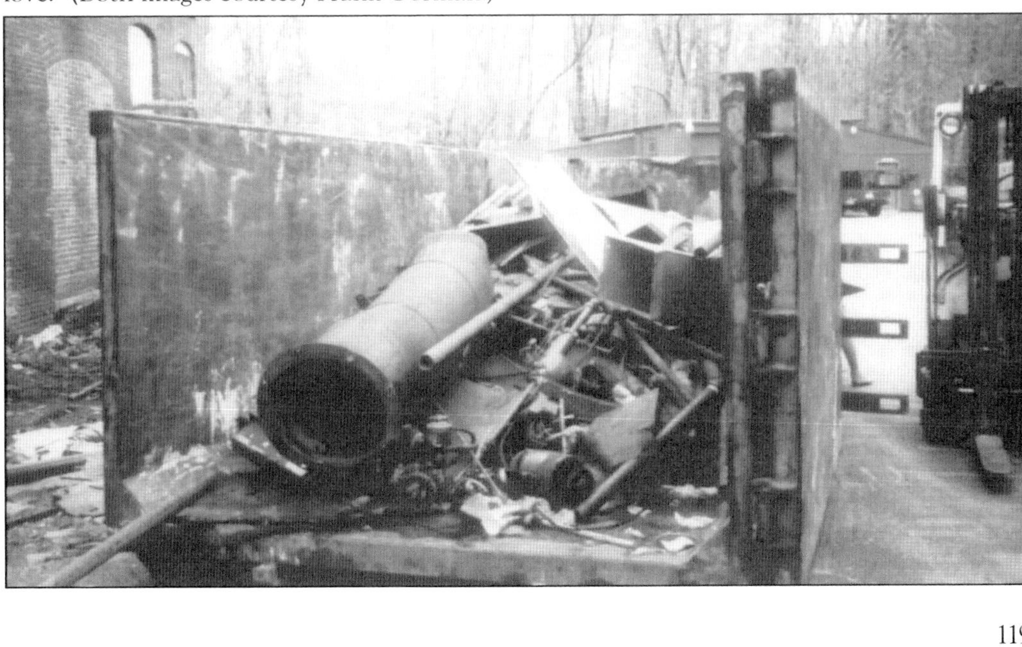

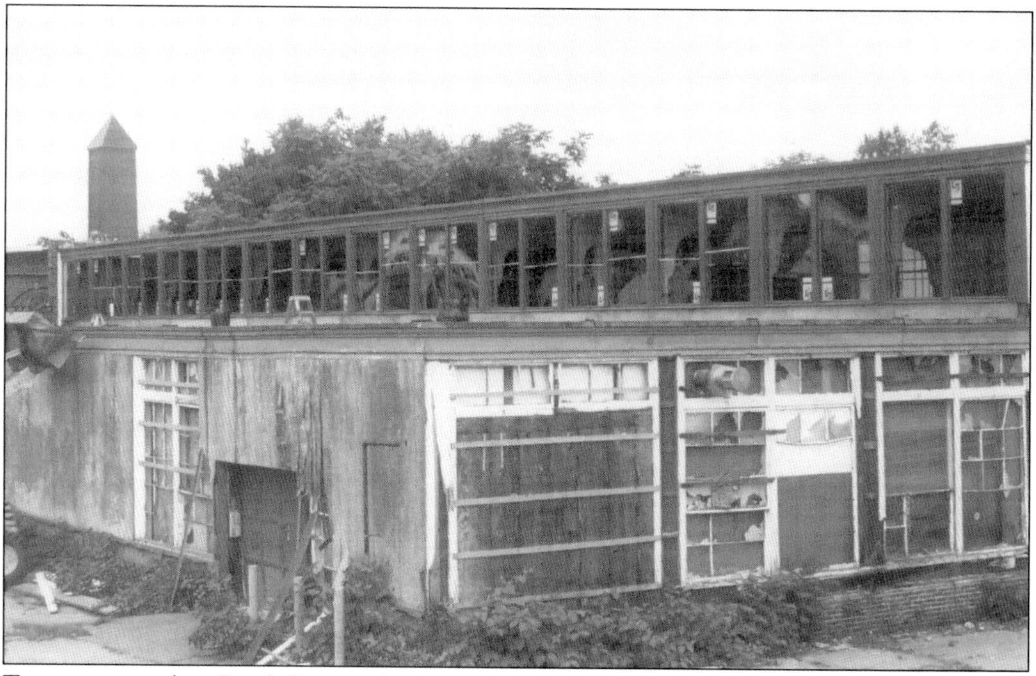

Ten years ago, when Frank Gorman began renovating the Beaver Brook Mills, the building was in disrepair. Today, this part of the complex is thriving and home to Owen & Ollie's Restaurant. The *Sun* called Gorman's work at Beaver Brook "The Crown Jewel of Dracut" in a 2006 article published just before the project was completed and open for business. (Courtesy Frank Gorman.)

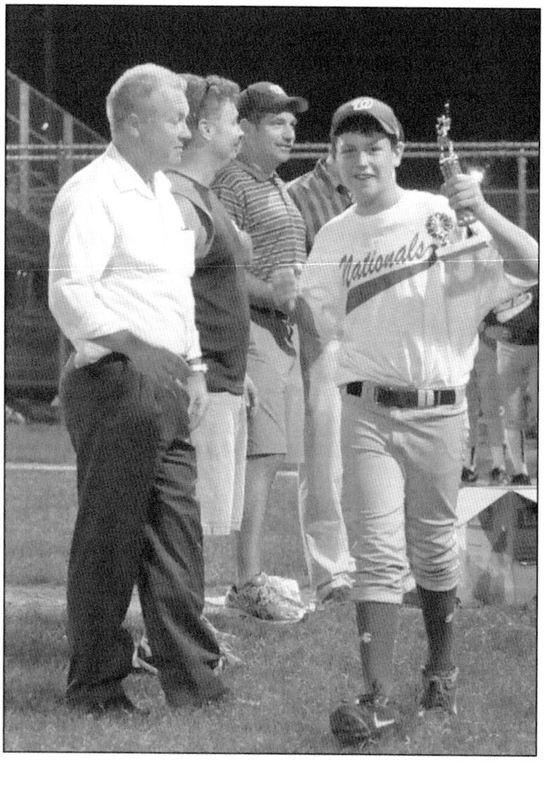

The Dracut Baseball Association is one of the more successful athletic organizations in Dracut, with over 700 children participating. This photograph was taken in July 2011 at the junior high school field. Colin Scano is seen receiving his end of year trophy. (Courtesy Harry Curtis.)

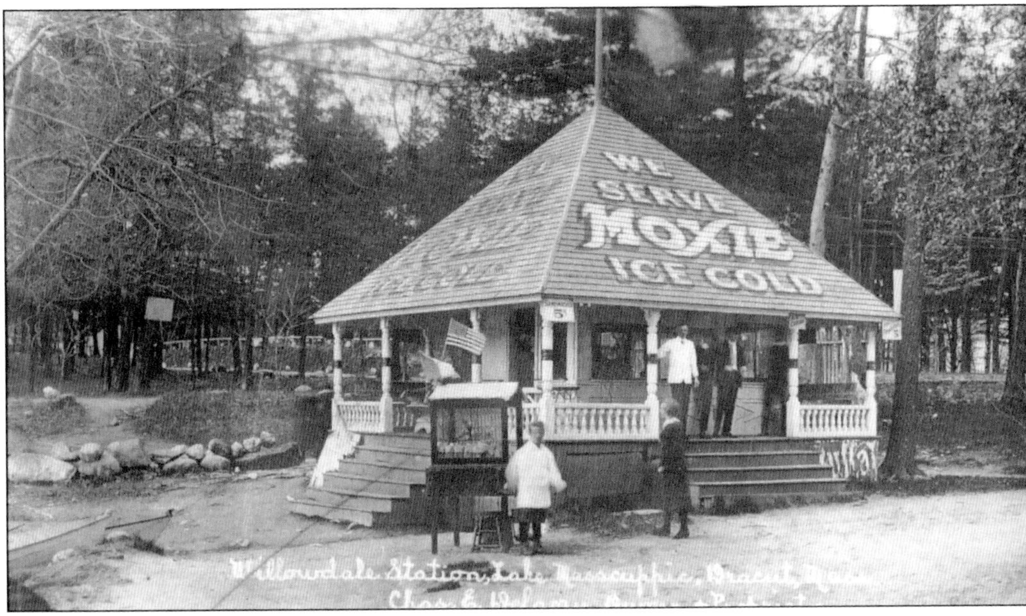

While significant changes have happened in the school department and at the Beaver Brook Mills, the same can be said about Lake Mascuppic and Lakeview Park. Picturesque scenes such as these are long gone. Apartment buildings and other small businesses now dot the coast of the lake. (Courtesy Paul Dumont family.)

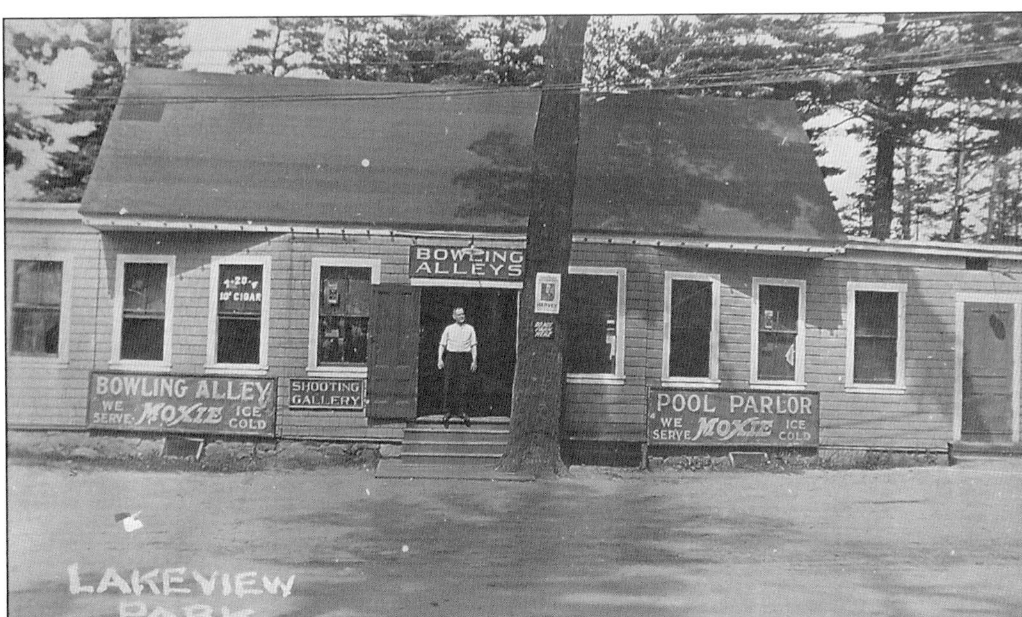

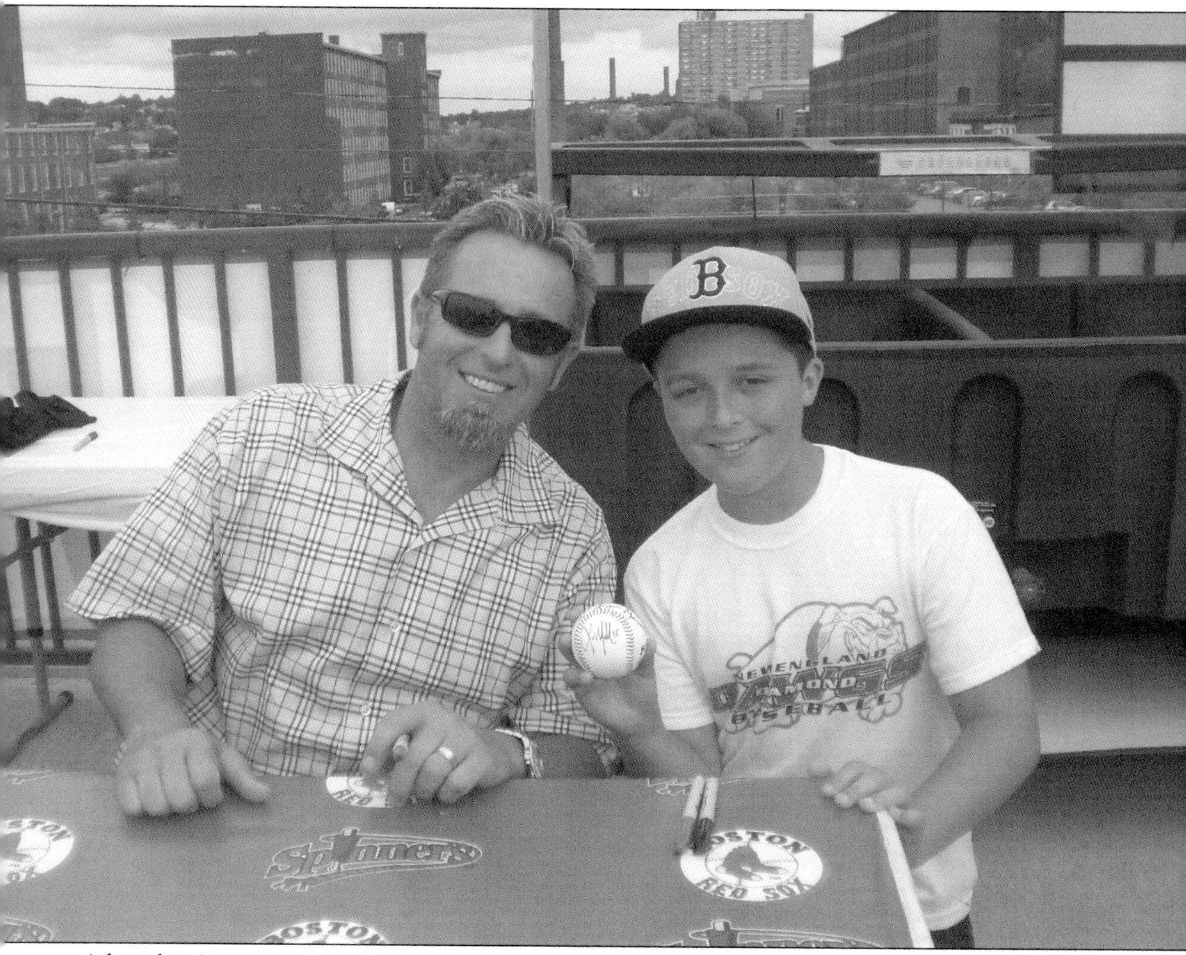

After the American Revolution, the Marquis de Lafayette visited Dracut to see his old friend Louis Ansart. Ansart was another French nobleman, like Lafayette, who helped Washington during the Revolution. Unlike Lafayette, Ansart remained in the United States and settled in Dracut. His house still stands in what once was Dracut, and is now Pawtucketville in Lowell. In the 1930s, Miss America paid a visit to Lakeview Ballroom. Celebrities still occasionally visit the area. This photograph was taken in July 2011 at LaLecheur Park in Lowell, where Dracut resident Joshua Gonzalez met former Red Sox first baseman Kevin Millar at a Lowell Spinners game and got his autograph. (Author's collection.)

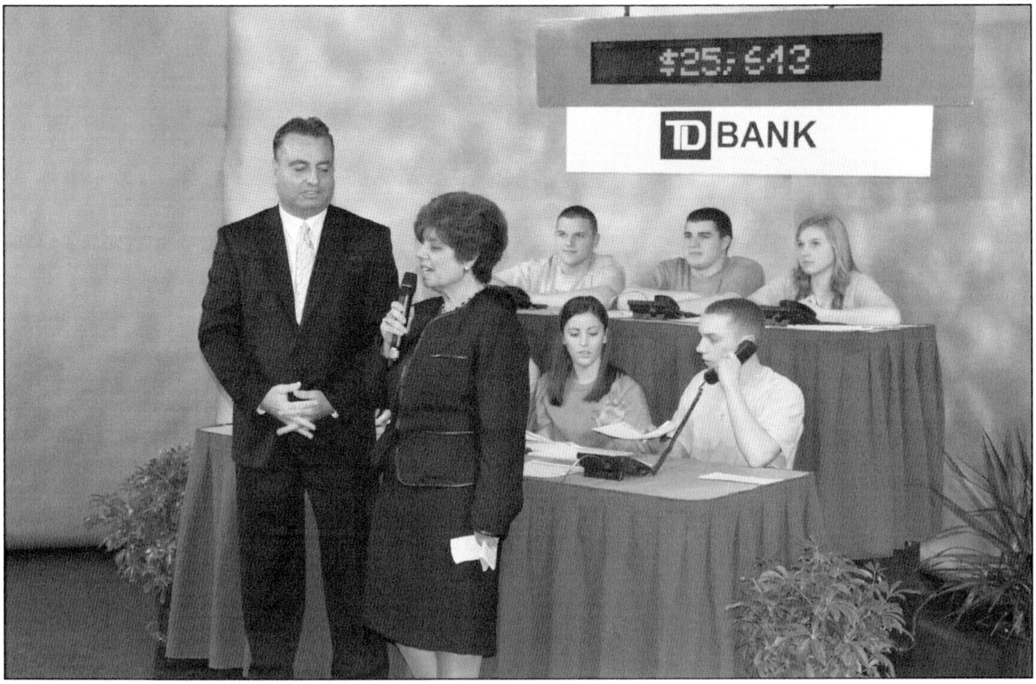

The Dracut Scholarship's Telethon each March has been very successful for almost 30 years. It is a town-wide event and pictured above at the 2006 telethon is then DSF president Mike Sancartier and Supt. Elaine Espindle. During her 10-year tenure as superintendent, Espindle was very supportive of school events and was seen at virtually every school activity. Pictured below is the auction board that displays items viewers can bid on during the four-night telethon. (Both images courtesy Lenny Proposki.)

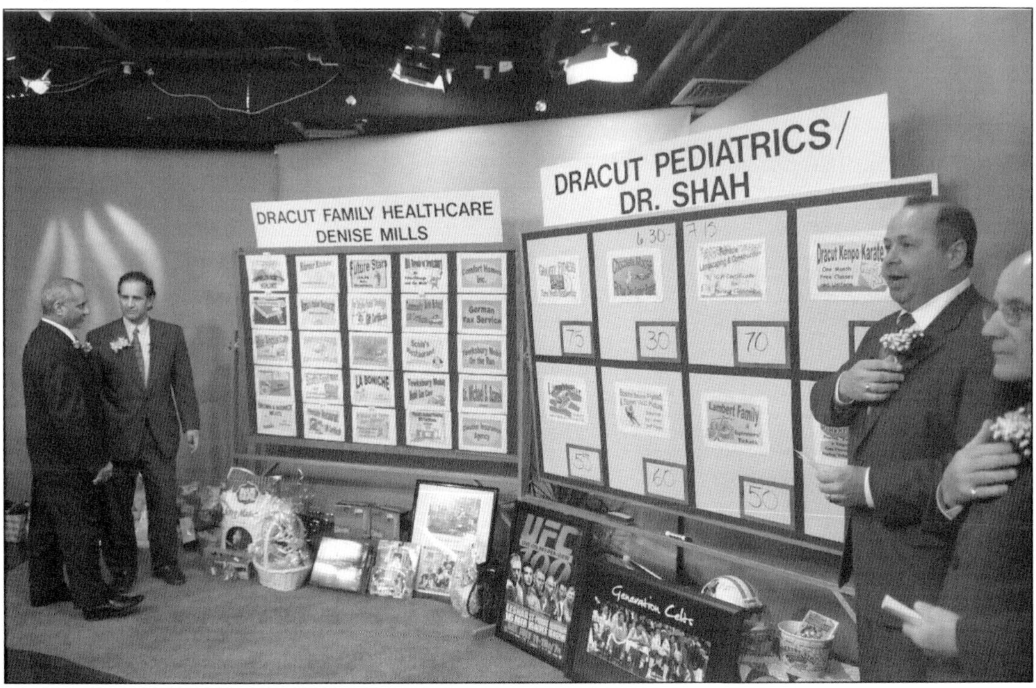

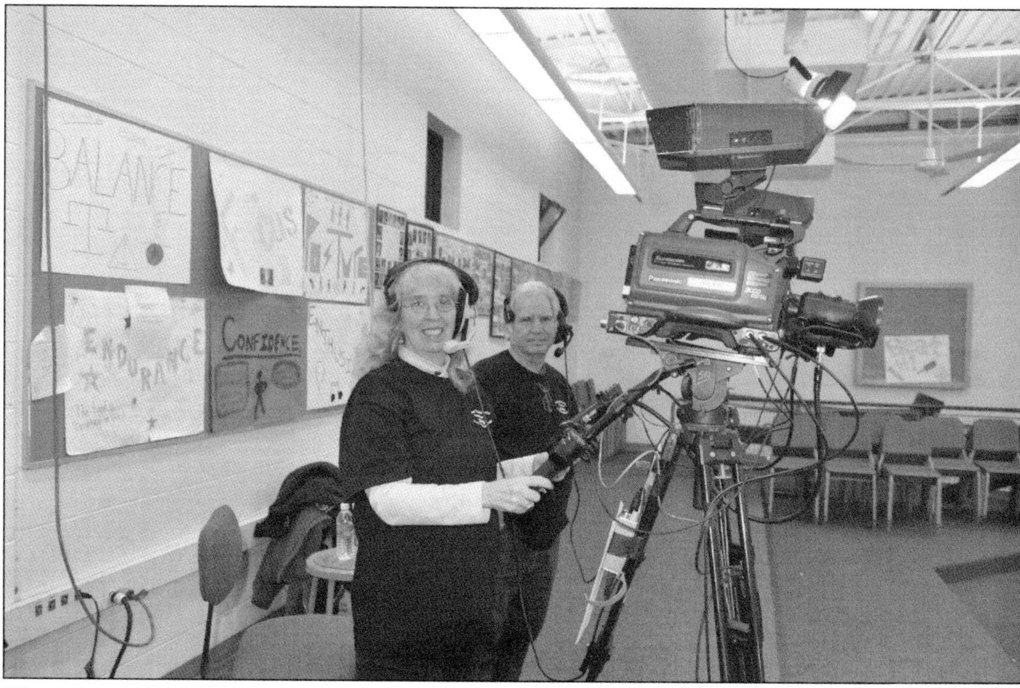

The annual telethon is as successful as it has been due to the dedication of many. Bob and Gay Corey, pictured above, are very active volunteers at Dracut Access Television (DATV) and help to televise the telethon each year. In addition, Gary Meuse, the telethon's producer, has a dedicated group of graduates that come back faithfully each year to help with the technical aspects of the production. Pictured below are members of the 2012 School Committee. From left to right are Matthew Sheehan, Bonnie Elie, Ron Mercier, Michael McNamara, and Michael Miles. Each year, the School Committee participates in a "game show" at the telethon called *Are You Smarter Than a DHS Senior?* (Both images courtesy Lenny Proposki.)

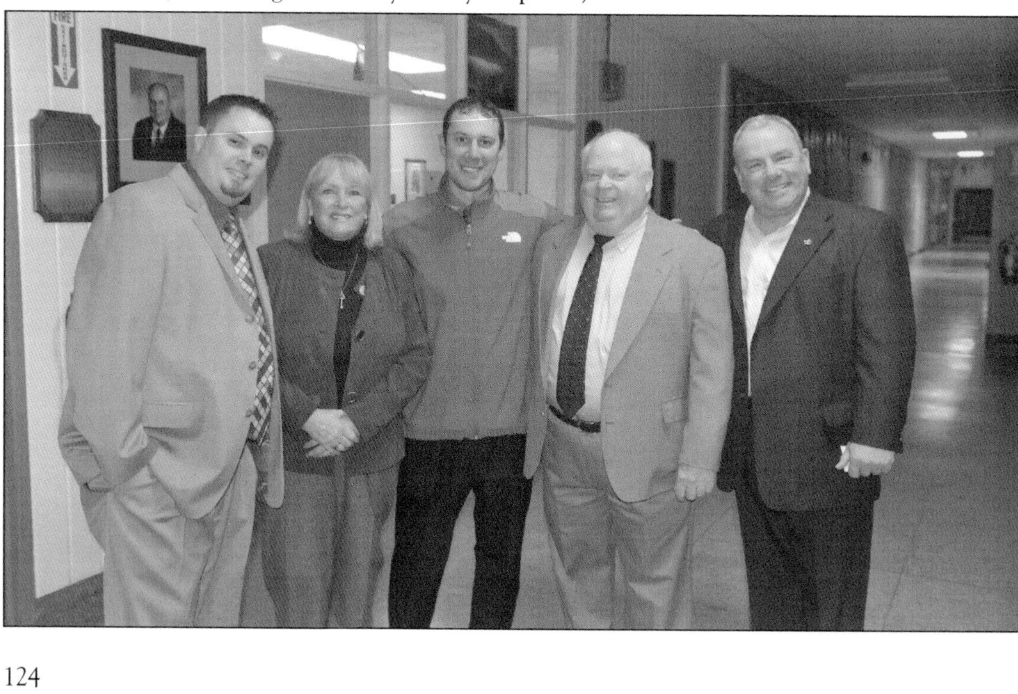

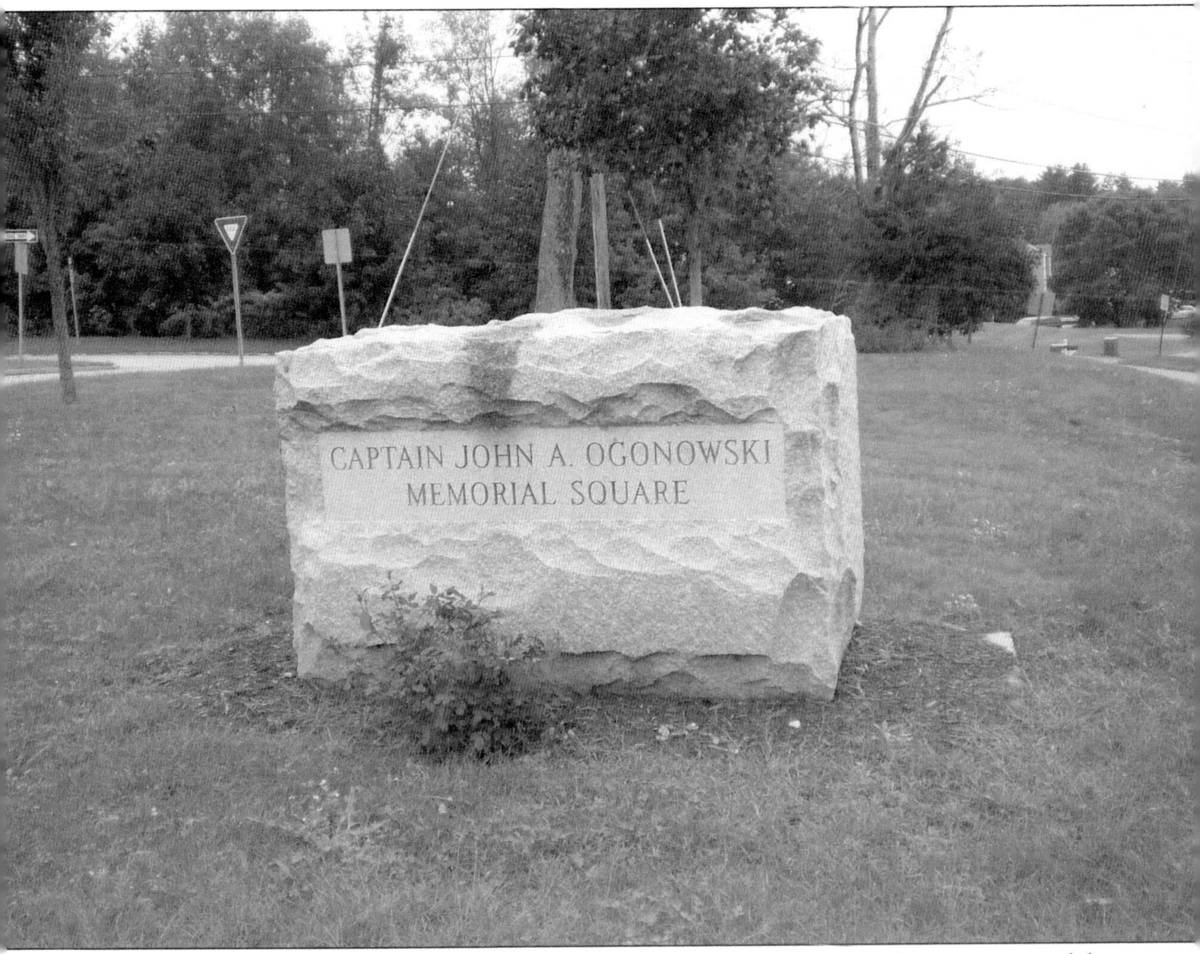

This photograph of the Ogonowski Memorial Square was taken on the 10th anniversary of the September 11th tragedy. (Author's collection.)

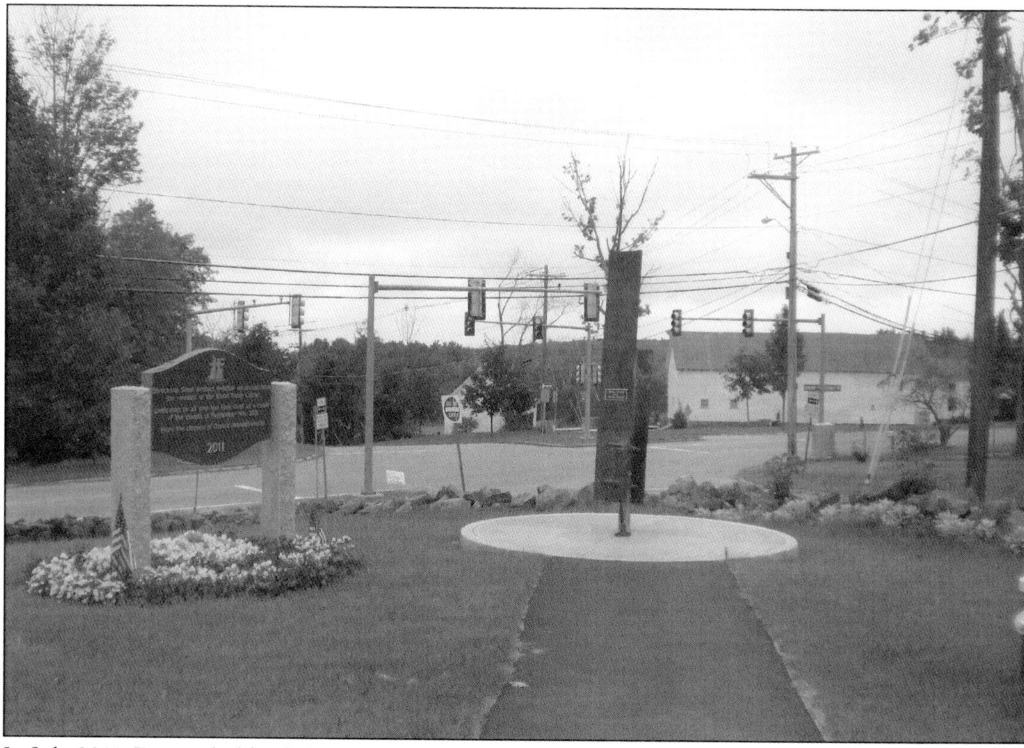

In July 2011, Dracut held a dedication ceremony for a new September 11th memorial on the lawn on the Jones Avenue Fire Station. Dracut received a steel beam artifact from the World Trade Center site. The beam faces the Ogonowski Farm across the street. (Both images, author's collection.)

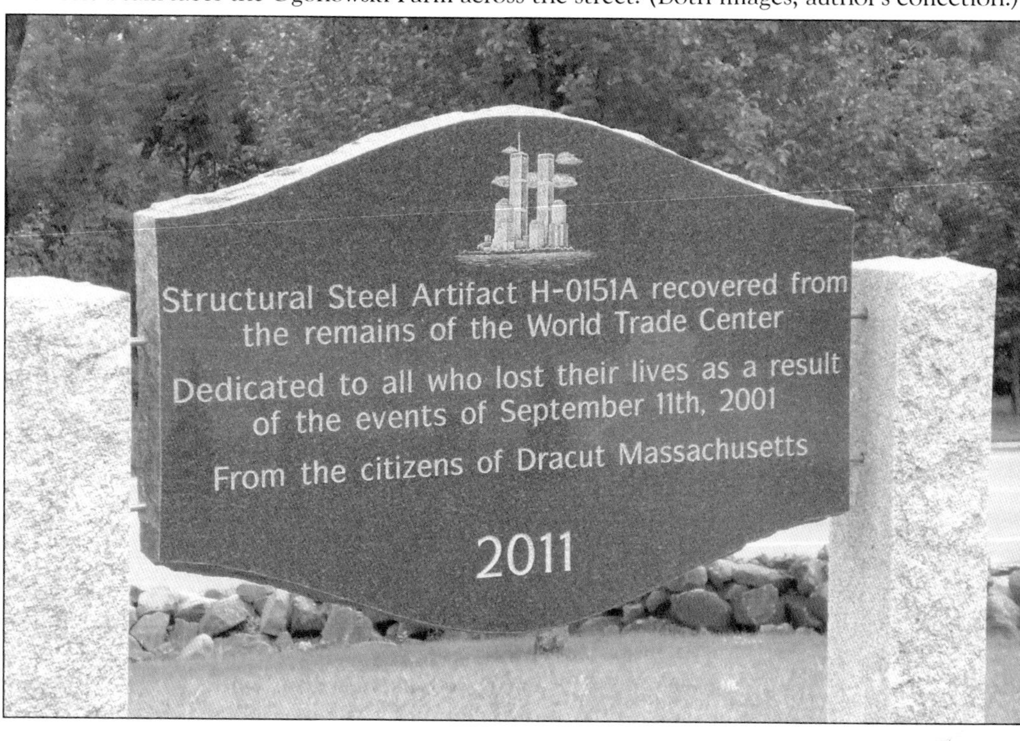

BIBLIOGRAPHY

Bright, William. *Native American Place Names of the United States*. Oklahoma City, OK: Oklahoma University Press, 2007.

Coburn, Frederick William. *Moses Greeley Parker, M.D.* Boston: Harvard University Press, 1921.

Coburn, Silas R. *History of Dracut, Massachusetts*. Lowell, MA: Courier-Citizen Company, 1922.

Goldsack, Robert. *A Century of Fun: A Pictorial History of New England Amusement Parks*. Nashua, NH: Midway Museum Publications, 1993.

Lowell Historical Society. *Lowell: The River City*. Portsmouth, NH: Arcadia Publishing, 2006.

Paquet, Donat. *A Photographic History of Dracut*. Lowell, MA: Dracut Historical Society, 1982.

Pendergrast, John. *Dracut*. Charleston, SC: Arcadia Publishing, 1997.